LETTERS TO MY FATHER

SOUTHERN LITERARY STUDIES

Fred Hobson, Editor

William Styron at age twenty-four, in the fall of 1949.

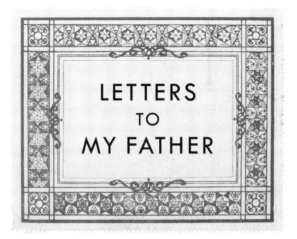

LETTERS
TO
MY FATHER

William Styron

Edited by JAMES L. W. WEST III

With a Foreword by ROSE STYRON

LOUISIANA STATE UNIVERSITY PRESS
BATON ROUGE

Published by Louisiana State University Press
Copyright © 2009 by Louisiana State University Press
All rights reserved
Manufactured in the United States of America
First printing

DESIGNER: Michelle A. Neustrom
TYPEFACES: Bodoni Old Face BE, Tw Cen BT
PRINTER AND BINDER: Thomson-Shore, Inc.

LIBRARY OF CONGRESS CATALOGING-IN-PUBLICATION DATA

Styron, William, 1925–2006.
  Letters to my father / William Styron ; edited by James L. W. West III ; with a fore-
word by Rose Styron.
    p. cm. — (Southern literary studies)
  Includes index.
  ISBN 978-0-8071-3400-9 (alk. paper)
  1. Styron, William, 1925–2006—Correspondence. 2. Novelists, American—20th
century—Correspondence. 3. Fathers and sons—United States. I. West, James L. W.
II. Title.
  PS3569.T9Z48 2009
  813'.54—dc22
  [B]
                                                                              2008031562

Remember to write to me . . .
    not as to a father, but without reserve as to a friend.

—Lord Chesterfield to his son
January 3, O.S. 1751

Contents

Illustrations

Foreword

LETTERS FROM POP

WILLIAM CLARK STYRON, SR., was a true southern gentleman—a gentle man—of uncommon dignity, intelligence, uprightness, cultivation, courtliness, and caring. The affection between "Dear Pop" and his son was the lynchpin of Bill Styron's young life. This is obvious in the letters they wrote to each other after Bill left home for prep school and then college. Pop suffered from depression after his wife Pauline died in 1939. I always believed that my husband's extremes of pessimism stemmed from his long childhood anticipation of her death, and the confirmation of his fears.

Through Bill's college days at Davidson and Duke, his time in the Marine Corps, and then his sojourns in New York, Brooklyn, Durham again, Valley Cottage, Greenwich Village, Paris, Rome, and Ravello— at least until Bill and I married—they corresponded constantly. WCS senior and junior were, as Bill noted later, "partners in spirit." Long distance, they discussed everything from bad grades and good school pals to books and music—their shared passion—to matters of morality, politics, money (always the need for at least a small handout, readily sent), details of Bill's writings and his decision to be a writer, progress or painful lack of it, triumphs and failures in academe and in the larger worlds of work and literature, through the publication of short stories, *Lie Down in Darkness,* and, during his European journey, the *Discovery* edition of *The Long March.* Bill was aware that without Pop's advice and encouragement, he would not have succeeded so early. Pop's idealism, his empathy for the less fortunate, and his hatred of racial prejudice and meanness and hypocrisy became Bill's.

When, after our years in Italy, we returned to the States, Bill and I went to Newport News for a visit. On that first trip Pop, from his verandah, pointed out the sights of the Tidewater Virginia shore, instructing me in the history of Hampton Roads and the battle of the *Monitor* and the *Merrimac* exactly there. He was a welcoming host and a fine storyteller. Pop was wonderful to me, as my Mom had always been. Bill and I felt blessed in having parents we admired, who stood by us and then by our own children.

I was actually introduced to Pop, and continued to receive insightful bulletins about his life over the decades, via *his* letters to his son. Alas, most have not survived for this collection, but I'll note a few I recall well. They invariably were bookended between "Dear Son" and "Your Devoted Father."

The first letter from Pop that Bill read to me, pre-Christmas 1952, was opened in Paris. It was mailed to Peter and Patsy Matthiessen, who had left it for our arrival on the bed we sat on in the little *pensione* they had found for us near their apartment, not far from the first office of the *Paris Review*.

The letter began: "Dear Son, What kind of trouble are you in? You can tell me. A gumshoe from Washington came down on the boat and is asking questions about us from all our neighbors. Son, you can tell me. It's okay." At that instant I suspected correctly that my mother had sent the detective. I remembered that she had once checked on a potential fiancée of my big brother's and on several of my big sister's. Like Bill, none were from Baltimore. In Paris, Bill and I were young and embarrassed and angry. But Pop understood: it was a different time, and Mom, a wise widow, felt she had the right to be sure her impulsive youngest daughter was marrying into a "good" family.

Bill Styron had proposed to me a few weeks earlier (at the bar of the Hotel Flora on the Via Veneto in Rome, before we drove to Paris), and I had accepted. Now I told him there was no way I could let him marry into a suspicious family like mine, and he agreed. We went on to have a great time in Paris, cementing friendships with the *Paris Review* gang, which included Peter (first and always), George Plimpton, John Marquand, and Billy du Bois. But soon after returning to Rome I moved to Florence with the intention of breaking up with Bill forever. Less than two months later, Bill's friend from the American Academy, the sculptor Bobby White, came to Florence and persuaded me to return to

Rome for a weekend visit. The first night he and his wife, Claire, produced Bill. I never went back to Florence.

Instead in that early spring of 1953, Bill and I moved to Via Angelo Masina 5B, a tiny basement apartment adjacent to the grand American Academy, which had been designed by Bobby's grandfather, Stanford White. Letters came, many from Pop—delivered by Giuseppe, the Academy doorman, huge and impressive in his long gold-buttoned coat with its shiny epaulets. He'd descend the steps, knock, smile, and give us our mail, plus news from Janiculum Hill.

The first letter from Pop that we received there arrived the same day as a bill from the London publisher Hamish Hamilton for £127 that they said Bill's first novel hadn't earned back from the advance. Bill was hurt and wrote his father immediately. At that moment his nearly lifelong Anglophobia began, mitigated forty-eight years later by the splendid Covent Garden production of the opera of *Sophie's Choice*. Bill was stunned and overwhelmed by the applause for him on opening and closing nights. Lunch at Claridge's with the opera's star, Angelika Kirchschlager, was a highlight of his later life.

The next letter I remember arrived soon after our wedding on May 4, 1953. Tom Guinzburg and Irwin Shaw had moved from Paris to Rome and had become special friends of ours. Irwin gave us our wedding reception at his Parioli apartment, swelling the Academy guest list with not only the *Paris Review* guys he had telegraphed, commanding them to come ("DON'T YOU REALIZE A MAN ONLY GETS MARRIED TWO OR THREE TIMES IN HIS ENTIRE LIFE?"), but with blacklisted McCarthy-era writers living abroad—most memorably, Lillian Hellman. The letter came to Ravello, where we'd begun our eight-month honeymoon. It described Pop's taking the boat from Newport News to Baltimore in order to meet my mother. The letter was glowing. He described her as lovely, elegant, welcoming. The two developed a lifelong friendship, enhanced by other trips he made to Baltimore when Bill and I and the children descended on my mother's house at 2707 Lawina Road for one holiday or another.

Back in the States, unable to stay in the New York apartment we had sublet because it was too noisy to permit Bill to write, we bought fourteen acres with an old farmhouse and cottage in Roxbury, Connecticut, and lived in it for fifty years. Soon Pop appeared. I remember him sitting on the lawn in the morning sunshine holding baby Susanna, Bill on the grass smiling happily. Seven cows from the adjacent farm watched at a nearby stone wall. When I'd sit there nursing Susanna, I sometimes wondered if their milk was swelling too.

Three springs later, I recall a steady grandfather approaching on the precarious walkway from the road to the farmhouse that we were re-modeling. We'd move in when Polly was born. Little Susanna stretched up to hug him. That night we opened a bottle of champagne, and Pop entertained us with a tale of Bill's participation in the champagne-bottle-breaking launch of a warship built in his Newport News shipyard. Bill would memorialize his paper route and a sad car ride from those years in *A Tidewater Morning* (1993). It was perhaps the only time his readers got a glimpse of his mother. Pop talked of her with love, but Bill rarely did, except now and then as we listened to Mozart in the evenings. He'd rhapsodize about her singing, and they often sang together. Music had cemented Pop and Pauline's romance in Virginia as, in a way, it did Bill's and mine in Rome. Surely her voice inspired her son.

On one of Pop's visits I discovered his obsession with genealogy. He arrived with a huge copy of a multicentury family tree as a gift. After laughing over names like "Lovey" and "Nicey," we spotted Cousin Arthur on one branch, born in Roxbury in 1890. We had met him, Roxbury's own defrocked Episcopal priest, by chance. Perhaps the only other Styron north of the Mason-Dixon Line, he and Bill's father had corresponded on literary matters. Pop had congratulated him on the publication of *The Last of the Cocked Hats*, a biography of President Monroe, and had told him about his son's success with fiction.

I cherish other childhood memories of Bill's, good and bad. How Pop woke him up when he was little to watch strong black workers standing in the water to launch a ship that Pop, an engineer, had helped to build. The only time Pop punished him was the time he made him stay in a cold woodshed for hours when he didn't get home from school to stoke the fire for his ill mother, so he'd know how she'd felt. When the local doctor several times came to pierce his infected eardrums—and his mother would go to a neighbor's where she couldn't hear his screams. Bill remembered, too, putting cotton in his own ears so he couldn't hear his mother's screams before her new dose of morphine came.

I recall fondly how Bill and Pop would sit chatting by the fire while I fed the kids and oversaw their homework. Then the three of us would have a late dinner, and Pop would go upstairs to the room-and-bath we'd added with his visits in mind. Also, once, indelibly, I remember

Pop, Bill, and I, side by side on the den couch watching JFK's funeral on TV, mourning, mourning.

Pop had been a quiet but active liberal all his life. He talked proudly of his many black and Jewish friends. "Jewish people are the salt of the earth," Pop would tell Bill. He left the Presbyterian Church because he thought they were racist and became a devout elder for the Episcopalians. Although Bill was not a churchgoing adult, we had all the kids christened—the fourth by the Reverend William Sloane Coffin. I took them to church in Roxbury and sang in the choir for Pop's sake.

Bill wanted all his friends, South and North, to know Pop. They thought him extraordinary and Bill lucky. Pop liked Bill's friends immensely. Carlos Fuentes, whom Bill particularly cared for, dedicated *The Old Gringo:* "To William Styron, whose father included me in his dreams of the American Civil War." John Marquand, Bennett Cerf, Tom Guinzburg, James Jones, Reynolds Price, and Tommy Peyton were Pop's favorites among Bill's men friends. As to women, Pop might have been a gentleman, but he was not above giving a couple of my girlfriends an extra squeeze when they danced together at our nighttime soirées.

Pop visited Roxbury frequently. Mike Carlisle recalls how our house vibes changed when Pop would visit. I was often, it seems, the speaker of the house of chaos in my enthusiasm for activities with our children. Bill slept late or worked in his studio. Everything calmed down later in the day, and we were all together. If Pop decided to cook "chitlins" in our kitchen, I'd flee, unable to stand the odor, but he cooked well, and Bill junior's gourmet leanings (and later splendid chefdom) must have started at home.

Then I remember vividly Pop's letter to Bill years later—after his second wife, Elizabeth, had died. Elizabeth had been formidable. Perhaps feeling that Bill was her rival, she had let her disapproval of his slack ways be felt. Bill tried for Pop's sake to be kind and to make her like him, but his lack of effect might be inferred from an astonishing letter Elizabeth wrote me while I was still in Rome, strongly warning me not to marry Bill. Eventually, after we visited Newport News as a family, she softened.

My favorite letter came after Elizabeth's death. Pop did not go into seclusion then but went immediately to Florida. He told Bill he was going to visit an old friend. The next week another letter, also to Bill only—he thought I would not approve so soon after Elizabeth's death—

detailed how he had tracked down his early love, Eunice. He'd kept tabs on her for fifty-odd years. Her husband, head of the Florida stock exchange, had died a short time earlier.

Soon there was another letter—ecstatic—enclosing Eunice's letter to him after their southern motel rendezvous: "Dear Darling Dynamite," she wrote, "Your brand of dynamite has kept me in a daze for days (no pun intended). Ever since you knocked gently on my door (BLAM, BLAM!) I've thought only of you. . . ." He also enclosed a letter of his that Eunice had kept for decades. In October 1914, Pop had written a regretful letter congratulating her on her marriage. He had appended some lines from Tennyson's "Tears, Idle Tears."

They married a couple of months later at a church in Goldsboro, North Carolina, where Eunice had an old home—a small, white-pillared house, the last private dwelling on a highway between a Burger King and a Pizza Hut. Pop and Eunice were sitting on the front porch glider when we arrived for the wedding. After the church ceremony, at the Downtowner Motel, where the marquee boasted "Lunch 95¢, Dinner $1.65," guests assembled at a long formal dinner table, but Pop and Eunice sat at a table for two in the corner, holding hands.

One more memory, this of a phone call from Pop in 1968: "Son," he said, "Elizabeth just came in from the kitchen. She was making Shake 'n' Bake chicken. She heard on the radio that you won the Pulitzer Prize! It's the proudest day of my life!" Years later Bill recounted this story to his friend Marcia Smilack. Then he quipped: "That and every other day of my life."

ROSE STYRON

Acknowledgments

FOR PERMISSION TO PUBLISH these letters I am grateful to Rose Styron, to the Estate of William Styron, and to Duke University Library. Robert L. Byrd, director of the Rare Book, Manuscript, and Special Collections Library at Duke; Linda McCurdy, head of Research Services; Will Hansen, assistant curator of collections; and Elizabeth Dunn, Research Services librarian, provided useful advice and assistance.

For reading this book in manuscript and offering helpful suggestions I thank Robert Loomis, Jackson R. Bryer, Gavin Cologne-Brookes, and Peter Coveney. My colleague Nick Joukovsky in the Department of English at Penn State assisted with a Wordsworth question; Barbara Alfano of the Department of Spanish, Italian, and Portuguese helped on two matters involving the Italian language.

I am grateful to Susan Welch, dean of the College of the Liberal Arts at Penn State; to Ray Lombra, associate dean for research; and to Robin Schulze, head of the Department of English, for their continuing support. For assistance with annotation, transcription, and proofing I thank Jeanne Alexander Nettles, Audrey Barner, Gregg Baptista, and Andrew Seidman.

J.L.W.W. III

Introduction

BETWEEN 1943 AND 1953 William Styron wrote a remarkable series of letters to his father. The earliest ones were written from Davidson College, where young Styron, a freshman, was very much unsure of himself and of his prospects in life. By the last few letters, however, much had changed. Styron had chosen writing as his calling, earned an officer's commission in the Marine Corps, lived through the Second World War, and taken his degree from Duke University. He had published two substantial works of fiction—a novel, *Lie Down in Darkness* (1951), which had won the Prix de Rome of the American Academy of Arts and Letters, and a novella, *The Long March* (1953), which had solidified his reputation as one of the most promising young authors of his generation. He had spent an expatriate period in Europe and had married the woman he loved. He was now ready to return to America and take up the life of a working writer. The letters, over one hundred in number, read like an epistolary novel, with movement from location to location and changes in voice and language. The narrative is a classic one, from youthful insecurity to artistic self-discovery, capped by recognition and success. There are complications along the way—poor academic performance, shortages of money, a syphilis scare, writer's block, and temporary frustration in romance—but the difficulties are overcome and the problems mastered. William Styron emerges as a confident young writer, ready to tackle his next novel.

Most readers of this volume will be familiar with the outlines of William Styron's life.[1] He was born in 1925 in Newport News, a busy ship-

---

1. For a book-length account, see James L. W. West III, *William Styron: A Life* (New York: Random House, 1998).

building town situated at the mouth of the James River in the Tidewater region of Virginia. He was educated at Christchurch School, Davidson College, Duke University, and the New School for Social Research. *Lie Down in Darkness* was published in September 1951 to excellent reviews and strong sales. In the spring of 1952, Styron traveled to Paris, where he wrote *The Long March* and helped to found the *Paris Review*. That fall he moved on to Rome to take up a fellowship at the American Academy; the following spring he married Rose Burgunder, an aspiring poet from Baltimore. He and Rose spent a long honeymoon in Ravello, the scene of his second novel, *Set This House on Fire* (1960). They returned to the United States in the fall of 1953 and settled permanently in Roxbury, Connecticut.

Styron went on to become one of the most celebrated writers of his time. *The Confessions of Nat Turner* (1967) was awarded the Pulitzer Prize for Fiction and the Howells Medal; *Sophie's Choice* (1979) won the American Book Award and sold over three million copies. After a bout with severe depression in the mid-1980s, Styron published *Darkness Visible* (1990), an account of his descent into madness and his subsequent recovery. He continued to write, primarily in the autobiographical mode, through the 1990s. He and Rose remained married until his death in November 2006.

Styron's father, William Clark Styron, was a native of North Carolina, born in 1889 in Washington, a small town on the Pamlico River in the eastern part of the state. He earned a degree in 1910 from the North Carolina College of Agriculture and Mechanic Arts (later known as North Carolina State University). His inclinations were toward literature and the arts, but his training at the A&M was in industrial engineering and mechanical drafting. For the nine months immediately following his graduation, he worked as an oiler and deck engineer on a transatlantic freighter. He traveled to Mexico, the Netherlands, Germany, and Great Britain but decided that he was not suited to a life at sea. In 1911 he took a job as a draftsman at the Newport News Shipbuilding and Drydock Company, about one hundred miles north of his home town. He lived in Newport News and was employed at the shipyards for the rest of his working life.

In 1918, at the end of the First World War, William C. Styron met Pauline Margaret Abraham, the general secretary of the Newport News YMCA. She was a northerner, the daughter of a prosperous coke-plant owner in Uniontown, Pennsylvania, and had come to Virginia to help with the war effort. Gifted in music, Pauline had studied voice and piano in Vienna before the war. It was music, in fact, that drew her to her future husband; he had a good tenor voice and an extensive layman's knowledge of classical music and opera. They enjoyed singing in church and going to concerts together.

After an extended engagement, Pauline Abraham and William C. Styron were married in September 1921. In the fall of 1924 she became pregnant and on June 11, 1925, gave birth to a son, whom they named William Clark Styron, Jr. He was a bright child with an active imagination, a strong interest in words, and an early love of reading. During his first year of grammar school his parents purchased a house in Hilton Village, a small community several miles upriver from the shipyards, built by the U.S. government just after the war to provide affordable housing for defense workers. Billy Styron spent his childhood in Hilton Village in a small house at 56 Hopkins Street. The house was two blocks from the James River; the presence and proximity of the great river were central elements of his boyhood.

In 1927, two years after her son's birth, Pauline Styron discovered that she had breast cancer. She underwent a double mastectomy, which temporarily arrested the progress of the disease. Eventually, however, the cancer returned. Billy was not told of his mother's illness as a small child, but at about the age of ten he was informed of her predicament and began to understand, as well as a child of that age can, that she would not live much longer. Pauline's final years were cruelly painful: she fell and broke her leg in 1937 and spent what remained of her life in a heavy leg brace. During her last few months, in the spring and summer of 1939, her body became emaciated and intolerant of the morphine that had been keeping the pain at bay. She died on July 20, 1939, a month after Billy had turned fourteen.

Thereafter he and his father grew increasingly close. They went to musical events and ball games together and took their meals at inexpensive restaurants in downtown Newport News. They talked about colonial Virginia and the Civil War and visited historic sites in nearby Jamestown, Williamsburg, and Yorktown. One of their pleasures was listening to music on the radio together—the Metropolitan Opera broadcasts on Saturdays and the NBC Symphony on Sunday afternoons. Father and son had similar temperaments and tastes and were at ease in each other's company. They were not pals or buddies—an element of formality was always present in the relationship—but there was much unexpressed love and affection between them.

About a year after Pauline's death, the senior Styron began to keep regular company with Elizabeth Buxton, the sister of Russell Buxton, the physician who had treated Pauline during her final illness. As a young woman Elizabeth had been trained as a nurse; she was now in her mid-forties and had risen in her profession to become a teacher of nurses. Eventually she would be head of the Virginia State Board of Nurse Examiners. Elizabeth had not married and probably had not expected to. She was a strong-minded and orderly woman, accustomed to obedience from the nurses she trained and intolerant of indolence and carelessness.

It was inevitable that she would have difficulties with young Bill Styron—a thin, rebellious teenager with a talent for sarcasm. He had turned fifteen and was now attending Christchurch, an Episcopal boys' school on the Rappahannock River, about fifty miles north of Newport News. During October of his last year at Christchurch, his father married Elizabeth Buxton. The couple settled in Elizabeth's family home at 139 Chesapeake Avenue, a large stone dwelling that faced Hampton Roads, the broad harbor that lies to the north of the James River. Bill and Elizabeth quickly developed an antipathy for one another: she criticized him for his messiness and poor grades, and he bridled at her assumption of authority over him. Fortunately he was not at home often; he spent most of his time at Christchurch and contrived to visit school friends during holidays.

On Sunday, December 7, 1941, halfway through Bill Styron's last year at Christchurch, the Japanese bombed Pearl Harbor. The United States declared war on Japan and her allies the following day. Along with most of the other boys of his generation, Bill would be drawn into this war. He was graduated from Christchurch in May 1942, still only sixteen years old, and began summer school almost immediately at Davidson, a Presbyterian men's college near Charlotte, North Carolina. The following February, at the beginning of the spring semester at Davidson, he enlisted in the Marine Corps.

At this point he began to write letters to his father. The first few are unremarkable. He gives a sketchy account of his activities, defends his mediocre marks, and asks for money. The atmosphere at Davidson was unsettled, he reported, and no one was studying much. Most of the students had enlisted in the armed services and were waiting for orders to report elsewhere for training. As a Marine Corps enlistee, Bill was transferred to Duke University in Durham, North Carolina. He went there in June 1943 and was assigned to the V-12 unit, a program designed to hold the youngest navy and Marine Corps officer candidates in college until they were old enough to be sent to boot camp. Bill wrote to his father regularly from Duke: he described his training exercises, reported on what he was reading, and mentioned his fledgling compositions in prose, for he had decided to become a writer. He had fallen under the influence of William Blackburn, a fatherly professor who taught courses at Duke in creative writing and in Elizabethan and Jacobean literature.

Late in 1944 Styron was sent to boot camp. He survived its rigors and passed on to officers' training school, where he earned his commission and was pronounced fit for warfare in the Pacific. Like thousands of other GIs, however, he was saved from combat by the atomic bombs dropped on Hiroshima and Nagasaki in August 1945. He was discharged from the Marine Corps but later enlisted in the reserves. Back now at Duke he finished his degree and landed a beginner's position in publishing in New York City—a dull office job at McGraw-Hill. He waded through unsolicited manuscripts by day and, by night, attempted to make a beginning on his novel. His letters to his father during this period are stiff and consciously literary. The novel was going slowly, he admitted, and the office work was dispiriting. Styron eventually lost his job and, down to his last few dollars, was rescued by his father, who sent money and encouragement.

Unemployed now, Styron drifted down to Durham in July 1948 and attempted without much success to reconnect with college friends. The following May he moved back north and rented a room in the Flatbush section of Brooklyn. Then, in a stroke of good fortune, he was offered a place to live and write in Valley Cottage, a village north of New York in the Hudson River valley. There he finally broke through on his novel, now called *Lie Down in Darkness*, and developed a plan for completing the manuscript. He returned to New York in June 1950 and finished the novel while living in a basement apartment on West 88th Street—working feverishly, because he had been recalled into the Marine Corps for the Korean War. In May 1951 he reported for duty at Camp Lejeune in North Carolina and began training exercises, but a defect in his eyesight (a congenital cataract in his shooting eye) saved him from service in Korea, and he was given a permanent medical discharge in late August. He returned to New York in September in time for the publication of *Lie Down in Darkness*. Positive reviews and the Prix de Rome followed; Styron traveled to Europe and began an extended *Wanderjahr*. He took a bride: he and she established their marriage on a long honeymoon in Italy and prepared to return to the States. There the letters end.

These letters concern every major piece of fiction that Styron would produce during his long literary career. They document the composition of *Lie Down in Darkness* from start to finish; they record the experiences at Camp Lejeune on which *The Long March* was based. The honeymoon in Ravello gave rise to *Set This House on Fire;* a letter to his father from Paris dated May 1, 1952, establishes his intention, very early in his career, to write a novel about the Nat Turner Rebellion. The period in Flatbush, described in two long, ruminative letters, provided the background for *Sophie's Choice.* The letters demonstrate how Styron, as a young writer, built up a fund of literary capital on which he drew for the rest of his life.

The most important letter in this volume is the one written by Styron to his father from Paris on May 1, 1952. "I've finally pretty much decided what to write next," says Styron, "—a novel based on Nat Turner's rebellion." This slave rebellion occurred in 1831 in Southampton County, Virginia, across the James River from Newport News. Styron had become curious about the rebellion as a teenager, and his curiosity had persisted. Now he meant to write a novel about the "Southampton Insurrection," as it was called. In this letter he asks his father, an amateur genealogist with experience in library research, to gather information on the rebellion and, more generally, on "life around the Southside–Caroline Border country of Virginia in the 1820–1850 period." Styron notes that he has written for help also to J. Saunders Redding, a professor at Hampton Institute whom he had talked with the previous Christmas. Both Redding and Styron's father supplied Styron with historical materials on the rebellion. Styron gathered additional information on his own during the late 1950s and early 1960s. He began composing his novel in 1962 and published it as *The Confessions of Nat Turner* in October 1967. The novel was later attacked as opportunistic— as an attempt by Styron to seize upon current racial problems in order to produce a best seller. This letter from Paris and another that follows, dated May 20, 1952, demonstrate that Styron's serious interest in the rebellion began some fifteen years before he published his novel. His plan to write about Nat Turner was not opportunistic: *The Confessions of Nat Turner* had a much longer period of gestation than some of his critics later supposed.

The present volume contains all surviving letters written by William Styron to his father between 1943 and 1953. The senior Styron donated these letters to Duke University Library in 1969; they are published here for the first time. A few more letters, also at Duke, survive from the late 1950s and the 1960s, but Styron was living in Roxbury by then and kept in touch with his father mostly by telephone. These later letters, which concern married life, children, and career, belong in an edition of Styron's selected correspondence, now in preparation. The letters from 1943 to 1953 constitute a separate narrative, independent and self-contained.

This volume includes, in appendix 1, three letters written by the father to the son. Styron attempted to save his father's letters, but in his frequent movement from place to place as a young man most of them were lost, along with many early manuscripts and much other correspondence. The three letters in appendix 1 are among the few that survive; they are newsy and informative, affectionate but not effusive, full of support and paternal concern.[2] Appendix 2 presents a biographical sketch of the son, written by the father for the Duke alumni office. In this sketch we hear the voice of the older man, writing about a child of whom he is proud. Appendix 3 is a selection of the young author's apprentice work—the compositions that he mentions in his letters home. These writings were published in the Duke literary magazine and in two clothbound collections of student work from the New School, where Styron took seminars in fiction-writing from Hiram Haydn. Styron's fledgling efforts show a gift for words and an early instinct for artistic control. Most student writing is self-absorbed and emotionally overwrought; Styron's early writings are marked by restraint in technique and feeling.

2. Styron included fictionalized letters written to Stingo by his father in Chapter 2 of *Sophie's Choice* (New York: Random House, 1979), 29–32, 44. For a portrait of Styron *père* as Peter Leverett's father, see *Set This House on Fire* (New York: Random House, 1960), 10–19.

Letters to My Father can be thought of as a book written by William Styron, not simply as a collection of letters. Styron produced this book in increments, over a period of ten years, as he grew from adolescence into manhood. Toward the end of his life he considered publishing these letters himself, with discursive annotations and explanatory bridge passages in which he would juxtapose his mature voice, ruminative and humorous, against the eager, youthful voice in the letters. It would have been a remarkable book, duplicating the double voicing of Stingo, young and old, in *Sophie's Choice*. Styron pondered the idea for several months in 2001 and 2002 but finally decided not to undertake the project. The present book is now as close as we can come to what he might have published.

There is no other extended series of letters like this one, son to father, in all of American literature. The letters tell their own story, a narrative of ambition, drive, and commitment to literature. Many people help the young author along his way—teachers, mentors, and friends—but the constant presence in his life is his father, steadfast and unfailing. William Styron was a gifted young writer, but without his father's support he would almost surely not have persevered and won through to his first success.

J.L.W.W. III

Note on Editorial Method

THE TEXTS OF STYRON'S LETTERS to his father are presented in full. Headings are regularized; return addresses are omitted after the first appearance; dates in the headings are given in month-day-year style. Inferential dates, established from postmarks or from internal evidence, are placed within brackets. Ellipsis points are Styron's, from the original letters. No attempt has been made to impose consistency in spelling, italics, or the rendering of compound words. If a letter was written on printed stationery or letterhead—for the Marine Corps or Whittlesey House, for example—that fact is noted in the heading. All of the letters were handwritten with the exception of the two on Whittlesey House letterhead, dated July 24 and August 20, 1947, which Styron pecked out on a typewriter. The letters have been numbered for ease of reference. Closings and signatures are rendered as in the originals.

LETTERS TO MY FATHER

1 / January 1943–July 1944

DAVIDSON AND DUKE

Styron entered Davidson College in the summer of 1942. That fall he pledged with Phi Delta Theta during the fraternity rush season. In January 1943 he began his second semester in college; he would enlist in the Marine Corps in February.

1. DAVIDSON (fraternity stationery)

[January 1943]

Dear Pop,

We are having the fraternity initiation on Wednesday. It is necessary that I have a check for $45 by Wednesday noon. Everyone in the pledge class is getting initiated, and I don't want to get left out. Because of the war the fee is being reduced from $65 to $45, or a $20 reduction. Please see if you can send me a check by Special Delivery as soon as possible. It certainly means a lot to be initiated, and I'd really appreciate it.

I am enclosing an article on the latest Davidson war situation. There is a rumor, unconfirmed, to the effect that all freshmen and sophomores are going to be sent to another school. I don't know.

Your son,
Bill

2. DAVIDSON (FRATERNITY STATIONERY)

February 16, 1943

Dear Pop,

I am enclosing a blank for you to fill out for my enlistment into the Marine Corps Reserves. Please sign it, have it notarized, and send it back with

Bill Styron
Phi Delta Theta
Davidson College

Dear Pop,

We are having the fraternity initiation on Wednesday. It is necessary that I have a check for $45 by Wednesday noon. Everyone in the pledge class is getting initiated, and I don't want to get left out. Because of the war the fee is being reduced from $65 to $45, or a $20 reduction. Please see if you can send me a check by Special Delivery as soon as possible. It certainly means a lot to be initiated, and I'd really appreciate it.

I am enclosing an article on the latest Davidson war situation. There is a rumor, unconfirmed, to the effect that all freshmen & sophomores are going to be sent to another school. I don't know.

your son, Bill

Styron's initial letter to his father, January 1943, from Davidson College.
Courtesy Estate of William C. Styron, Jr.

the following: *three* citizens of Newport News recommendations as to my character; my birth certificate. The people whom you get recommendations from must be of no kin, and must have come in contact with me during the past few years. Please have these letters typewritten, and don't forget my birth certificate. I have decided on the Marine Corps as I think, as far as immediate call goes, it is safer; although the quicker I go in service the happier I'll be. Yet I realize that I should stay in school and try and get as much education as possible.[1] You understand that this branch of the Marine Corps is the Class IIId or Officer's Candidate Class, and that I have a much better chance here than I would have in the Navy V-1 program for getting a commission.

I got your allowance money, and also the initiation fee, both of which I appreciate very much. It certainly is fine to have such a swell Pop. The last part of the initiation is to take place today, and I'll be a full-fledged Phi Delt, pin and all.

Pop, please don't forget those papers. Air Mail them if possible, as all Reserve Branches may close any minute. Give my best to Liza.

Your son,
Bill Jr.

3. DAVIDSON (fraternity stationery)

[March 6, 1943]
Saturday

Dear Pop,
I received your letter today, and was rather taken aback by it, as I am afraid that there are a few points which need clearing up.

Sincerely, Pop, I know that your psychology of my situation is vastly superior to mine, and I realize that my faults are many; however, entirely because I am closer to the "facts." I feel that I should strive to do some explaining, from an unbiased viewpoint.

1. I went to Raleigh, at my own expense, to take the exam for the Marine Corps because their orders explicitly stated that I report there at that time.

1. Davidson students were being urged to stay in college as long as they could, and to take as many credits as possible, before leaving college for training in the armed services. Styron wrote a satirical poem on the subject entitled "Get All You Can" and published it in the May 1943 issue of *Scripts 'n Pranks*, the campus humor magazine.

2. I am at fault for overcutting classes; however, I didn't take "many cuts." The penalty was imposed for taking *one* excess *tardy* in Bible class. Incidentally, that tardy cut occurred in the middle of last semester, and had nothing to do with my going to Raleigh. I was fully excused for that trip.

3. Regarding my entrance into the Marines, it must be remembered that I *did* join with the intention of staying in school as long as possible. If, though, they intend to call me before June 11 I shall have to go simply because I'm needed. There is just a possibility that they'll call me before I'm 18, but isn't that infinitely better than being drafted in June and having practically no chance at all to get a commission? After all, it would be practically a certainty that I would be inducted then, so what difference would a few months make? The faculty has also passed a ruling which states that a student leaving school after April 1st for military reasons shall receive full credit on the semester's courses, graded according to quality of work done in each course up until that time when he shall be called. So if I were called after April 1st I'd receive full credit for the semester's work.

4. As to joining the fraternity, I can only stress one point. That is because membership in a fraternity means so much in later life. If I return to college after the war it would mean the basis of a whole new beginning into campus life, and would be invaluable if I were to go to another school. When I "go out into the world," fraternity membership will mean everything in establishing contacts and associations. That, Pop, I think is about the greatest thing in a college fraternity—the "social jumping-off place" for life after college. I don't know if I made the meaning of that so clear or not, but I'm taking it from one of our brothers, Dean C. K. Brown.

5. Pop, I realize that I have done very little to further my "scholastic record," if you can call it that, either at Morrison, Christchurch, or Davidson. I also realize that you have expended a lot of money to keep your worthless son in school. The only consolation I have is that I have made no academic failing large enough to actually "flunk me out" of school. I have, by some means, maintained an "average average," which only seems worse when I consider how much better I could have done. But I suppose there comes a time in everyone's

life when he looks back with regret and misgiving. I am doing better this semester, and am gradually pulling my grades up. Incidentally, I made a *95* on a *Trig* review, unprecedented in my case, and this grade was among the highest in the whole class.

I hope you haven't considered this letter too much of an harangue. I've tried to shoot you the "straight dope" without offering too many excuses, and I hope you'll believe every word I have said as being sincere.

Please give my best to Eliza. Although we aren't getting a Spring Vacation, perhaps I may see you soon.

Your son,
Bill

P.S. In case I hadn't told you, I am now rooming with Sam Waddill, since the new movement caused much confusion and turmoil. Herman's now rooming out in town. I enjoyed rooming with him a lot, and I think Sam and I will get along fine together too.[2]

4. DAVIDSON (fraternity stationery)

[March 28, 1943]
Sunday Nite

Dear Pop,

Everything around here sure is in turmoil. About 115 boys left yesterday. Another dormitory, West, was evacuated, to provide for accommodations for 250 more Air Cadets. People are being drafted right and left. At present there are only about 225 boys left in school, which is quite a decimation, what? The morale is really quite awful. No one is studying much, and activities are at a minimum.[3]

I'm doing just fairly well in my lessons, to be quite frank. I completely missed the boat in R.O.T.C., as did everyone else, simply because of the fact that it is being forced upon us, and its practical value

2. Styron's first roommate at Davidson was Herman Walker, from Greenville, South Carolina, who remembered in later years that Styron tacked up maps of the world on the walls of their room and talked of joining the foreign service after graduation. Sam Waddill, a Newport News native, was Styron's roommate during the second semester. Waddill left Davidson at the end of that term and served with the navy in the Pacific during the war.

3. Styron wrote a humorous article about the situation for the student newspaper: "Writer Tells of Confusion in Migration," *Davidsonian*, February 25, 1943, 1.

is almost nil. I have made excellent grades on all my Math Reviews; however my daily grades have pulled me down a lot. My grade in Bible will be very low for mid-semester—but the Professor misplaced one of my reviews, and my make-up review will, I think, bring up my grade considerably. I have one of the best grades in Sophomore English, that is, in Professor Lilly's class. He and I see things in the same light and I think my English grade will be either a B or B+, which is, if I do say so, excellent for "the good doctor" Lilly. My Geography grade will be a C, but I'll bring that up easily next half-semester. My French mark will be either a C+ or a B.

Which all adds up to not much. I'm still holding that old "*average.*" But I promise you that my grades will be well above that "average" at the end of the year.

You know that the continual grind which my colleagues and I are going through is very unnerving. This business of five months' straight school without any break whatsoever is extremely unappetizing. If we knew that the five months were to be terminated with the world at peace, everything would be okey dokey; but to finish school and then go straight "in"—ah, 'tis a consummation not very devoutly to be wished. Pop, I hope you'll grant me a fairly free month of June before I go to Parris Island which, I've been informed, will be on July 1st.[4]

Jean Maclay goes to Salem College, and I go up to Winston-Salem about every free week-end I get. Last week-end Bill Sheely, a good Phi Delt brother from Elizabeth City, went up with me and we had a fine time.

Well, Pop, I must go now. Please write me soon. If you don't mind, please include an extra $2.50 in my allowance, as dues for brothers are $5.00, instead of the regular $2.50 for pledges. It won't be for long. Give my best to Liza.

Your son,
Bill, Jr.

5. DAVIDSON (fraternity stationery)

[ca. April 28, 1943]

Dear Pop,

I'm sorry I didn't write sooner, but I haven't had much time as at the present we are going thru an intensive period of reviews.

---

4. Most Marine Corps recruits from east of the Mississippi River went through boot camp at Parris Island, South Carolina. Styron was not sent there until October 1944, at the end of his fourth academic term at Duke.

About a week ago I took a set of exams for the Marine Corps. They were more or less an I.Q., and evidently they are trying to eliminate, from an intelligence standpoint, all men who are not officer material. Things change quickly in the Navy Department, and as I understand it now, we will be sent to Parris Island in July for a period of basic training, then to some college, probably the University of Virginia or West Virginia for advanced training.[5] From what I hear, we will attend school, including perhaps Quantico, for about five or six months, at Navy expense with pay and uniforms. Officer candidate material will be weeded out as we go.

I certainly enjoyed your piece on the paratrooper on the train. I showed it to Bill Lyman, the editor of the magazine, and he thought it was excellent. I think you missed your calling. You should be a writer. Incidentally, if and when I get my commission I think I'll transfer to the Paramarines. I think they're the best outfit in the Armed Services, and they get exactly twice as much pay.[6]

Regarding my "vacation" in June, I wonder if it would be all right if, instead of coming directly home, I could go up to Charlottesville for a couple of days and see T. Peyton.[7] Then I could come on down to Newport News. He invited me up and, since he's been down to visit me more than once, I think I should return the favor, n'est-ce pas? My exam schedule is arranged so that I get out on the 25th of May. I could be in Newport News on the 28th.

I am pulling up in all my studies, especially Bible. I think I'll pull through this term without any serious difficulties.

Remember me to everybody. It won't be long now before I'll be home, and boy I'm certainly looking forward to it!

Your son,
Bill.

P.S. If it's possible, would you mind sending my allowance sometime before Saturday, May 8th? Thanks a lot.

---

5. Styron was ordered to report to Duke University in June.

6. These parachute troops, trained for raiding and reconnaissance work, were used during beach raids (at Iwo Jima, for example) but proved difficult to equip and deploy. The Paramarines disbanded in December 1943; their personnel were reassigned to other combat units.

7. Tom Peyton, a fellow Virginian from Crozet, near Charlottesville, was Styron's best friend at Christchurch.

After a brief visit at home in Newport News, Styron reported to Duke University for summer school and the beginnings of his military training. He had been assigned to the V-12 unit at Duke, a training program for officer candidates in the navy and Marine Corps. Styron traveled to campus on a bus and was deposited at night in front of Duke Chapel. "Dark as they were," he later recalled, "the Gothic outlines of the campus loomed in the shadows most attractively and impressively; and the Chapel tower rose up against the night with formidable majesty and grace."[8]

6. DUKE (fraternity stationery)

[July 13, 1943]
Tuesday P.M.

Dear Pop,

Well, things have been going along pretty well so far. We got issued our uniforms last Saturday and they're pretty slick. They're regular G.I. issue, olive green, overseas cap and marine insignia. We also got underwear, socks, and two pairs of shoes. They really look good (the uniforms), and the Marines are so superior to the Army and Navy that it isn't even funny. You walk down the streets of Durham with that Marine emblem flashing and the sorry looking soldiers from Camp Butner just step aside.[9]

Boy, I don't know how long I'm going to last here. If Davidson was tough, this place is tougher. I don't mind the Physical program or getting up at six in the A.M.—but I've never seen such rough courses. That Physics tops them all. I think I may be able to maintain the required C average—but that's about all. I'm doing all right so far. My favorites, in order, are as follows: Political Science, English, History, Psychology, and Physics. I *am* studying, but this hot weather isn't conducive to concentration. So far I haven't made any startling grades, but I haven't dropped below C, which is okay. I have a Psychology test tomorrow and expect to pass it all right.[10]

8. From an untitled contribution by Styron to *Duke Encounters* (Durham: Duke University Office of Publications, 1977), 78.

9. Camp Butner, a 40,000-acre army installation near Durham, was used for infantry training from January 1942 until August 1943. Thereafter it became a prisoner-of-war camp.

10. Physics proved his undoing. He failed the course (required for the V-12 program) three times before earning a courtesy D on the fourth try.

We get paid on Saturday—$50 on the line in cash. That dough certainly will look good. This week-end Don Strotz (my roommate), Satan, and myself are going to Norlina to visit one of Don's cousins who has a plantation near there.[11] We get a furlough around the middle of October for about a week, and I certainly will be glad to get home. This place is all right, I guess, but it sure gets on your nerves.

Well, I've got to sign off now. Give my best to Eliza, and tell everybody hello. Hope everything is going along okay at home.

Your son,

Bill Jr.

7. DUKE (Marine Corps stationery)

August 23, 1943

Dear Pop,

No change here yet. Things are going on about the same. I got your letter and one from Auntie Elmer.[12] You all must have had a pretty good time in Philadelphia. Hope you did.

We have just finished our mid-term exams and have received some of our "semi-final" grades. I have maintained all passing marks. I got a D in Physics, D+ in French, C+ in Political Science, B+ in Psychology, B in History, and I think I got either a B or B+ in English, although the professor doesn't really give a definite grade in that course. That Physics course is really tough. The whole class average is about a D. To show you how hard it is—I have had two tests and made grades of 40 and 45 with an average of 43. That was automatically brought up under the "curve," or scaling system, to an average of 75—almost doubling my score.

Don't worry about my French grade, as I'll bring that up by final exams. GHQ figures that about 50% of the Marines will flunk out of

---

11. V-12 trainees were paid fifty dollars a month in pocket money. "Satan" is the nickname for Tom Peyton, the friend from Christchurch mentioned in letter 5. Norlina is a small North Carolina town just south of the border with Virginia.

12. Auntie Elmer was Mrs. Lynwood R. Holmes, a friend of Styron's mother who took an interest in him as a teenager. Mrs. Holmes (named "Elmer" by her father, who had wanted a boy) sent Styron his first stamp-collecting paraphernalia during the spring of 1938. He visited her and her husband, whom he called "Uncle Buck," at their home in Philadelphia in May of that year. Styron wrote to her regularly during his prep-school and college years; the letters are among his papers at Duke. See James L. W. West III, *William Styron: A Life* (New York: Random House, 1998), 47–49.

here or be shipped out through graduation by the end of October, but I won't be in that select percentage. However, even knowing how lucky I am getting an education and all, I sure wish I could do a little bit more to actually fight the war. I suppose, though, that the Navy knows what it's doing in sending us here.

So far I haven't gotten a single demerit. Eliza would be proud to see how neat we keep the room. We signed the payroll for our second pay which we'll get during the first week of September. We also got our second and last tetanus shot on Saturday. It didn't cause any ill effects at all, and Satan and I even took a trip to Lynchburg that night. We had a *very* good time.

We are taking swimming in Physical Training now, but go to jiu-jitsu next week. I am still looking forward with anticipation to our leave in October. Please write and give my love to Eliza.

Your son,
Bill, Jr.

8. DUKE (Marine Corps stationery)

September 15, 1943

Dear Pop,

Well, it's been a while since I last wrote you, but things have been just about the same around here. My grades, with the exception of Physics, are pretty good. Physics has thrown me and the rest of the Marines for a loop. To show you how hard the last test was: the average grade in the whole class of about 700 was *38;* I got a 21. History, still about B; Polit., up to a B; French up to a C; English still a B; and Psychology still a B. Which all in all isn't so very bad.

Right now I am writing my *chef d'oeuvre* in English. It's a short story about a woman evangelist in the deep South who is jilted in love. The theme of the Song of Solomon runs throughout. If it's good enough, I might try to get it published somewhere—as the editors of most magazines need material badly. One of my stories is being considered for publication in the *Archive*, the Duke literary magazine. If it's accepted, I'll send a copy to you.[13]

---

13. The manuscript about the woman evangelist does not survive. The story submitted to the *Archive* was probably "Where the Spirit Is," published in the January 1944 issue of the magazine.

We're studying boxing, wrestling and jiu-jitsu. They're all very educational—especially jui-jitsu. My partner is the son of a Marine officer who was stationed in Japan before the war—just my luck! I am continually being thrown on my can.

Still getting up at six o'clock for exercise. The "cadet" system is still in effect. They rotate officers, and any day now I expect to be made a platoon leader or something. Hope I don't get nervous giving those "right and left flanks." By the way, you can tell Eliza to have no fear of my oversleeping, as the early morning routine has now become pretty much of a habit.

I still have hopes of getting home in October. I may bring Don Strotz, my roommate, but I'll let you know later. In the meanwhile, I'll content myself with occasional trips to Durham and dates with the newly arrived girls on East Campus.[14]

Write soon and give my best to Eliza.

Your son,
Bill, Jr.

9. DUKE (Marine Corps stationery)

September 28 [1943]

Dear Pop,

I got your letter and enjoyed it very much. I'm glad you had such a fine time on your vacation. I know you and Eliza must have painted the town red. When at Davidson I saw "Arsenic and Old Lace" and if the New York production was as good as the Davidson one (I doubt if it could equal the Wildcat Dramatic Society), you all must have been rolling in the aisles. It certainly was funny. I heard that "Watch on the Rhine" was excellent, but I suppose it'll be a long time before it gets to Durham.[15]

---

14. The dormitories for female students were on the East Campus of Duke—the original campus of Trinity College, which had been incorporated into Duke University in 1924.

15. Styron's father and stepmother saw the original stage production of *Arsenic and Old Lace*, a comic thriller by the American playwright Joseph Kesselring. The play opened on Broadway on January 10, 1941, at the Fulton Theatre, and was transferred to the Hudson Theatre on September 25, 1943, a few days before the date of this letter. The film adaptation of *Arsenic and Old Lace*, starring Cary Grant, was released in September 1944. *Watch on the Rhine*, Lillian Hellman's anti-fascist drama, had opened to good reviews in New York in April 1941 at the Martin Beck Theatre. By the fall of 1943 the play had ended its run; the Styrons would have seen the 1943 Warner Brothers film version, based on a screenplay by Dashiell Hammett and starring Paul Lukas and Bette Davis.

I told all the guys about your unique toast to all the states in the Union. They said we'll have to try the same toast before Durham runs out of beer.

So far Duke has played two games and won two. We have scored 101 points, beating Camp Lejeune 40–0 and U. of Richmond 61–0. Pretty good, eh?

Lately I've been reading a lot—mostly Thomas Wolfe. I think he's the greatest writer of our time. I read "Of Time and the River" and "Look Homeward, Angel" and am starting on "The Web and the Rock." Did you know that Tom Wolfe worked in Newport News during the last war? He speaks of the old home town, not too complimentary, in a couple of his books. He even worked in the Shipyard for five minutes, but was kicked out because he knew too little about carpentry—even for a Carolinian. He· was born in Asheville and went to U.N.C. In his novels, the saga of Eugene Gant (which is really an autobiography), he speaks of the University at "Pulpit Hill," the sprawling Tobacco Town of "Exeter" (Durham), and Sydney (Raleigh).[16]

I got a letter from Aunt Edith and she sent me ten bucks. Also asked me to come and visit her on my furlough. Should I?[17]

I certainly appreciate you and Eliza sending me the candy. It tasted good on those "hungry nights."

Write soon, and give my love to Eliza.

Your son,
Bill, Jr.

Like many colleges and universities during World War II, Duke offered courses for its military trainees on an accelerated academic calendar. As a member of the V-12 unit, Styron took classes on this calendar, while the other students followed a conventional semester system. Styron's first term at Duke ended in mid-September 1943; he took a brief holiday in Newport News and returned toward the end of the month to begin his next semester of classes. It was during this semester that he began to take classes from William Blackburn, who is first mentioned in letter 13.

16. See Styron's reminiscence "'O Lost!' Etc.," in *This Quiet Dust and Other Writings* (New York: Random House, 1982; rev. ed., 1993), 73–86.

17. Edith Abraham Crow (the only sister of Styron's mother), lived in Uniontown, Pennsylvania, with her husband, a physician. Styron corresponded with her during his teens and twenties.

10. DUKE (Marine Corps stationery)

[November 3, 1943]
Wednesday

Dear Pop,

Well, here I am again. I got into D.U. at about 5:00 Friday morning and I've done nothing since. We got in three days ahead of the sailors, and since there was nothing for us to do, we've been just loafing. Classes start today, and I have a pretty rough schedule, namely, Math, Physics, Political Science, Engineering Drawing, and English. Physical Training consists this time of hand-to-hand combat, basketball, football, and swimming. That is quite an improvement over last semester's course in running, tumbling, boxing and the like.

The Marines shipped out over two hundred men on Monday,—110 officer candidates to Parris Island, and about 100 "flunkees" (guys who failed) to San Diego for general duty and combat training.[18] Too bad. Don Strotz, my ex-roommate, was in the latter group.

By the way, I've changed my room and, of course, my roommates. I'm rooming with "Doc" Chandler from Chattanooga, Tenn. and Lee Strasser from Wheeling, W.Va. Both are good guys.

Well, there really isn't much else in the way of news. I hope that I'll be sent to O.C.S. after this semester in March.[19] I'm getting very tired of Duke and the food is no better.

Although I failed Physics last semester, I am consoled with an A in History (one out of six A's in about 400 History students), and a B+ in English.

Write soon, and give my love to Eliza.

Your son,
Bill

P.S. I'll send you a genuine G.I. stainless steel razor soon.

11. DUKE (fraternity stationery)

November 23, 1943

Dear Pop,

I'm sorry to be so late in writing you, but I've been reading a lot lately and I'd get so engrossed in a book, planning to write all the time, that

---

18. V-12 candidates who washed out of officer training were sent to boot camp in San Diego and from there into the Pacific war as enlisted men.

19. O.C.S.: Officer Candidate School.

Styron with his father in Newport News, Virginia, at age five. No other photograph of father and son together is known to survive. Courtesy Estate of William C. Styron, Jr.

when I had finished reading I'd have to go to bed and postpone the letter.

Things, as usual, are about the same. I'm making out all right in my studies, nothing spectacular, but about par. So far we haven't had any quizzes, so I can't evaluate my grades.

I've been reading some good books—Hemingway, Wolfe, Faulkner, Dos Passos and short stories by Balzac, Thurber, de Maupassant, Joyce, Poe, and others. "U.S.A." by John Dos Passos, while rather long, is especially good. It's the writer's attempt, through fiction, to portray America and its people. Mentions Newport News and Norfolk, and the *Northern Neck*—to quote: ". . . you'd ride slowly home hating the goddam exhausted land and the drought that wouldn't let the garden grow and the katydids and the dryflies jeering out of the sapling gums and persimmons ghostly with dust along the road and the sickle-shaped beach where the sea nettles stung you when you tried to swim out and the chiggers and the little scraps of talk about what was going on up to the Hague or Warsaw or Pekatone and the phone down at the cottage that kept ringing whenever any farmer's wife along the line took up the receiver to talk about things to any other farmer's wife and all down the line you could hear the receivers click as they all ran to the receiver to listen to what was said. . . ."[20]

Sounds just like the Northern Neck and Dolph Chowning.[21] Brings back old memories.—About that story I wrote I was telling you about: It's scheduled to be published in the Christmas issue of the *Archive*.[22] The Editor said it would have won the prize in their short story contest, but I didn't know anything about it (the contest), so I didn't win. They were going to run another story of mine, entitled "Home Again," but the MS. was lost, and I didn't feel like doing it over. We get three

20. Styron is quoting from the section entitled "The Camera Eye (21)" in John Dos Passos, *The 42nd Parallel*—the first novel in the *U.S.A.* trilogy. Styron has likely been reading *U.S.A.* in the Modern Library edition of 1937, which includes all three novels. (The other two are *Nineteen Nineteen* and *The Big Money.*) The passage that Styron quotes is printed on pp. 261–62 of the Modern Library edition.

21. The Northern Neck of Virginia lies between the Potomac River on the north and the Rappahannock on the south. Randolph Chowning was a friend from Styron's prep school, Christchurch, which is situated on the Rappahannock fourteen miles upriver from the Chesapeake Bay.

22. "Where the Spirit Is."

days leave Xmas so I'll see you then. Write soon and give my best to everyone.

Your son, Bill Jr.

P.S. I enjoy Mech. Drawing very much. Take after Pop, eh?![23]

---

12. DUKE (Marine Corps stationery)

January 18, 1944

Dear Pop,

I got the box you sent me some time ago, and it will please you to know that the picture of my illustrious papa holds a commanding station now atop my dresser. The room now fairly radiates dignity. Thanks also for the stationery.

Things are as per usual down here, with conditions still as monotonous and routine-full. My work, while far from Phi Beta Kappaish, is being maintained with mediocrity and fair promise of passing. I'm afraid that scholastically I'm pretty much of a border-line case. But then, I never was much of a student.

Pop, please send me $5 when you write next. I'm not broke, but I gave Tommy $15 to keep for me to prevent my spending it, since we're going to take a trip to Charlottesville on the 29th. He won't give any of it to me until that date, and I can see my funds are going to be exhausted. Also please send me Molly Dickson's full name and address.

The *Archive* with my story will be out on Jan. 24th and I'll send you a copy then. Best to all, and write soon.

Your son,
Bill

---

13. DUKE (fraternity stationery)

March 12 [1944]
Sunday

Dear Pop,

I got your letter a few days ago, and I certainly enjoyed it. I was glad

---

23. The senior Styron had been a mechanical draftsman at the Newport News shipyards during his first few years there.

you enjoyed my story. Another one of my opuses (or operas, I think, is the plural) is going to appear in the April issue of the *Archive*. It is, appropriately enough to my faculty for picking primitive subjects, a story about a lynching, and the psychological effect of it on a young boy. The title is Delta Night.[24]

Dr. Blackburn, in his comment on the story said: "I take great pride in your progress this term. While I don't usually urge undergraduates to make writing their livelihood, you are definitely one to be encouraged . . . you have grown . . . in both strength and wisdom. This story is the strongest you have done."

My studies are coming along pretty well. We've had no tests as yet, so consequently I've gotten no grades. But I'm coming along.

We got paid this week, and I got $45. So I suppose I'm all set financially, for the time being anyhow. Incidentally, I was 45 minutes late coming back from furlough, so I was put on a week's restriction, that is, no liberty at night, having to sign in at the N.C.O. "every hour on the hour." That's O.K., though; I won't spend so much money.

Leon is now at Miami Beach, taking pre-flight training.[25] I hope he makes out O.K. But I think he will.

Last week-end, four of us went to Danville and had dates at Averett college. We came back Sunday night, starting out at 10:30 hitch-hiking. We got stuck in Yanceyville, N.C. for four hours, and we just barely made reveille at 6:30. I almost froze to death! What a detail!

Am now rooming with Art Katz of Memphis, and Claude Kirk of Montgomery, Ala.[26] Both are transfers from Emory, and they're good guys.

Give my regards to Eliza. Write soon.

Your son,

Bill, jr.

24. Published as "The Long Dark Road" in the March 1944 issue of the *Archive* and first reprinted in *One and Twenty: Duke Narrative and Verse, 1924–1945* (Durham: Duke University Press, 1945), a collection of work by students in William Blackburn's writing seminars. The story is reprinted in appendix 3 of this volume.

25. Leon Edwards was a boyhood friend from Hilton Village with whom Styron kept in touch through college and into the early years of his married life. Leon is mentioned in the senior Styron's August 2, 1952, letter, published in appendix 1.

26. Claude Kirk eventually became governor of Florida (1967–1971). He was a candidate for the Republican presidential nomination after leaving office.

14. DUKE

[April 3, 1944]
Monday

Dear Pop,

Please excuse this stationery, but I'm writing this in Shakespeare class, which is a very boring class, so I reckon you'll understand.

Last weekend John Carson, Chet Stull, and I went up to Danville and dated at Averett college. We had quite a time. I have been dating this girl Doreen Stanley from Queens Village, L.I. She's 18 and very nice looking, intelligent, and her father is Sales Manager for National Distillers, Inc. (Old Grandad, Old Overholt, Wilson's, Black & White, etc.)! In these days of liquor rationing it might not hurt to date the daughter of a whiskey magnate! No kidding, we had a fine time up there. Stayed at a tourist home for $1.00 and ate at the college, which made things very inexpensive.

While I was up at the school, the girls put on a Palm Sunday musical service. It was very good, and I noticed especially a choral piece for women's voices entitled, "Look Homeward, Angel." It was taken from a chapter of the book by Thomas Wolfe and the music was arranged by a gentleman by the name of William Schuman. It was beautiful, and I was very surprised. Specifically, the passage was the one which begins: "A stone, a leaf, an unfound door; of a stone, a leaf, a door. And of all the forgotten faces. Naked and alone we came into exile. In her dark womb we did not know our mother's face, etc." It ends beautifully like this: "O waste of loss, in the hot mazes, lost, among bright stars on this most weary, unbright cinder, lost! Remembering speechlessly we seek the great forgotten language, the lost lane-end into heaven, a stone, a leaf, an unfound door. Where? When? . . . O lost, and by the wind grieved, ghost, come back again." Only the girls had to pervert the whole thought of the passage by inserting "O lamb of God" in the last line. That rather irritated me.[27]

The gym instructor really got rough with us this morning. We had hard calisthenics for forty minutes, which included push-ups, pull-ups, deep knee-bends. When we were all but completely exhausted, we had to climb a 30-foot vertical rope *twice*. But that wasn't all. *Then* we had to work out on the parallel bars for ten minutes. I was pretty well pooped out when we finished. But, as they say, "That's where they separate the men

27. Styron heard Schuman's *Prelude for Voices* (1939), the text for which was taken from the opening lines of Thomas Wolfe's *Look Homeward, Angel* (1929).

from the boys." If you don't completely pass out, I suppose you're a man.

I got a letter from Leon saying that he is now a Qualified Air Cadet. That's what he was aiming for, and he's pretty happy about it. Right now he's in the Base Hospital at Miami recovering from a cold. Nothing serious, he says.

I might have told you before, but I just finished reading Schopenhauer's "Studies in Pessimism." It's not very long, and it's very good, although I don't agree with or understand many of his ideas. I've started on Kant's Basic Thoughts, including "Critique of Pure Reason." I fear that this boy Kant is just a little bit too profound for yours truly. I may, however, be able to struggle through it.

We get paid tomorrow, and I'm really going to need it. I owe about $15, which won't leave me much from the $35, since we'll probably be compelled this month to pay the $5 athletic fee. But, that's the way it goes. "Always Broke" Styron, that's me!

My second *Archive* story will be published this week.[28] You said that you had entered a subscription, so it won't be necessary for me to send you a copy. It's not a bad story, but on the other hand it's not as good a story as I set out to write. I suppose, though, that no story is exactly what the author intended to write.

Is it okay if John Carson comes home with me on furlough? We don't plan to stay home more than two or three days, since we have a big party scheduled up in Urbanna.[29] This is planning right far ahead, I know (furlough begins 17 June), but I just wanted to know if it meets with your approval. Carson's father is a captain in the Navy and is commander of the U.S.S. Boston, probably based now at Kwajalein atoll. When Pearl Harbor came, he was operations officer for the southwest Pacific area, and sent the submarines and P.T. boats to Bataan to take off MacArthur and his staff. John's lived practically everywhere. He graduated from N.M.M.I., and went two years to the Univ. of New Mexico. Also he's a swell guy.[30]

---

28. "The Long Dark Road."

29. This would have been a party with friends from Christchurch, which is situated across Urbanna Creek from the town of Urbanna. Styron and his friends dated the "Urb girls" on weekends during their prep-school years.

30. The USS *Boston*, a heavy cruiser, earned ten battle stars in the Pacific war. Captain John H. Carson commanded her from August 1943 until June 1944. Kwajalein is an atoll in the Marshall Islands. Styron's friend attended New Mexico Military Institute in Roswell, New Mexico.

Well, I'd better close now. Give my love to Eliza, and write soon.

Your son,
Bill, jr.

15. DUKE

[June 13, 1944]
Tuesday

Dear Pop,

Well, exams are coming up starting Friday, and so I expect I'll have to be getting "on the drive." On Friday I have Physics, preceded tomorrow by a Mapping exam, which I will pass easy enough. No exams Thursday, Saturday, or Monday; my last two—Shakespeare and Math—are next Tuesday. I think I'm going to pass everything, or at least enough to get me by. However, I'm not sure. I'm up a tree, like I was last semester, and I can bank on nothing for certain. I know this—that I'll be here at Duke for one more semester, *if* I pass. If I don't, I'll go to San Diego. The same old story. It all rests, though, on whether I pass Math or not, and I'm pretty sure I'll be able to pass it, even if it is Analytic Geometry and tough as hell.

I'll be home on Wednesday, by myself, since John is staying for a couple days in Richmond. I'll get off from Wednesday until the 3rd of July, which makes about 12 days furlough. Don't make any plans for me, because I probably won't be home all the time. Peyton and Carson and I have decided to go to Urbanna the weekend of the 24th, and we might stay for a few extra days. If anything comes up to change my "sailing date," I'll wire you.

On Sunday two other marines and myself went over to Dr. Blackburn's house and listened to his records. Heard *Eroica* and Brahms' 1st. It was great.

Aunt Edith sent me $10 bucks for my birthday, which adds greatly to my bankroll.

Give my love to Eliza.

Your son,
Bill, Jr.

16. DUKE (Marine Corps stationery)

July 6, 1944

Dear Pop,

I'm all safely back at "dear old Duke" now, ready to pile into another semester's work. I'm sorry I didn't get to see you before I left, but I thought you were going to wake me up on Sunday morning. Anyway, I hope you had a good sail.

I had a fine time while I was at home, and had a good time also in Richmond. Capt. Carson had some business in Washington, so John and I went with him. We stayed with another Captain in Chevy Chase. We had a couple of dates with two WACs, and went to a night club Friday night—the Lotus—an opulent, gaudy Chinese "cabaret" on K street—which really cost us. However, we enjoyed it.

I'm taking three English courses this semester, namely, Victorian poetry, Romantic period literature, and 19th century prose. Also I'm taking a Religion course, Philosophy, and Physics (as usual). Although they aren't too easy, they shouldn't prove terribly rough. So I imagine I'll come through fine this semester.

When I get paid, I'm going to send you and Eliza part of the money I owe you.

Give my best regards to Eliza and write soon.

Your son,
Bill, jr.

17. DUKE

[ca. July 26, 1944]

Dear Pop,

Please excuse the long delay in correspondence. I've been rather busy of late. My three English courses have been keeping me on the ball. Not only do we have to read the prescribed text, but we also have to do outside reading and, while interesting, it eats up the time considerably.

I've just finished another story. It's real short, and while it's not nearly as good as I had hoped it would be, it is an incident taken from "early childhood" and might prove of some interest to you.[31] If I can find a large envelope I'll send it and the other short sketch I was telling you about to you.

31. "Sun on the River," published in the *Archive* issue for September 1944 and reprinted in appendix 3 of this volume.

I've just about decided not to write any more. Each time I sit down to write I usually have a good idea in mind, but the idea turns up flooie and the story consequently ends up in a lot of drivel.

In reading a biography of Wordsworth, the author mentions that in Wordsworth's village there were two thieves, very brutal characters. One was a doting old man of 90, the other was his grandson—aged 3. They would steal slyly hand in hand into the fruit market and stealthily steal all sorts of fruit and candies. Unknown to them, the villagers were watching their every move and, of course, instead of condemning them, looked upon their malefactions with gentleness and pity. As an idea for a story, I don't think this has ever been worked upon and, if I get sufficient incentive, I think I'll try my hand at it. I can think of no more touching or pathetic a scene.[32]

Things around here are about as usual. Eat, study, sleep.

I'm doing very well in all my subjects. Made a "B" in the last Physics quiz which, I think, will take me off the black list.

I'd better sign off now. Why don't you send me the plot of that story you were telling me about?

Give my love to Eliza.

Your son,
Bill jr.

18. DUKE

[ca. July 27, 1944]

Dear Pop,

I got your letter this morning, and agree with you that the plot has opportunities for greatness, if handled properly. However, there are a few very tough obstacles which must be eliminated. Since Mary, or "Jenny Field," as I have named her, is a female and the central character, and I'll have to handle the narrative from her point of view, it may prove extremely difficult to get the feeling of her character from the introspective male's point of view. Christopher Morley did it excellently in "Kitty Foyle," and I think I can do it too. I've started on the outline, and plan to do it in this manner: Make it a short novel of about 20,000 words

32. Styron likely read this tale in George McLean Harper's *William Wordsworth: His Life, Works, and Influence* (London: John Murray, 1916), 1:38. Wordsworth's poem "The Two Thieves, or The Last Stage of Avarice," published in the second edition of *Lyrical Ballads* (1800), is based on the story of the old man and the boy.

(about the length of "Goodbye, Mr. Chips"), dividing it into 10 chapters of approximately 2,000 words each. The story, as I see it, should fall into three parts, namely, (a) Jenny at home in Guinea, (b) her life, and the various conflicts that arise at the hospital, and (c) the finale in the South Pacific.[33]

But still more complications arise. In a novel of this sort, one must obey the certain rules of technicality which crop up. Not ever having been a nurse, or overseas, I would hesitate to describe life in either place. So I'll have to do some research. First, find out from Elizabeth the following things:

(1) How does a prospective nurse make application for a hospital career in nursing?

(2) What courses do the nurses take, and later, what specific courses would an anesthetist take? How long would all this take?

(3) How would a girl make application for becoming a Navy nurse?

(4) What are some of the duties of the student nurse, and of the Navy nurse?

The rest, I think, I can find out from the library and from my friends at Duke Hospital.

Right now, the plan as a whole seems to be taking good form in my mind, and I think that if I do a good job on it, work hard, it might turn out to be something. However, I won't know until I've finished it. I'll start on the first part, and you send me the information. With careful revision, it should be finished in a month and a half.

Thanks a lot for the idea, and I'll keep in touch with you as to my progress.

Your son,
Bill jr.

Ask Eliza to tell you of any typical classroom incidents which have reflected the general ignorance of a country girl. Please tell her also, that *anything* she can tell me about nurse training I can use.

33. Styron's attempt at a novel does not survive. Christopher Morley's *Kitty Foyle* was a 1939 best seller, told from the point of view of its title character, a young working-class woman from Philadelphia. Much of the text is rendered in interior monologue. *Kitty Foyle* was attacked by book critics and newspaper columnists for its frank treatment of sex and abortion. *Goodbye, Mr. Chips,* a popular 1934 novel by James Hilton, is a heartwarming story about a teacher at Brookfield Academy, a fictional English boys' boarding school. It was made into a film in 1939.

2 / November 1944–July 1945

PARRIS ISLAND, CAMP LEJEUNE, QUANTICO

Soon after his arrival at Parris Island for Marine Corps boot camp in October 1944, Styron was called into the base dispensary and was told that his blood sample had tested positive for syphilis. Styron was confined to the urinary ward of the base hospital—known to the marines as "the clap shack." He was kept there for a little over two weeks; he informed his father of his predicament via a long-distance telephone call. It turned out that Styron had trench mouth, probably caused by unsanitary conditions in the dining halls. The spirochete that causes trench mouth (Borrelia vincentii) *is almost identical in appearance under a microscope to the bacterium that causes syphilis* (Treponema pallidum). *While in the hospital Styron received an admonitory letter from Elizabeth Buxton Styron, his stepmother. The letter below, addressed to his father, should be read with that fact in mind. Styron wrote about the clap shack experience twice: first in the play* In the Clap Shack *(New York: Random House, 1973) and again in the personal essay "A Case of the Great Pox,"* New Yorker, *September 18, 1995, 62–75, reprinted in* Havanas in Camelot *(New York: Random House, 2008), 19–64.*

19. PARRIS ISLAND (Marine Corps stationery)

[November 25, 1944]
Saturday

Dear Pop,

I received your letter today, and was very glad to hear from you. I have not yet gotten the underwear, but I imagine that they will arrive in a day or two.

Today I fired the M-1 rifle for the first time, and I am now firmly convinced that it is without a doubt the finest small-bore weapon in the world. Its accuracy and power are unbelievable until you actually fire one. The M-1 has a chamber pressure of 32,000 lbs. per sq. inch, and yet it has a very slight recoil. It gives one almost a sense of exhilaration to fire one—the sense of power it gives you is uncanny. It is semi-automatic, and will fire as fast as the trigger is pulled (squeezed, I mean); it fires, extracts, ejects the cartridge, and reloads in 1/40 of a second. Of course by now we've learned the nomenclature and functioning backward and forward, but it is rather complicated. Even as complicated as it is, though, we can field strip completely and reassemble the rifle in less than a minute. Another interesting feature of the weapon is the fact that it not only fires a clip of eight rounds as fast as the trigger is pulled, but automatically ejects the empty clip after the eight rounds are fired. While I've gotten off to an excellent start, I think, in learning my positions, trigger squeeze, windage, etc., it's going to take quite a bit of practice before I can fire expert.

I'm glad you wrote me what you did in your last letter. Frankly, I was very worried when I was in the hospital for fear I had syphilis; and of course I was very relieved when I heard that the positive Kahn came as a result of trench mouth.[1] If I had had the disease, I wouldn't have known where it could have come from, for, although I'm not exactly what one could term an angel, I have always taken extreme precaution about what sort of women I went out with. Last night when I first started to write this letter, I wrote a couple of pages attempting to explain my views on the idea of morality. After rereading it, I tore it up because it really makes no difference to you or anyone else what my moral philosophy is. I'm probably not old enough to have such a philosophy. I know this for a fact, though—that the morality which we have in a so-called "moral" society is the weakest leg that civilization has to stand upon. The religion of the Church, which is the basis for morality, is a religion of hypocrisy, and each man should realize that the good life is a life of *Good Will*, a life of Love and Loneliness (as Thomas Wolfe would say), and not the fanatical adherence to a Book, most of which is

---

1. This laboratory test, developed by the immunologist Reuben Leon Kahn (1887–1979), was the standard test for syphilis in the 1940s. It was quicker to perform than the Wassermann test but often yielded false positive results.

a gruesome melange of cruelty and pagan cosmology. The Bible begins with the fantastic story of Adam and Eve, continues through countless bloody anecdotes of "religious" warfare, torture, and human sacrifice, and ends with St. John's laudanum dream of an absurd and impossible Apocalypse. In parts the Bible is a literary masterpiece. Nothing finer has been written than the story of Job and the sermon of Ecclesiastes, and I believe that if Christ was not the son of God, he approached such a divine kinship as nearly as any man ever born. But it is impossible for me to cling to a Faith which attempts, and succeeds in too many cases, in foisting upon the multitude a belief in so much which is utter fantasy. And it is such a religion which, throughout its history of corruption and strife, has promulgated its own standard for morality behind a thin veil of cant and hypocrisy. I have my own personal religion, *and* I believe that I am as steadfast in it as any one of our Baptist Fundamentalists. I am far from believing with George Santayana that religion is the "opiate of the poor"; but I do believe that an overdose of religious activity, in which people tend to take the syrupy tenets of the preacher and the vindictive dogmatisms of the Old Testament at face value, both deadens the mind and makes life a pretty sterile and joyless affair.[2]

I have probably not made myself very clear (which makes little difference), and I imagine you are not a little disappointed in knowing that your boy, after all those years of Sunday School, has not "turned out right"; but please don't think that I have sunk into the slough of degeneracy. I have never as yet done anything which I was really ashamed of. After the war I'm going to write a book and tell people what I think. Carlyle, I think it was, said that the real preachers are not those who stand behind the pulpit, but who sit behind a writing desk. In the meantime I'm going to keep on thinking, loving Life as much as I can in a world where the value of life is only the value of the lead in a .30 calibre bullet, and loving my fellow man (which the greatest Preacher said was the finest virtue of all).

Well, I hope you don't think what I've said sounds ostentatious for one who has not quite reached his 20th birthday. I might still be a college boy know-nothing with a sophomoric attitude, but I still think quite unreservedly that I have more understanding than quite a few people of my age.

2. Styron has in mind Karl Marx's maxim that religion is "the opium of the people," from his *Critique of Hegel's Philosophy of Right* (1843–44).

I won't be home for Christmas. I am now in the real Marine Corps, and there is no redundance of furloughs. When and if I get to Quantico, though, I think I'll be able to get home fairly often. I'm almost positive I'll get a furlough before I get shipped overseas.

I'd better close now. Please give Eliza my love, and I certainly hope she's feeling better by now.

Your son,
Bill jr.

20. PARRIS ISLAND (Marine Corps stationery)

[December 31, 1944]
New Year's Eve

Dear Pop,

Please excuse the delay in correspondence, but we've really been busy lately. All during the past week we practiced for record day—which we fired on Friday. I don't know yet whether I qualified or not. I fired left-handed, because of my weak right eye, and found that my left eye— none too strong—hindered my marksmanship considerably. However, I think that the boys pulling the targets might have given me enough extra points to qualify.[3]

I enjoyed Christmas very much—thanks to the swell box you all sent me. This pen, as you can see, writes excellently—and I appreciate it very much. Aunt Edith sent me a check, as did Aunt Adelaide and Aunt Juliet. Hugh and Melissa sent me a couple of extra fine handkerchiefs.[4] Considering everything, it was a nice Yuletide season for me, and I hope it was the same for you.

We leave the Range tomorrow for the Main Base, and we are due at New River next week. I think that I will be accepted for Japanese Language

3. Styron had a congenital cataract that blurred the vision in his right eye (his shooting eye). The condition, in the 1940s, could not be corrected by lenses or surgery. In order to pass the vision test at the induction center for the Marine Corps in February 1943, he had cheated by memorizing the eye chart as he waited in line to take the exam. He learned to fire the M-1 rifle left-handed, but the weapon—designed for right-handers— ejected the spent shell almost into the eye of a left-handed shooter. This defect in Styron's vision would later lead to a medical discharge from the Marine Corps during the Korean War. See *William Styron: A Life*, 90, 198–99.

4. Aunt Edith is identified in letter 9. The other names in this passage belong to members of his father's family.

New Years Eve

Dear Pop,

Please excuse the delay in correspondence, but we've really been busy lately. All during the past week we practiced for record day – which we fired on Friday. I don't know yet whether I qualified or not. I fired left-handed, because of my weak right eye, and found that my left eye – none too strong – hindered my marksmanship considerably. However, I think that the boys pulling the targets might have given me enough extra points to qualify.

I enjoyed Christmas very much – thanks to the swell box you all sent me. This pen, as you can see, writes excellently – and I appreciate it very much. Aunt Edith sent me a check, as did

Styron to his father, December 31, 1944, from boot camp at Parris Island. Courtesy Estate of William C. Styron, Jr.

School, which is now at Lejeune. I certainly hope so, because I think I would like the work of an interpreter. It is a hell of an intensive course of 10 weeks, after which the "graduates" are immediately assigned to Intelligence units. So, if things work out right, I'll be talking to the Japs before Summer.

Well, I've got to start packing. Thanks again for the pen, and give my best to everybody.

Your son,
Bill, jr.

21. PARRIS ISLAND

[January 1945]

Dear Pop and Eliza,
Enclosed you will find a rather belated Xmas present. Anyway, I hope that it will help make your post-war trip to "the ruins of Germany" more enjoyable.

Love,
Billy
(*Pfc.* in one week)

22. PARRIS ISLAND (Marine Corps stationery)

February 14, 1945

Dear Pop,
I received your letter, and letters of recommendation, and also the long letter you wrote me—which came belatedly through the devious channels of the Marine Corps mail system.

I especially enjoyed the letter you wrote me—the one in which you enclosed the letter from Mr. Fleet. Naturally I was very happy to learn that my story was accepted so favorably by the Virginia Writers' Club, and I am only sorry that my inevitable redundance of adjectives kept me from winning the prize.[5] However, it is almost impossible for me to

5. Styron's father had entered one of his son's manuscripts in a short-story competition organized by the Virginia Writers Club. The manuscript was praised by the judges but was disqualified for exceeding the word limit announced in the contest rules. The senior Styron compiled three scrapbooks of memorabilia relating to his son's life and donated them to Duke University Library in 1967. The letter from Beverley Fleet, chair of the judges' panel, dated January 8, 1945, is pasted into the first of these scrapbooks.

become what you termed *swellheaded* over any of my so-called literary achievements. Although I'm no scholar, I have read enough to know that my stories are very insignificant compared to what people have written, are writing, and what I myself would one day like to write. Especially during wartime, as I am beginning to find out, the futility of writing, art, of most everything—becomes more apparent. As you said, there is a story around every corner, and I see a million potential stories around me all the time. Now the crux of the situation lies in the fact that, to the writer, war is a gigantic, inexorable, relentlessly terrible panorama which, although at every hand fraught with mists of beauty and pathos, swirls about him so swiftly and chaotically that he is unable to find a tongue to utter his thoughts. And after the war, if he has extricated himself from the whole mess with a sound mind and body, he is usually so terribly cynical and embittered that those golden words turn to dust. To be platitudinous, it changes one's viewpoint immensely. Like Wolfe's Eugene Gant I see "Time, dark time, flowing by me like a river"—and that is all one can say. I intend to write some more, whenever I get a chance. That story that you have an idea for sounds very interesting, and I would like to hear the details.

Whenever I get a chance I'm going to write to Mr. Fleet and thank him for his kind words. I was astounded at the impressive array of judges who liked the story, and until I read Mr. Fleet's letter I had no idea what competition I was up against. I also enjoyed Eliza's letter, and please tell her I will write at length when I find time.

My application for O.C. has not gone through as yet, and I am still in a state of confusion.[6] This company is due to ship out for California (dread word!) sometime around the 23rd of this month, and I fully expect to ship out with everyone else, unless a miracle happens. I'm sure that, with a little prodding, the application would go through and be accepted (since I passed the physical), but at present it is lying dormant somewhere in the sergeant-major's office—while the hour of departure fast approaches! I don't mind going to the West Coast and points beyond if I am definitely out of O.C., but I fear that all is lost if I get to San Diego without having had any action taken on the application while I was here at Lejeune. If you have any friends who are friends of Forrestal or any of the other Navy-Marine Corps gods, it certainly wouldn't

6. OC: officer candidacy.

hurt to give them the word, as I am beginning to think that I have been kicked around enough.[7]

If we are all not restricted to the base this week-end, I will try my very best to get up to see you. It may be the last time for quite awhile, so I will try and get a pass. If I do get off, I'll wire you beforehand, giving time of arrival, etc.

Well, I had better close now. Again, I appreciate the fine letter; and that "pardnership of Styron and Styron" is okay with me! Please write soon, and love to all.

Your son,
Bill

P.S. You should have seen me throwing TNT grenades today. Quite a thrill!

23. CAMP LEJEUNE (Marine Corps stationery)

March 8, 1945

Dear Pop and Eliza,

I received your letters a few days ago, and—as usual—enjoyed them very much. Since I've arrived in O.C. my letters (outgoing) have been very few—mainly because I find it extremely hard to get the time to squeeze any correspondence in.

Today was a typical day—let me give you an idea:

We got up at 5:00, swabbed and cleaned the barracks, and after breakfast at 6:00 we put on packs and rifles, got into trucks, and went out into the swamp. Out there we studied defensive combat for four hours—which means we did nothing but dig foxholes; dig, dig, dig! At 11:30 we knocked off for chow—which means we ate K rations. K rations are the most vile tasting replicas of food ever devised. I had a "dinner" unit—as differentiated from "breakfast" and "supper." The "dinner" unit, as do the other two units, comes in a waxed cardboard box about 7" × 2" × 2". It contains, to wit, one small can of cheese; two packs of horrible tasting vitaminized biscuits; one packet of lemon extract which, when mixed in a canteen, produces a fluid which tastes somewhat like paregoric; a package of bone-dry pellets which ostensibly

7. James V. Forrestal (1892–1949), secretary of the navy from 1944 until 1947, is credited with organizing naval battle groups around aircraft carriers during the Pacific war.

contain life-giving energy in the form of dextrose; one stick of chewing gum; and four Fleetwood cigarettes. After chewing the gum (the rest of the ration invariably goes into the campfire), we started hiking the five miles back to the barracks. Now the average fast marching rate for infantry troops on a level highway is 2½ miles per hour. So when I say that we covered 5 miles of rough, sandy terrain in 1 hour and 7 minutes, you may imagine how we felt when we arrived back here. To top that off, we double-timed the last quarter-mile! It's pretty cold here, but I was soaked through to my dungaree jacket from sweat—I mean perspiration. That was just the beginning. As soon as we got back we had to fall out for classes. These classes ran for three hours—from two until five—and covered English, Estimate of the Situation, and Leadership. Then one hour for supper, and two more hours tonight of mapreading.

Outside of the above-described daily schedule—everything's quite okay. We get off-base liberty this Saturday, and another ex-Duke marine and myself are planning to go to Durham. We *might* get a couple days' leave on Easter. If so, I'll try to get up to N. News. Its been since July when I was home last, and I certainly would like to get a little furlough.

I'd better sign off now, as I only have fifteen minutes before lights out. Another big day tomorrow out in the field. Schedule: offensive combat under simulated gas attack. Lots of laughs!

Don't forget to write soon.

Love,
WCS, jr.

24. CAMP LEJEUNE (Marine Corps stationery)

April 15, 1945
Sunday

Dear Pop and Eliza,
I received both of your letters recently, and also Helen's nice note; and I'm glad that everything is going well at Styron Manor.[8]

8. Helen Buxton was Elizabeth Buxton's sister. Helen was mentally retarded; she served as the model for a preliminary rendering of Maudie Loftis in *Inheritance of Night*, an early version of *Lie Down in Darkness*. See the facsimile edition of the surviving typescripts, *Inheritance of Night: Early Drafts of "Lie Down in Darkness,"* ed. James L. W. West III (Durham: Duke University Press, 1993).

Things are still rough here, and as you suspected, getting rougher and rougher. We had four days in the field this past week. Monday we marched out to the demolitions area, a distance of 12 miles, to watch a demonstration of high explosives. They set off 100 pounds of TNT in a small pond about 25 yards from where we were sitting, and the entire pond—mud, water, and all—came pouring down on us. It was terrific. Later we made and threw TNT grenades. The march back was hot, fast, dirty, and extremely arduous—since we double-timed the last mile.

Tuesday we made a "bridgeless stream crossing" with packs and rifles. The stream was about 25 yards wide, and deep. We crossed it tactically—which means that we crossed it as we would under actual combat conditions. I was fire-team leader of the first squad, so I was the first man across. I never swam so hard in all my life, since the extra 30 pounds I was carrying didn't help buoy me up at all. My rifle got wet and muddy, so the ramrod you sent me helped quite a bit when I finally got back to the barracks (the ramrod, by the way, is very fine, and I thank you a lot).[9]

Friday we ran the obstacle course, and I fell off of a log and got wet again. It's amazing that none of us have any broken bones! Here's a diagram of the course (looking down):

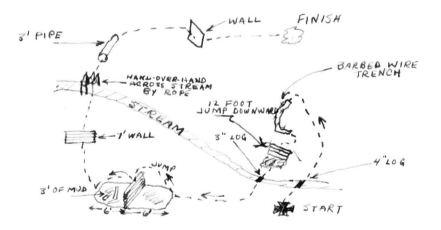

9. Styron means a cleaning rod for his rifle. He suffered an injury to his neck during this training exercise when he was caught beneath a cable stretched across the stream. The injury caused a slow deposit of calcium in his neck and eventually required an operation, during his seventies, to relieve pain in his neck and right arm.

Everyone was shocked to hear that President Roosevelt died. The flags, of course, are all at half mast, and on Saturday afternoon in the beer hall there was a five minute period of silence. Even though it was a great loss, I have a feeling that Truman might make a good president.

You perhaps read of the death of Maj.-Gen. Maurice Rose in Germany, killed by German machine gunners as he surrendered his troops.[10] Well, his son is in my platoon, so it was of special interest to us. His son took it pretty well, though, since there was nothing he could do.

We have another hard week ahead of us—mess duty. It's very tiresome work, I hear, but we have no classes or field work, for which I am thankful.

I expect that I'll be going to Quantico in another five weeks; so perhaps I'll be able to see you all and Aunt Edith at the same time. I hope so.

Write soon.

Love to all,
WC jr.

25. QUANTICO (Marine Corps stationery)

May 24, 1945

Dear Pop and Eliza,

Well, I'm finally an honest-to-goodness, bona fide Officer Candidate. It's taken two years, but I'm finally at the real "Quantico."

We came over from the refresher school yesterday, and started our classes today. The course looks pretty hard, but with some luck I think I can make it. We have a platoon leader who seems to be a pretty nice guy, and I don't think he'll be too hard on us. If everything goes all right I'll get my commission on the 12th of September but, to reverse a metaphor, a lot of water has to flow under the bridge before then. We went down to the PX last night and got fitted for officers' uniforms. They're very pretty, but it seems that one has to be an heir to an asbestos fortune to pay for a complete outfit. An entire set—the minimum requirement (green suit, khaki suit, and overcoat)—costs $270. The government gives you a $260 uniform allowance, but doesn't seem to account for the various accessories—caps, shoes, bars, belts, ornaments, etc.—which must come from each new officer's own pocket.

---

10. General Rose, commander of the Third Armored Division, was killed in Paderborn, Germany, on March 31, 1945, while attempting to surrender to a German tank commander.

I received the shirts and found them in good order. The collars were a bit wrinkled, but I ironed them out quickly, since the Corps kindly provides each barracks with five or six irons. Thanks a lot for getting the chevrons sewed on for me, as it would have taken me quite a while to get them done on my own hook.

I'm planning to come down to Newport News again on the weekend after this (the 2nd of June)—that is, if its okay with you all. I want to bring a friend, and I'll be sure to let you know this time what hour I'll be in.

I'd better close now. My address is on the envelope, so write soon. Love to all.

Your son,
Bill S. jr.

26. QUANTICO (Marine Corps stationery)

[June 12, 1945]
Tuesday

Dear Pop,

Thought I'd write a line and let you know how everything is, and that I made it back to Quantico okay after the nice visit with the "folks."

We had a very busy week last week, and this one wasn't, or isn't much better. We covered the Browning Automatic Rifle in three days— quite a feat—and have started on the Browning Machine Gun. As I told you before we don't have quite as rough a time here physically, but the mental strain is pretty arduous. The Marine Corps seems to have a penchant for throwing seven or eight consecutive hours at you, all on one and the same subject—which isn't such a good idea.

I had a swell time while I was home weekend before last. It was good just to relax, eat some real home cooking for a change, and just take things easy in general. Tell Eliza that she's an A-1 cook in my opinion, and also in other respects she's A-1.

Went to Washington last weekend, and had a pretty good time. The beer in D.C. has this Marine Corps brew beat a dozen ways.

I haven't received the shirts yet, but rather expect that they'll get here soon—that is, if you've sent them yet. I sure hope they arrive pretty quick, as my wardrobe is running low.

I was color bearer in the parade yesterday, and as we were walking past the Ordnance School somebody spoke my name, and it was Buddy

Hayes. Told him out of the corner of my mouth that I'd see him tonight. He's the tallest man in the Marine Corps, I do believe.[11]

Well, I'd better close now. I'll try and get down to see you again in a couple of weekends, but will let you know first.

Love to all,

Your son,
WCS jr

27. QUANTICO (MARINE CORPS STATIONERY)

[June 25, 1945]
Monday

Dear Pop,

It's been quite a while since I wrote last, which must be laid to the fact that things are pretty busy now.

We're still out at Camp Barrett, having completed one half of our bivouac—the whole thing lasting two weeks.[12] Last week was taken up entirely with the Machine Gun—Range Firing, Technique of Fire, Fire Orders, Tactics. I flunked my first test, which isn't too bad, since most everybody has flunked at least one. The week before that we fired 60 and 81 mm mortars, which is just about the only weapon I've ever seen that I like. When I go overseas I'd like to get into a mortar section.

As to how I'm "making out," I don't know. I don't think I'm deficient, although I might have been put on the list since the last one came out. I certainly hope I get to stay here the whole 16 weeks, since one doesn't find liberty (week-end) like this many other places in the Corps. Getting a commission doesn't mean too much to me, although I would like to get the bars.

This coming week will be taken up in Scouting and Patrolling (Snooping and Pooping), and from all reports it's pretty rough. We have two all-night compass marches, which are not designed to make the troops too happy. On Wednesday 50 civilians are coming out here to

11. Buddy Hayes, who stood six feet six inches in height, was a friend from Styron's boyhood in Hilton Village. Buddy's mother, Sally Cox Hayes, taught Styron to read before he entered the first grade. He stayed with the Hayes family during his mother's final illness in the spring and summer of 1939.

12. Camp Barrett, a separate training facility for officer candidates, is located eleven miles west of the main base at Quantico.

stay for a week. I don't know who they are, except that they're moving one of us out of each tent to make room for them. I think they're social workers or congressmen, or industrialists or somebody who just wanted to see how rugged this Marine O.C. can be. They'll find out, by god.

Next weekend we're restricted to the Camp for "Potomac Watch," an anachronism now, since it was designed early in the war to protect Washington from a Nazi U-boat invasion. But they sell beer out here, so it won't be too bad.

Write soon, and give my love to Eliza.

Your son,

WCS jr

28. QUANTICO (MARINE CORPS STATIONERY)

July 9, 1945

Dear Pop,

I received Eliza's letter Saturday telling about Uncle Al and your being sick.[13] It certainly wasn't a very joyous 4th of July for you, but I hope you're up and feeling okay by now.

I am doing pretty well, and think that I have safely passed my first eight-week "semester," which means that all I'll have to do is keep my nose clean for eight more weeks and I might conceivably become a lieutenant. The classes and tests are becoming tougher, but the situation is of course alleviated by the weekend liberty in D.C. I have been dating a girl in Washington, Barbara Taeusch, who used to be with me in Blackburn's class at Duke.[14] We get along very well together. You may rest assured that I'm not spending my money in the wrong way when I say that last weekend my largest expended sum was $5.50, which I spent in buying this young lady an album of records—Brahms' 1st Symphony, to be specific.

Most of our time is being spent in the field these days. We are studying the Rifle Squad in Attack and we execute practical work in the form of Troop Leading Exercises. Whoever is selected to lead each exercise acts as squad leader, issues his orders, and proceeds to take a woods,

13. Al Styron, a paternal uncle.

14. Barbara "Bobbie" Taeusch was Styron's first serious love. They continued their romance in New York, after graduation from Duke, but decided finally not to marry. See *William Styron: A Life*, 105, 108, et passim.

house, or hill full of Japs. The leader usually has two or three courses of action, but gets graded badly if he doesn't get the preferred solution of Marine Corps Schools. Buddy Hayes was a Jap sniper the other day (he's now in Training Battalion) and I think he took a few pot shots at me. I talked to him during chow time and he told me where all the guys were, Joe Lawson, Pete Preston, et al.[15]

There's not much other news that I can think of. I hope to get home in a couple of weekends, if we get out early enough.

Write soon, and give my best to Eliza and Helen.

Your son,
WCS jr

15. Boyhood friends from Hilton Village.

3 / March 1946–March 1948

DUKE AND NEW YORK

Styron completed his training at Quantico and, in late July 1945, was commissioned a second lieutenant in the Marine Corps. Had the war continued he would likely have participated in the assault on mainland Japan. On August 6 and 9, however, nuclear bombs were dropped on Hiroshima and Nagasaki. Japan surrendered a few days later. Styron was given temporary duty as commander of a guard platoon at the naval prison on Hart's Island in Long Island Sound. He completed his duty there in November and was discharged from the Marine Corps in Portsmouth, Virginia, in December. No letters from Styron to his father survive from this period; when he returned to Duke in March 1946 he resumed the correspondence.

29. DUKE

March 8, 1946
Box 4571, Duke Sta.

Dear Pop,

I just now went down and got the money order, which I appreciate very much. I will attempt to keep track of all my expenditures. For two days I was flat broke, but borrowed a few dollars from a friend of mine, Ben Williamson, who is a medical student here.

My trunk just got here, too. They held it for some time—why, I don't know—down in Durham. So all last week I slept on a bare mattress (which I've done many times before) and used my overcoat for a blanket. I presume that I have a roommate—most of his clothes are on an empty bed and the man at the rooming office told me I had a roommate—but he certainly hasn't showed up yet.

I spent my first night here with Prof. Blackburn, and the next day he helped me make out my course card. He advised me to take the minimum number of subjects, so that I may have time to write on my novel. He's fully expecting me to write one, it seems; and although I want to—and probably will—I don't see *now* one in the offing. However I'm going to start pitching in and see if I can't finish one in six or eight months.

I'm taking Russian history, Psychology, Geology, and—of course—Composition under Prof. Blackburn.[1] The Russian course and Psychology both look very interesting, and the Geology—for a science—doesn't look too hard.

Duke is the same old Duke, full of vacuous looking Long Island *nouveaux riches,* and odd-looking persons, dressed exquisitely in the latest in male and female fashions, who, I surmise, are here because they couldn't get into Princeton or Vassar. It's a shame, I think, that the current situation prevents me from going to Columbia or U.N.C., but I don't suppose it will be too bad here.

I find that I only know two or three people here—mostly medical students whom I knew at Davidson—but, if my present judgement is correct, I don't care to know too many of these noisy oafs.

There are three things which I wish you would try and find for me. First, a desk lamp. Duke, naturally, doesn't provide a study lamp. Also a record player and typewriter. I don't necessarily need a typewriter (for I can't type) but I do need the lamp. If you can also find a second-hand record player combination, it would be fine, for I really feel the need of good music at times.

Write me a letter. Take care of yourself, and give my best to Eliza and Helen.

Your son,
WCS jr

1. The "Composition" course with Blackburn was a seminar in creative writing.

30. DUKE

[May 6, 1946]
Monday

Dear Pop,

I am enclosing a notice from the Dean's Office which was sent to all students in reference to entrance here next Fall. As you can see, it will be necessary to pay the $25 fee—which will be refunded to veterans—or else one loses all right to a reservation.

Please send me a check for that amount before May 10. Although it's true I might get into Carolina, I still don't think I'd better take any chances, do you?[2] Professor Blackburn, anyway, has suggested that I sweat it out here at Duke for another semester—since that's all I'll have to go. He said that the very fact that I dislike Duke might be a greater incentive toward my finishing the "novel," since if I went over to Carolina the atmosphere might be too distracting. I think perhaps he's right.

I got a letter from Crown Publishers today, which is headed by Hiram Haydn, ex-professor of English at W.C.U.N.C. Blackburn wrote him about my projected book, and Mr. Haydn wrote in return that he'd be glad to read it when I finished it. So, with Rinehart, that makes two publishing houses that I know will at least give the ms. consideration.[3]

I'm not progressing too fast on the ms., but I don't mind since I think it's best to take my time. It'll probably take a year or more, including this summer.

I received the $65 and the clippings, both of which I appreciate very much.

Give my best to Eliza and Helen.

Your son,
Bill jr.

2. Styron thought briefly of finishing his degree at the University of North Carolina in Chapel Hill (Thomas Wolfe's university, it will be remembered), but he decided to remain at Duke.

3. Blackburn had sent copies of *One and Twenty*, the anthology of writing by his students, to various editors in New York, including Hiram Haydn, with whom he had become friendly while Haydn taught English at the "Women's College" of the University of North Carolina in Greensboro—which Styron refers to here as "W.C.U.N.C." Two of Styron's stories ("Autumn" and "The Long Dark Road") were included in the anthology. This promotional activity by Blackburn brought Styron a letter of inquiry from John Selby, an editor at Rinehart who had visited Duke earlier to talk to the students in

31. DUKE

June 9, 1946
Sunday

Dear Pop,

I received the Concerto Friday and have played it a few times on a record player I borrowed and it sounds very good. I'm going to take it around to the Blackburns' tomorrow and I'm sure they'll like it. I saw Dr. Blackburn yesterday and we had a short talk. He seems to have enjoyed your visit last weekend very much and told me to tell you to come and see them again if you're down this way again.

I'm having two stories typed now—"Autumn" and the one in the last issue of the *Archive*—which I'm going to send to Middlebury College as part of my application for the Bread Loaf Writers' Conference in August. I'm pretty sure I'll be accepted, as long as their enrollment isn't too full already.

This coming week is the last week of classes this semester. Exams start next Monday and I leave the following Friday. I don't know what my grades will be yet but I'm pretty sure of two or three "A's," which should boost my record somewhat. As I told you, I am going to N.Y. with Jack Smith. I think I'll have enough money to make the trip, but if I find that I'm running short I'll let you know and you can relay some extra cash.

Bobbie hasn't written me since I told her I was coming up, but I imagine she'll be there that weekend. Women, I have found, are very unreliable when it comes to writing letters—unreliable about a lot of things. I can't figure them out.

When you get this letter, I'll be 21 and a MAN.[4] Write soon.

Your son,
Bill jr.

---

the writing classes. And a letter arrived from Haydn, who was then an editor at Crown. Haydn would become Styron's mentor at the New School and his editor for *Lie Down in Darkness,* published by Bobbs-Merrill in 1951.

4. Styron turned twenty-one on June 11, 1946.

32. DUKE

[June 10, 1946]
Monday A.M.

Dear Pop,

I received your letter and telegram, both of which I enjoyed very much. In regard to your encouraging telegram, I can only say that I don't know how "gigantic" a stature I can ever realize, but I hope I will always have the assiduousness and will-power to learn, and to work toward doing the very best I can. As each day goes by I acquire more and more introspection into my own make-up, and I know that I have many faults and weaknesses—some of them very bad—but I hope to fight toward conquering these weak spots and foibles to the best of my ability. It's a hard job, but I can succeed.

I have two more exams, and then I leave for New York; but I'll be back on the 26th or 27th. It will certainly be a pleasure to see Aunt Edith again, won't it? It's really been a long time . . .

I don't know what I'm going to do for the remainder of the summer—outside of going to Middlebury—but if I stay at home I fully expect to establish for myself a definite schedule for reading and writing. By establishing such a schedule I'll go at least part of the way toward conquering my chief fault—*laziness.*

I wish you would send me $25 for the trip before this Friday P.M., as I may need some extra money. I think I'll have enough money anyway, but I would like to have $25 "just in case." In case I don't use it, I'll return it. I'll see you soon. Give my best to everyone.

Your son,
Bill jr.

In July 1946 Styron sailed to Trieste as a deck hand on the Cedar Rapids Victory, *a cargo vessel carrying livestock to Yugoslavia on a postwar relief mission. His story "A Moment in Trieste," based on this experience, is reprinted in appendix 3 of this volume. When he returned in August, Styron attended the Bread Loaf Writers' Conference in Vermont for two weeks. No letters are extant for these months; Styron began writing again to his father when he returned to college in the fall.*

33. DUKE

October 21, 1946

Dear Pop,

It'll be necessary to send in with my application for the Rhodes Scholarship State committee (I passed the local board) (a) a *statement* certified by you before a notary public that I was born on June 11, 1925, and (b) the names of *two* citizens who can attest to my character, sobriety, virtue, and all that sort of thing. I don't have to have the statements, but merely the *names* of two reputable and fairly prominent people who will be *willing* to write a short panegyric if called upon by the Committee. However, I have to have the application in by November 2nd, so please send these to me as soon as possible. My chances are mighty slim in getting anything out of this deal, but I don't suppose it'll hurt to try.[5]

I've still got some money left from the check you sent me, but not much. My check from the V.A. will undoubtedly not get here until the first of next month, food still costs $1.50 a day, and Bobbie is coming down on Nov. 2 for the homecoming game. Please send me $15 with the letter, as I fear I shall be in desperate straits before the end of the month. At that, I'll probably have to ask for more if my Veterans' check doesn't come before Bobbie gets here.[6]

I'm fed up, disgusted, and totally out of sorts with Duke University and formal education in general, for that matter, and I hardly see why I'm taking a crack at this Rhodes scholarship when I'm such an execrable student. Only the fact that this is my last semester keeps me from packing up and leaving.

I've come to the stage when I know what I want to do with my future. I want to write, and that's all, and I need no study of such quaint American writers as Cotton Mather or Philip Freneau—both of whom we are studying in American Lit—to increase my perception or outlook on literature and life. For a person whose sole burning ambition is to write—like myself—college is useless beyond the Sophomore year. By that

5. Blackburn, who had been a Rhodes Scholar and who was on the selection committee for the state of North Carolina, was urging Styron to apply. See Styron's reminiscence "Almost a Rhodes Scholar," in *This Quiet Dust and Other Writings*, rev. ed. (New York: Vintage, 1993): 317–22.

6. Styron finished his degree under the G.I. Bill, which paid college expenses and provided fifty dollars a month in pocket money for unmarried veterans of the war. Styron's monthly checks were issued to him from the Veterans Administration.

time he knows that further *wisdom* comes from reading men like Plato and Montaigne—*not* Cotton Mather—and from getting out in the world and *living.* All of the rest of the scholarship in English literature is for pallid, prim and vapid young men who will end up teaching and devoting 30 years of their sterile lives in investigating some miserably obscure facet of the life of a minor Renaissance poet. Sure, scholarship is necessary, but its not for me. I'm going to write, and I'll spend the rest of my days on a cattle-boat or jerking sodas before I'll teach.

So far, though, I'm making good grades and I hope to get out of here *soon.*

Give my best to everybody,

Your son,
Bill jr

34. DUKE

December 15, 1946

Dear Pop,

I have a short story to tell you. It's not an altogether happy story, but in some respects it's pretty successful and encouraging. It happened this way: last Thursday I, along with three other guys from Duke, went over to Chapel Hill to go before the State Rhodes Scholarship Committee. The competition was stiff; there were 18 very bright boys over there, most of them Phi Beta Kappa, and all of them exceedingly well "on the ball." But I was elected from that group, with two others (one from Davidson, the other from U.N.C.), to go to Atlanta for the District, and final, committee. I thought that for me to be elected at the State board was incredible, but it seems that—along with all my qualifications—I made a good personal impression. So that night, or rather early Friday morning, I got on a plane at the Raleigh-Durham airport and flew to Atlanta. I arrived there at about 8:00 Friday morning and slept all day, then went to a movie that night. On Saturday morning the committee met at the Atlanta Biltmore Hotel, and I again was interviewed and, as was intimated later by one of the committee members, I comported myself very well.

But after waiting all day (in a perfect agony of uneasiness) I found out that I didn't make it. However, this has its brighter aspect. There were 18 again, from the Southeast, who were interviewed. Six of these were elected by the committee, after the interviews, in a 2-hour long private session. After the results were announced, Dr. Harvie Branscomb, who was on the committee and is now president of Vanderbilt Univ. after having been head of the Duke Divinity School, took me aside and informed me that during the 2-hour discussion the committee had, fully one-half of the time was taken up discussing me and my merits, faults, and potentialities.[7] It was, he said, a toss-up between myself and a fellow from Florida, and they finally decided to give it to him instead of to me because of the three very black "F's" which I received in Physics. This fact was corroborated, too, by another committee member after the session. So, though it's somewhat disappointing, I think you can see that the whole thing is in the nature of a moral victory. I was also encouraged very definitely by the committee to try again if I ever go to Graduate School and boost my marks. And upon coming back to Durham today, Blackburn told me that I had made the best showing of any Duke man since 1930. So you may see that—against Phi Beta Kappa's and Ph.D.'s, M.A.'s and straight A averages—Styron didn't show up too badly.

That's the short story. What do you think of it? I wish you'd please inform Mr. Harrison and Mr. Ferguson of the results, and thank them for me for writing the letters of recommendation. They were, I'm sure, very helpful.

I think my own greatest debt of gratitude is to Dr. Blackburn. I've never seen such a kindly and charitable person. He drove me over to Chapel Hill for the meeting on Thursday, and I'm sure his presence on the committee helped immeasurably. When I learned that I was elected he not only lent me $40.00, but drove me all over town getting checks cashed. He also lent me a white shirt, a book, and drove me to the library to get another book. I'll never be able to repay him, although I, of course, will have to pay him the money as soon as possible. In this regard, I wish you'd take $50 out of my account and send it down here, either by special delivery air mail or wire, before Friday noon, which is when I leave for home. When I left for Atlanta I had $20, plus the $40 that Blackburn gave me. The plane fare was $20, train fare back $10, and I spent about $15 for hotel, meals, etc., which leaves me $15.

7. Branscomb was chancellor of Vanderbilt University from 1945 until 1963. Styron sent an inscribed copy of *Lie Down in Darkness* to him after the novel was published, and Branscomb responded with a letter of congratulation on October 30, 1951. The letter is among Styron's papers at Duke.

The Rhodes committee is going to reimburse me for transportation, but I suppose (as with my other check) I won't be getting it until after Christmas. But I do want to pay Blackburn back as soon as possible, so please send it *tout de suite*.

I'll be home probably sometime in the small hours of Saturday morning, as I think I'll be taking the Norfolk and Western which gets into Richmond at 11:00 P.M. and from Richmond will take the bus. Then a taxi out to the house.

Don't forget to thank Mr. Ferguson and Mr. Harrison and tell them I did better than I expected.

Your son,
Bill jr.

Styron was awarded his degree from Duke at the end of the winter term of 1947. He enrolled briefly in the graduate program in English but after only a few weeks decided to withdraw. In March he wrote to tell his father of his decision.

35. DUKE

[March 2, 1947]

Dear Pop,

Of making many books there is no end, and much study is a weariness of the flesh.[8] Therefore, taking a sudden and rather desperate inspiration from Ecclesiastes, and from mine own turbulent mind which for quite some time has been rebelling against the academic cloister—such as one may call a cloister at Duke—I have decided to throw it all up and go elsewhere for my wisdom. In other words—I should be blunt—I'm leaving Duke as soon as I settle my affairs.

There is, I think, little need for rationalization. After four trying years of college I finally have my degree (an end, I think, in itself) and I can only foresee a modicum of knowledge to be gained from three stretched-out and ineffectual months at Duke. I am doing nothing here now but boring myself, drinking beer, and wasting time better wasted somewhere else. Duke, as you know, in all of its aspects, has pained me

---

8. Ecclesiastes 12:12.

to a certain degree always, and I have only been happy in this environment through a suspension of reason and through the utmost exertion of will. Consequently, having obtained the much sought-for sheepskin, I see little reason why I should irritate myself any longer. In short, I quite frankly think that I'm wasting my time now in, for the most part, unattractive surroundings and that—though my mental bewilderment and unrest is not contingent upon Duke alone—I should definitely begin to try my luck in another and perhaps more auspicious climate.

So I will be home sometime within a week—will wire you the exact time. I realize, as you do, that my being at home for any length of time is a rather nervous and uncertain business, so I hope you'll believe me when I say that I hope to get a job lined up elsewhere soon. I also hope, though, that it'll be all right if I can plan upon staying at home until I *do* get straightened out.

This move I am making—though I perhaps, egotistically, exaggerate its import—is not conventional and is, at the same time, an important decision. But it is not impetuous. I have given it good thought.

Without, I believe, having approached the neurotic stage, my mind is in as much a ferment as it ever has been or ever shall. Though the seer saith "The Kingdom of God is within thee," I know I need a change of some sort; therefore I'm leaving Duke in the vague hope that in a different place—wherever that may be—I may gradually gain the perspicacity enough to sit me down and read and write, become mature in *mature surroundings,* and do those things which, undone, shall make me live only partially. I mean *writing,* a field in which I know I can become supreme if I can only develop the discipline and strength and love.

I'll see you soon and I hope I'll be able to explain things further. I'll see Dr. Blackburn tomorrow, who I'm sure will greet my decision with some dismay, and equivocal mumblings, and who will give me his dear and always cherished benediction.

Your son,
Bill

After a short stay in Newport News, Styron traveled to New York City in late March and, through John Selby, the editor at Rinehart who had written to him while he was at Duke, landed a position as a junior editor at Whittlesey House, the trade-book division of McGraw-Hill. A month into his job he came down with a case of hepatitis, probably from bad hygiene at one of the cheap New York restaurants he was patronizing. He was hospitalized for almost two weeks at the French Hospital on West 30th Street.

36. NEW YORK

[May 1947]
Saturday

Dear Pop,

I have just about recovered from my illness now; I'm up and around, and will be going back to work on Monday. The doctor informs me that I was lucky to have a very mild case, because the convalescence period for the average case is usually two or three months—enough to make anyone lose their job! As it is, the people at Whittlesey House have been very nice in telling me to stay in bed until I was completely well, and in bringing manuscripts every other day or so up to Bobbie's apartment for me to read. I've read a lot of interesting mss, but not one yet to really crow about. The novels are for the most part consistently bad and it's rather encouraging to me when I reflect that I can do 100 times better than 99% of them. I'm in the process now of writing a short story which, if it ever turns out all right, I'm going to try to market. Again I find writing an utterly exasperating process and I wish there was some easy way to accomplish it, but there isn't. I suppose it's a matter of trial and error, plugging and plugging, like anything else that brings results.

Bobbie's going away for the summer and will return sometime next fall, but in the meantime I plan to take over her apartment, since her roommate will be away too. I don't yet know exactly how things will work out, but I find my present room on 11th street a completely depressing affair and I know I'd go mad if I had to stay pent up there for long. I also don't plan to stay in N.Y. for the rest of my life, for many and obvious reasons, and I'm going to start angling around for a way to get to France or Italy, sometime next year, I hope. Such is not mere escapism, because I really feel that I should do my traveling in Europe when I'm young and it'll do me good. I still love the good old U.S.A., but I would, for a while, like to see a country completely free of neon, "Funlands," drugstores, and cheapness.

One interesting ramification of my illness is the fact that the doctor has forcefully suggested that I not drink more than a beer a day for the next few months—certainly no whiskey. I expect to follow his orders assiduously, since I don't want to go back to bed again, and I trust you approve.

A friend of mine here, Tom Hedges—recently graduated from Cornell Med. School—has a wife in the hospital and since Bobbie is away this weekend in Newport, R.I. visiting her brother, I've been spending the evenings at the hospital (N.Y. Hospital, 69th at the East River). Ann, Tom's wife, was operated on for a displaced disk in her spine and has recovered nicely, but has had an exasperating post-operative effect in that she has had complete urine retention for two weeks with no signs of let-up. She is, of course, catheterized, but Tom, being a doctor, is even more concerned than Ann, and I am his prop and bolster in these days of trial. Last week they had every bit of clothing stolen from them, which didn't help things any. Fortunately, they were covered by insurance.

I'm glad Eliza is up and around, and I hope you had a pleasant time out in W.Va.

Give my best to everyone, and write soon.

Your son,
WCS jr

37. NEW YORK (typed on Whittlesey House letterhead)

July 24, 1947

Dear Pop,

I received your letter and the check a few days ago, and enjoyed the letter and thank you for the check. I have put the money in a savings account at the Clinton Trust Company and I hope to augment it in the near future, although at my present salary I just about break even each month, what with New York prices being what they are.

Everything is progressing as usual up here. The work is about the same, much manuscript reading, brightened up occasionally by interviews with prospective authors and now and then a few letters to write. The novels I read still remain uniformly bad or, at most, mediocre; and I am gaining comfort at least from the slightly invidious fact that I can do so much better than the majority of these *opera*. I have been reading William Faulkner on my own time lately and find him just about the most stimulating writer I have read in a long time. I have secured

WHITTLESEY HOUSE A DIVISION OF THE McGRAW-HILL BOOK COMPANY, INC.

EDWARD C. ASWELL, *EDITOR IN CHIEF*

McGRAW-HILL BUILDING
330 WEST 42ND STREET
NEW YORK 18, N. Y.

July 24, 1947

Dear Pop,

I received your letter and the check a few days ago, and enjoyed
the letter and thank you for the check. I have put the money in
a savings account at the Clinton Trust Company and I hope to augment it in the near future, although at my present salary I just
about break even each month, what with New York prices being what
they are.

Everything is progressing as usual up here. The work is about the
same, much manuscript reading, brightened up occasionally by interviews with prospective authors and now and then a few letters to
write. The novels I read still remain uniformly bad or, at most,
mediocre; and I am gaining comfort at least from the slightly invidious fact that I can do so much better than the majority of these
opera. I have been reading William Faulkner on my own time lately
and find him just about the most stimulating writer I have read in
a long time. I have secured the Viking Portable edition of Faulkner,
in which the editor, Malcolm Cowley, has set out to show how Faulkner's depiction of Mississippi life is in reality a cycle or saga,
dating back to 1830 and embracing a whole mythical county and many
families. I have often thought I might do the same thing with a
North Carolina or Pennsylvania family or families (Abraham, Rush,
Styron, Clark, et al) and I am beginning to appreciate your interest
in genealogy and ancestral history. The average historical novel
can be pretty deadly, but with the touch of Faulkner it can indeed
become a wonderful thing.

Styron to his father from Whittlesey House, the literary division of McGraw-Hill.
Styron was fired from his position there in October 1947 by Edward C. Aswell,
whose name appears on the letterhead. Courtesy Estate of William C. Styron, Jr.

the Viking Portable edition of Faulkner, in which the editor, Malcolm
Cowley, has set out to show how Faulkner's depiction of Mississippi life
is in reality a cycle or saga, dating back to 1830 and embracing a whole
mythical county and many families. I have often thought I might do the
same thing with a North Carolina or Pennsylvania family or families
(Abraham, Rush, Styron, Clark, et al) and I am beginning to appreciate
your interest in genealogy and ancestral history. The average historical
novel can be pretty deadly, but with the touch of Faulkner it can indeed
become a wonderful thing.

Friday I'm going down to Washington to see Tom Peyton. A couple
of his friends are going to be there, and we might even venture as far
as Urbanna, although I doubt it. Peyton just got back from Cuba, and
in August he's going to Venezuela for the company he works for, after a

two weeks' reserve officers' course at Quantico. He seems to be pretty active these days. Bobbie and her roommate are still in New England, and I've received a couple of cards from Bobbie saying that she enjoys everything fine. I was up at Bill Bowman's house in Hartsdale Sunday at a birthday party which Mrs. B. held for him. It was quite enjoyable, and I met some nice people.[9]

I have sent an order to Simon & Schuster for "Peace of Mind" and when I get it I'll send it on to you.[10] By the way, when I get settled—and if I get settled—in roomier quarters, I'll probably be asking you to send my record player up. I think that it's out of order at the present, but I can have it fixed up here. I'm feeling better each day now, although I'm still not fully strengthful, and I don't think that the jaundice will bother me any more.

I'd better close now, since I have a very dreary-looking novel to read. Give my best to all, and write soon.

Your son,
Bill jr.

38. NEW YORK (typed on Whittlesey House letterhead)

August 20, 1947

Dear Pop,

I hadn't realized that time passes so fast, for when I looked at the date on your last letter I found that our last communication was nearly three weeks ago. Life is progressing here about the same. New York has been fiercely hot during the past few weeks but has moderated during the last couple of days. The weatherman, however, promises that a two-day heat wave will begin anew tomorrow. I haven't made definite plans yet, but think I might run down to see Bobbie in Washington tomorrow for the week-end. But, since I had planned to see her Labor Day week-end, I don't know if I'll splurge to the extent of seeing her both times. Bill Bowman wants me to go down to Urbanna with him on Labor Day, and

9. Bowman was a friend from Christchurch School; he and Styron were drinking beer together on the day Pearl Harbor was bombed. See the reminiscence "Christchurch" in *This Quiet Dust,* rev. ed., 309–12.

10. *Peace of Mind,* a work of applied psychology by Joshua Loth Liebman, was published by Simon and Schuster in 1947.

I'm considering that, too. I haven't been down to the old place in a long time, now.

New York can get painfully monotonous, especially on Saturday and Sunday, when there's no place especially to go. Most of the people I knew here when I first came up have flown the coop, so I have to more or less shift for myself when it comes to entertainment. But then some wise man said that an educated man is one who can (1) entertain a new idea, (2) entertain his friends, and (3) entertain himself. The last is the hardest to do for me, but with the aid of things like books I am gradually developing to the point that I don't of necessity need people around me all the time—or beer! At the present I'm reading a new novel *Under the Volcano*, by Malcolm Lowry, which got excellent reviews. I haven't gotten far enough into it to deliver any opinion, but it certainly looks, so far, as if it's really something.[11] The books I've been reading at Whittlesey House have been uniformly bad—or mediocre. I had the pleasure the other day of delivering an opinion on a book by Walter B. Pitkin ("Life Begins at 40") which he sent in as a possibility. It was a manuscript called ON YOUR WAY AT 20, directed toward young boys who, denied college, have to get out on their own. Mr. Schaeffer, the editor, wanted my judgement of the book, and I wrote what I thought—a platitudinous pep-talk, full of the same worship of spurious values which made LIFE BEGINS AT 40 such a success. Mr. Larned, the director, read the report, liked it, and I'm pretty sure that Mr. Pitkin's phony blandishments are doomed as a result of my report, at least as far as Whittlesey is concerned.[12]

No results on an apartment yet, although Bill Bowman and I have signed up together for an apartment in Peter Cooper Village, Metropolitan Life's new development on the East River.[13]

They didn't promise us anything over there, but said that we stood a fair chance of getting something before Christmas. I don't think I'm a

11. Lowry's novel had recently been published by Reynal and Hitchcock.

12. Pitkin's *Life Begins at Forty* (which, as Styron suggests, is filled with bromides) had been published by Whittlesey House in 1932. No sequel appeared under the Whittlesey House imprint.

13. This residential area on the Lower East Side, built by the Metropolitan Life Insurance Company in the late 1940s and early 1950s, provided apartment housing for low- and middle-income New Yorkers. Styron's plan to live there never materialized.

complete sybarite, but I believe that even a Jesuit would find it gloomy business living in the box I live in. Imagine a room the size of the big bathroom upstairs at home, ill-lighted, decorated with muddy wallpaper, and subjected to a ninety degree temperature all summer, and you'll get an idea of my nocturnal mode of living.

Continuing our genealogical discussion, I would be most happy if you would send me any information or anecdota concerning Beaufort County, the Clarks, Styrons, or anything else that you think might form germinative thoughts in my mind and get me started on a saga of Eastern North Carolina. I've got lots of ideas and theories but, like Sinclair Lewis, I'll have to search through records to find a family framework upon which to hang my story.

I see in the papers that the Terminal Leave bonds of veterans may be cashed any time after September 1st. You are holding one for me, I believe, and I wish you would send it to me some time before that date so I may add it to my savings account. It's written out for about $225—with a picture of Carter Glass on it—and I'd rather cash it and add it to my account, since in the form of a bond it doesn't pay interest, as the War Bonds do.[14]

That's about all the news for now. I'm glad to hear that you are coming up in November, and I'll see that you are properly feted, as they say in the society columns. Tell Eliza that I'm glad she is continuing on with the story, and hope she sends it to me. I'll write her soon.

Your son,
Bill

P.S. *Peace of Mind* is gratis. After all, *we* in the publishing business have to get *something* at discount.

39. NEW YORK (typed on Whittlesey House letterhead)

September 19, 1947

Dear Pop,

A belated letter finally, and I'm sorry that I didn't write sooner. I have been deluged by mss since Mr. Aswell took over—seems like every beginning author in America wants him to be their editor, so I have to

---

14. Carter Glass (1858–1946), a native of Lynchburg, Virginia, was secretary of the treasury under Woodrow Wilson from 1918 to 1920—hence his printed image on Styron's bond. Glass served as a U.S. senator from Virginia from 1920 until 1946.

do the dirty work.[15] The quality is improving greatly, too, so that I have to concentrate a little harder on work that was formerly merely weeding out the trash.

The weather here is much better, and it's positively amazing but I feel that a great load has been lifted from my shoulders. The heat here was enormous during the dead of summer—almost a palpable thing—and I'm beginning to realize now that what I thought was a hangover from the jaundice was really the sun and the humidity. But Autumn is a wonderful season anywhere, I suppose.

My social activities have been somewhat circumscribed of late, but I'm gradually coming to meet some genuine people. Prof. Blackburn—I don't know if I told you or not—came through here on his way down from Boston and I, of course, was greatly calmed and pleased by his conversation. We're kindred souls, I believe. Bobbie has been up here for a week—she's staying with a friend of hers in the Village—and we have had a pretty good time together. Last night I went out to Jamaica to see Hank Simons and his family, had dinner, and thoroughly enjoyed myself. Dr. Simons, incidentally, is submitting us a ms on the diseases of the kidneys, written for the layman. I've read portions of it, and think that we might publish it.

I'm still on the scrounge for an apartment, and the prospects are looking better. Ed Hatcher, a Duke friend who is now working at Bobbie's old job at Carbide, and I are collaborating to get a place, and have a sure thing that we may occupy on Oct. 15th—a 25 x 17 room on west 84th street with kitchen and bath—only the price is fairly steep—$100 a month—and we hope to get something better before then.[16] I firmly believe that I'll be able to write something once I have a place to stretch out in. That, I suppose, is rationalization, but I still believe it. *One* incentive I know I'll have is the fact that I have enrolled at the New School to take a course in Creative Writing under Hiram Haydn who, as you

15. Edward C. Aswell had become editor in chief at Whittlesey House in September. Aswell had been Thomas Wolfe's editor at Harper and Brothers in the late 1930s, after Wolfe had left Scribner's. After Wolfe's death in 1938, Aswell had assembled three books from his literary remains—*The Web and the Rock* (1939), *You Can't Go Home Again* (1940), and *The Hills Beyond* (1941). Styron gives a fictional portrait of Aswell as "The Weasel" in *Sophie's Choice* (New York: Random House, 1979), 15–20.

16. Hatcher, a native of North Carolina, roomed with Styron during this period and remained friendly with him through the 1950s and early 1960s. Bobbie Taeusch had been working at Union Carbide in the city.

may remember, is Blackburn's friend and Editor over at Crown publishers. He taught writing at W.C.U.N.C. for a while, and when I wrote him asking to be allowed to take his course, he wrote back saying that Blackburn had already told him of my record, and that I *Belonged* in the course. Since I'm taking the course under the G.I. Bill, I'll have to keep my grades up to get a reimbursement and, by the same token, will *have* to do some writing.

I received Eliza's Chicago letter, and am glad to hear that she finds the city fairly agreeable at least. Tell her I will write her soon.

I wish I knew where I was going to be ten years from now; I suppose everyone does. The world situation doesn't tend to make one sit down and write deathless prose, but I suppose that with the passing of the years, with effort, I'll be able to figure at least part of the things out that bother me now. Right now I have the feeling that I'm about to undergo a change which will put me more at rights with the world. Perhaps I'm changing right this minute. At any rate, I know that I will never compromise when it comes to my ambition to put something down on paper that is true and meaningful. Perhaps, when I understand more fully my capabilities, my aspirations will not be so vaunted, ethereal, and vainglorious, but at least they will still be there.

I should close now. Give my regards to everyone, and write soon.

Your son,
Bill

40. NEW YORK

October 10, 1947
1453 Lexington Ave.
New York 28, N.Y.

Dear Pop and Eliza,

I received both of your letters lately, including the one Eliza wrote from Chicago, and I enjoyed them both very much, and I'm sorry I haven't written sooner, except that a number of odd circumstances have prevented me from having too much extra time.

I may as well start from the beginning, and not be equivocal about it. First, I am no longer working for McGraw Hill. I shall be quick to state—lest you have any apprehensions along that line—that I was *not* dismissed for any reason other than the fact that Aswell did not think that I had the age or experience to qualify for my title or position. It was strange luck that got me the job in the first place and by the same token it was strange luck that had Aswell, a few months later, step in and plan for expansion—an expansion, the plans for which my rather menial duties as manuscript reader were not needed. There were no hard feelings and Mr. Larned, the director, hastened to tell me that I was leaving there with his, and the other editors', highest recommendations. But, as Lois Cole—a very nice lady who is one of the editors—told me before I left, the publishing business is a strange, cutthroat game and there are very few people in the racket who are not hired and fired half-a-dozen times. Aswell obviously has his mind on someone whom he has worked with, and who is older, more experienced, and has all sorts of "contacts" with agents, authors, and so forth—necessary accoutrements for an associate editor. Still, though I realize and appreciate his position and my own relative inadequacy, I still bear a half-hearted resentment against the cold, pudgy little man who so abruptly dismissed me and I'm sure *he'll* never publish any of Styron's immortal and lucrative prose. No matter what the circumstances, getting fired is a fairly bitter experience. But, I say I only bear *half-hearted* resentment toward Aswell, because in reality I believe he's done me a favor. This is not "sour grapes" when I say that I'm glad I've left Whittlesey House, and that my joy at leaving the publishing business, even after so short a time, is genuine. Because, after observation, I've concluded that most publishing people are really frustrated writers and, beyond this, that it is practically impossible to combine a writing and a publishing career. There is actually very little glamour in publishing and my job at Whittlesey House, though occasionally interesting, would have become, I can see now, very dull—perhaps not as dull as bank clerking or accounting, but dull nonetheless. I would have for years, as I do now, wanted to write, but would have instead become more and more involved with *other people's work* until the actual *will* to write would have vanished and I would have nourished many regrets. This is not rationalizing. I know it to be the truth; and all the editors, friends of mine at Whittlesey House, wished me godspeed and were frankly and sincerely rather envious, because they too, when they were my age, wanted to write but got enmeshed in publishing, which is only a counterfeit, a reflection, of really creative work.

But you might be asking now, just what do I plan to do? I plan to sit down in this place I'm now living in and do exactly what I want to do—

which is to write. I have a little bit of money in the bank, and for nearly a year I can get $20 a week from the Veterans Administration. Right now I'm fairly sure I could get a job at Thomas Y. Crowell as associate editor but, as I told you, I am going to steer clear of that sort of work from now on. What I'm going to do now is sit down every day for a set number of hours—five, at least—and see if I can't turn out something decent. For the past week I've been doing it—my first really concerted effort at writing—and I've been fairly successful. I've written a short story which I know is the best I've done since *Autumn* and, in many respects, better than Autumn. It's in Hiram Haydn's hands now and he's going to criticize it next week in class. Writing is a matter, really—that is, the *mechanics* of writing—of dogging both the idea and yourself to death, pacing about the room until you've wrung every possible drop of richness out of your mind and into the story. I'm going to try it honestly, even desperately, for I realize with a sort of blunt self-honesty that if I'm ever going to do anything with myself along literary lines I might as well start now while the trying's ripe, while I'm not saddled with too many practical responsibilities, and see if I can do it. If I find that I can't, then maybe I'll do something more harmless, like publishing. I wrote Brice,[17] at Duke, about all this and he said: "You may be at a dead end, but the only way to find out is to travel it to the end—something you obviously had to do. I'm glad that you aren't putting it off any longer." If Hawthorne could take 12 years to teach himself to write, I certainly can take a year or so, or however long it'll be.

Eliza, your story is being handled by a friend of mine who is an editor and, though she hasn't had any results yet, she's still trying. I hope you've written some more, and will send them to me.

I'm living now with a friend, Ed Hatcher of High Point, N.C., who went to Duke, in a house on Lexington Ave near 94th Street. We have the bottom floor and it's very nice and fantastically cheap, and Pop, you'll have to see it when you come up on November 12th. I'll be looking forward to the visit.

I don't think I'll have any financial worries for quite some time, since I'm not living "high" any more and spend most of my time writing anyway. Wish me luck.

Bill

17. Ashbel Brice, then an instructor of English at Duke and a friend of Blackburn's, later became director of Duke University Press.

41. NEW YORK

[October 20, 1947]
Monday Night

Dear Pop,

I have been terribly lax in my correspondence, I know, but I have been very busy—believe it or not—during the past weeks on a long short story, which I have just finished and which I have sent to the New School to Hiram Haydn, for criticism. I have intentionally delayed, too, writing you, because I wanted to wait and see if I got a reply from the *Atlantic Monthly*, concerning my "Trieste" story. It's been there for nearly a month and a half now, and I don't know whether they are really considering the piece carefully, or whether it has been merely lying idly upon some reader's shelf. I hope it's the former, but strongly suspect the latter. But I have received no reply to date, and don't know exactly what to think.[18]

The other story upon which I have been laboring so steadily is, I think, about my best to date—although I say that about everything I write. I think it probably shows more real maturity than any of my others, although I'll have to hear what Mr. Haydn says about it before I really know. It's on that long-belabored Hart's Island theme, and I think I've managed to incorporate the essence of the thought within a framework of a story which, though detached and objective, is still meaningful and rich. I'll let you know later what my plans for it, if any, are. At any rate, my progress on this story has encouraged me a great deal and I feel again—though I realize the story is no earth-shaker—that all is not lost.[19]

Barbara and I have come to the parting of the ways. She wrote me that another guy is interested in marrying her and that I should write her and tell her if I were interested in her any longer—that she was still interested in me, but she thought we should not mosey along together undecided any longer. So I wrote her, telling her that I was, of course,

18. "A Moment in Trieste" was rejected by the *Atlantic Monthly* and appeared first in *American Vanguard,* ed. Don M. Wolfe (Ithaca: Cornell University Press, 1948), 241–47. The story that Styron has submitted to Haydn for criticism is "The Enormous Window," first published in *American Vanguard,* ed. Charles I. Glicksberg (New York: Cambridge Publishing Co., 1950), 71–89. Most of the contributors to these two collections were students of Haydn's at the New School. Both stories are reprinted in appendix 3 of this volume.

19. This was Styron's first attempt to base a narrative on his experiences, just after the conclusion of World War II, as an officer at the U.S. Navy prison on Hart's Island in New York Harbor. He would return to this material in 1953. See letter 103.

still fond of her but that I was in not much of a position to get married any time soon. So that's that. Tom Peyton, who lives in D.C., wrote me the other day that Barbara called him a few days after receiving my letter and seemed pretty broken up about the thing, but I don't know.

I have bought a few albums and have had the record-player fixed. I have the Beethoven Violin Concerto, two concertos by Haydn and Bach, Handel's Water Music, and the Bach Brandenburg Concertos. So the nights are filled with music.

I enjoyed your visit very much, and am only sorry that we couldn't have done more in the way of "big city" entertainment. But I suspect that you, as I, enjoyed just sitting around talking, so it didn't matter.

I doubt very much whether I'll be able to make it down there for Christmas, and rather suspect that I'll have to postpone such a visit until later in the winter. I'm starting in on a very long short story which might even develop into a novelette, and it's pretty well absorbing most of my working time. I do want to come down there very soon, though, and as soon as I get my present plans wound up I want to come down for a long visit.

I owe Eliza a letter, so tell her I will write soon. Everything is going along well and I'll write again soon and let you know what Haydn has to say about my latest *opus magnum*.

Your son,
Bill jr

42. NEW YORK

October 28, 1947

Dear Pop,

I received your letter the other day, and was glad to hear that we are both coming into a little cash.[20] Your borrowing half of my share is perfectly all right with me—better, in fact, since it assures me, for a time, of a steady income each month. I am now listed with the New York State bureau as a "self-employed" veteran and will be receiving $80 a month from that department which, along with the $60 you send me, will make a tidy $140—about the same as my starting salary at McGraw-Hill.

I was also happy to hear that you are coming to N.Y. next month, and

20. At her death, Styron's maternal grandmother, Belle Abraham, left bequests to him and his father. Styron transformed this experience into the story of the slave Artiste in *Sophie's Choice*.

I'll certainly be on hand to give you a big welcome. I wrote Aunt Edith and told her when you are coming, and expressed the hope that she would be here at the same time, so we could all do the town together.

The story I mentioned in my last letter was read in Hiram Haydn's seminar at the New School. Haydn, as I think I told you, is editor of Crown Publishers and also editor of the extremely respectable *American Scholar,* journal of the Phi Beta Kappa organization. Haydn, who is a fairly harsh critic, said that the story was "terrific," "powerful," and "certainly publishable," all of which delighted me no end. I also sent a copy to Blackburn and Brice, both of whom thought the story was excellent. Brice suggested that I send the story to the *New Yorker,* which I have done (no answer yet) and then to the various literary quarterlies. The *New Yorker* is very particular about the names of their authors, and I doubt seriously if they will accept it; but both Blackburn and Brice are convinced that I can get the thing published somewhere so I'm going to keep trying until I get an acceptance.

I'm very glad that you see eye to eye with me about my present attitude concerning my attempts at writing, and about the loss of my job. I realize that I've finally come to grips with myself, and that the job was in reality merely a delaying action. Writing for me is the hardest thing in the world, but also a thing which, once completed, is the most satisfying. I have been reading the letters of Joseph Conrad, and really feel a kinship—if nothing but in spirit—with the late master, for one discovers in the letters that writing, for Conrad, was the most despairing, painful job in the world.[21] It most definitely is that way for me. But someone— I think it was Henry James—said that only through monstrous travail and agonizing effort can great art be brought forth from those who, like himself (James), are not prodigies or, like Shelley, spontaneous founts of genius. Anything less than unceasing toil will produce nothing or, at best, facility. I am no prodigy but, Fate willing, I think I can produce art. For me it takes much girding up of loins and an almost imbecile faith in my potentials—but I suppose that's part of the satisfaction.

I'd better close now. Give my love to Eliza, and I'll see you soon.

Your son,
Bill jr

---

21. Styron probably read Conrad's letters at the suggestion of William Blackburn, who was at work editing a volume of the author's correspondence during the 1950s. See Joseph Conrad, *Letters to William Blackwood and David S. Meldrum,* ed. William Blackburn (Durham: Duke University Press, 1958).

43. NEW YORK

[January 5, 1948]

Dear Eliza, and Pop:

I received the Christmas box in good order and was certainly pleased with the contents. The food, of course, will come in handy these cold winter nights—it has already been rapidly depleted—and *Atlantic Harvest* is fine.[22] I've already dipped into the contents and it seems like very good stuff. The essays (Whitehead, Havelock Ellis, et al.) seem especially fine selections. I also noted Sedgwick's autograph on the fly-leaf which, of course, enhances the personal value of the book. The razor's a beauty, Pop, and I'm sure it will serve to beautify many a hairy cheek in the years to come. Thank you both for everything.

I'm sorry to hear about your current indisposition, Pop, and I certainly hope that it's nothing that will seriously disable you. Take care of yourself, and let me hear how things develop. I know the *diet* must be something of a strain.

I spent Christmas Eve working on a short story (which I just yesterday completed), and then went out with Charlie, the landlord, and had a couple of beers before bed. On Christmas day I went over to Brooklyn and had dinner with Mac Hyman and his wife. Mac's a boy from Georgia, one of Blackburn's students, who came to N.Y. seeking his fame and fortune, as I did.[23] They're both nice folks. Later on in the day I took the train for New Haven where I visited Tom Peyton. Peyton's sister and brother-in-law live there, and the whole family was up from Crozet for the holidays. I stayed until Sunday and came on back to N.Y. It snowed 19 inches in New Haven and 26 inches here, which is about as much snow as I've ever seen, or shall ever want to see. Luckily, I haven't caught cold, and now feel about as good as anyone can feel, I suppose, in New York.[24]

22. Styron's father had sent him an anthology of writings from the *Atlantic Monthly* entitled *Atlantic Harvest*, ed. Ellery Sedgwick (Boston: Little, Brown, 1947). The volume contains writings by Thomas Bailey Aldrich, Mark Twain, Sarah Orne Jewett, Edith Wharton, Alfred North Whitehead, Ernest Hemingway, and D. H. Lawrence, among others.

23. Hyman eventually scored a success with his comic novel *No Time for Sergeants,* published in 1954 by Random House.

24. During the storm, while snowbound in his basement apartment, Styron had first read Robert Penn Warren's *All the King's Men* (1946). He recalled the experience, and the influence of Warren's novel on *Lie Down in Darkness,* in "Robert Penn Warren," *This Quiet Dust,* rev. ed., 267–70.

Hatcher and I are getting evicted from this apartment on the 15th of this month, due to the fact that the landlord, Charlie, is so in debt that he has to sell the house. Fortunately, however, we have found a large apartment *right next door*, at 1455 Lexington, and we're moving in early next week. So you may send any mail, until then, to this address. Incidentally, Bill Bowman, whom you both remember, is moving in with us, since it's a three-man apartment. Bill has a pretty nice job now, as reservationist with Eastern Air Lines. So old friends get together after all.

An extraordinary opportunity has come my way. Since you, Pop, read my story about Trieste I have written two others—both quite long. Hiram Haydn at the New School (editor of Crown Publishers, you remember, and also editor of the American Scholar) has read all three of them, and liked them so well that he has offered me an advance of a substantial sum of money if I write a novel. Of course, since I haven't written anything on the novel he can't offer me a contract right now. But he was so enthusiastic over the stories that he called me down to his office at Crown and told me that he had informed the publishing director (the big shot) at Crown that he had so much faith in my potentialities that he suggested that they break their rule (against giving advance-on-royalties to unknown writers) in my case. The publishing director finally agreed, after a lot of rhetoric by Haydn, so now all I have to do is write the damn novel. I have to write a first chapter and outline and Haydn said he'd do all he could to help me along with it so it would be met with approval by his associates. Of course all this doesn't mean that it's in the bag and I wouldn't like it to be rumored about that Styron has finished the great American novel, but it has inspired me with such confidence that I know I can write a good novel.

It was interesting to hear more about Barbara Bottom's progress through life. Luckily I haven't run into her here in N.Y. yet. Probably wouldn't recognize her if I did. Who's the new man?[25]

Eliza, have you written anything else in your "spare time"? I still have your story here, which this friend of mine sent to a few magazines. She got some very nice notes back about the story, but no checks. I suppose you're partly right—magazines nowadays (even the good ones) just don't seem to want childhood stories. Do you want me to send it

25. Barbara Bottom was the daughter of Cdr. and Mrs. Raymond B. Bottom of Newport News. Her father was the owner of the *Newport News Daily Press*. Styron based the character of Peyton Loftis in *Lie Down in Darkness* in part on Barbara Bottom.

back to you, or would you rather me try again? I'd still like to see some more stuff you've written, as I think it's mighty good.

Thanks again to both of you for your nice presents. Write soon.

Love,
Billy

44. NEW YORK

[March 31, 1948]
Wednesday Night

Dear Pop,

A much belated letter to let you know that I am still kicking and that everything is coming along all right. The little visit home, though short, was enjoyable and I'm only sorry that I couldn't stay longer. We are still having trouble with our landlady here—though nothing serious—otherwise the scene on the domestic front is okay. An evil brood, landladies!

I'm progressing well on the novel, although frankly it is a mystery to me how I am able to keep going from one section of the story to another. Haydn read the completed portion of the MS in class tonight and I am, to say the least, excited at what he told me (in front of the class) about the novel, to wit: "Although you can't really say anything positively, of course, until the novel is completed, this part seems to me to stand up beside *any contemporary American writer.*" I nearly fell over and, of course, walked home in a daze. He said something about the fact that I have a "tragic sense" of the place and the people I'm writing about and, after class, told me he thought what I had written was "terrific." I needn't have to tell you that I'm terribly encouraged, because I feel sure that Haydn's comments and criticisms are judicious and considered.[26]

I can't tell you how much this novel means to me. The process of sitting down and writing is pure torture to me, but at the same time I think about the book all the time and am in more or less a suspended state of worry and anxiety if I'm *not* writing. I worry, too, about the sincerity of my effort; if whether what I'm writing is not so much rhetoric, and it is only in my most now-self-critical mood that I can even come

---

26. Styron was working on *Inheritance of Night*, the early version of *Lie Down in Darkness.*

vaguely to realize that what I write does, in truth, have an element of truth in it and is, after all, a more faithful rendering of life than I believe it to be in my moments of doubt.

The world situation is such that I—along, I suppose, with everyone else—really don't know whether a novel, or a symphony, or anything else, is worth the trouble or not. But I suppose that if you relinquish your claim as an "individual," no matter what your endeavor might be, or in whatever state the world is in, you might as well cease living. So I'll go on writing, hoping that we will survive, and perhaps taking a measure of courage from the fact that in the face of disaster my story might become even more significant.

New York is beginning to wear on my nerves, and now that spring is coming I want to leave. The novelty has worn off; the city, with all its excitement and grandeur, is a terrible place. The tide swarms on; how people manage the pretense of humanity in such a jostling, surly antheap is beyond me. The eye bends down from the jutting skyscraper—man's material achievement—to gaze in horror on the pawing mess of Broadway at lunchtime and the greasy, muttering squalor of the interior of a subway car—surely the symbol of man's spiritual decay.

I hope I get an offer of an advance on royalties from Crown within the next few weeks; I think I will. And that Eastern Shore deal, if you still want to try and help me out, sounds good indeed.

Do you think that if people learned to love one another, that if the collective human mind could be conditioned to good-will and rich laughter, the resultant effect would be boredom? That mutual hatred, a natural antipathy for his own species, is a predetermined condition of the state of man on earth? Sometimes it seems that way to me.

Haydn's words still ring in my ears. Wish me luck!

Your son,
Bill jr.

P.S. Did you read the reviews of Haydn's *The Time Is Noon*? Last Sunday's *Times* and Tribune's were fine, and the daily reviews in the same papers even better. (see enclosed)[27]

27. On Sunday, March 28, 1948, Haydn's novel was given a mixed review in the *New York Times Book Review* (p. 7) and a positive notice in the *New York Herald Tribune Weekly Book Review* (p. 3). A review by Orville Prescott appeared in the daily *Times* on Monday, March 29 (p. 19); a review by Lewis Gannett was published in the *Herald Tribune* on that same day (p. 13).

4 / July 1948–June 1949

DURHAM AND FLATBUSH

Discouraged over his lack of progress, Styron had a long conference with Haydn and decided to return to Durham, where he had a circle of friends and where his money would stretch farther. He would be able to see William Blackburn regularly and to visit his father from time to time in Newport News. Styron packed his things and traveled to Durham in July. For the first few nights in the city he camped out at the home of Ashbel Brice. Then, with a friend named Bill Snitger, he moved into an apartment at 901 East Fifth Street, near the East Campus of Duke.

45. DURHAM

July 11, 1948
Sunday
c/o A.G. Brice
814 Sixth St., Durham, N.C.

Dear Pop,

Suzie sent all my stuff—records, books, etc.—down from New York, so I am now prepared to move into the apartment that Bill Switzer and I have rented.[1] The apartment, just in back of the Woman's College Campus, is in the first floor of a private home—two medium sized rooms, kitchen, bath, and large back yard, $40 per month. It is *not* furnished, and that is the big difficulty; we plan just to buy bare essentials at first—

---

1. Suzie was a New York girlfriend; Bill Switzer was a friend from undergraduate days at Duke. Styron ended up sharing the apartment with Bill Snitger (mentioned in the headnote above), who was working at a Durham radio station.

beds, chairs, kitchen utensils—and get the rest later. I'd appreciate it if you would send me a check for $150 as soon as possible, as I figure that is about what it'll take to supplement the money I already have to pay the first month's rent and buy a bed and maybe a lamp or two, besides food.

Switzer and I have, in the meantime, been staying with Brice. I have done some work on the novel, but I find it pretty rough going. I don't seem to have the innate confidence in myself or my work which I suppose is a part of genius; consequently I am diverted too easily into less favorable channels—like reading *Time* magazine. Every word I put down seems to be sheer pain, and although I often am a victim of sloppy writing I have nonetheless too much of what I suppose is called artistic integrity to put down something I know is not true or merely a half-truth. Because of that, I suppose my sessions at the desk are doubly painful in that where someone else might put something—some idea or word-picture—to paper merely for the effect, I have to ponder and ponder and reject anything I sincerely believe at the time hints of fraudulence. Even so, I know there are many things in the work I've already accomplished that I didn't mean to say. I think the crux of the issue is merely that I don't know enough yet about people to be writing a novel. But I'm at least giving it my earnest application, and trying hard to put myself on an inflexible schedule. I realize that I'm among the favored few, that there are not many people my age who've been given the sort of encouragement I have and that it would be both sinful and weak not to attempt to live up to the faith that has been put in me. I'll have a novel finished next year this time—I hope a good one.

Durham is an ugly town but many of the people I know here are very fine. Last night, for instance, Brice had Frances Gray Patton over. She's married to a Duke professor of history, is an O. Henry short story prize winner (see "One and Twenty") and is now a regular contributor to the *New Yorker*.[2] A very charming lady. She lived as a girl in Newport News. Her father was editor of the *Daily Press* and *Times Herald* in the early twenties.

Write soon, and please don't forget the check.

Your son,
Bill jr.

2. Patton (1906–2000) was one of the first professional writers whom Styron knew socially. Her short stories appeared in various magazines, including the *New Yorker, Mc-Call's,* and *Ladies' Home Journal.* Her best short fiction is collected in *Twenty-eight Stories* (New York: Dodd, Mead, 1969).

46. DURHAM

[July 21, 1948]

Dear Pop,

I just received your letter and, as your letters generally do, it greatly encouraged me and filled me with new resolve. I'm beginning to see and realize now that my trouble on this novel—in fact, my whole thinking—has been, as you pointed out, a matter of grasp rather than reach. A solemn and considered realization of one's capacities is one of the greatest assets. I don't want to be a Shakespeare or a Shelley. A Suckling or an Andrew Marvell or a Ben Jonson is just as nice, and more pleasant. I'll just do as well as I can.

You mentioned furniture in your earlier letter. I'd be glad to have whatever you can send me. We do need a table, silverware, and lamps badly. Also any pictures you might have that are stored away, to decorate the walls. If you could arrange to have them sent I'd be glad to pay whatever shipping and/or packing charges there might be.

Everything is going nicely here, only the heat is pretty cruel. Drop me a letter, and give my best to all.

Your son,
WCS jr

new address:
901 Fifth Street
Durham, N.C.

47. DURHAM

[August 3, 1948]
Tuesday night

Dear Pop,

It was nice seeing you the other week-end, and I hope you enjoyed it as much as I and the others did. You and Mr. Switzer seemed to have gotten along fine, struck a common chord. Bill said that he hadn't heard his father talk so much in years.

The novel is coming along at about its usual slow but steady turtle's pace. I read part of it to Dr. Blackburn and his class, and he seems to be immensely and sincerely pleased by what I've done so far. It's a tedious and agonizing process and I loathe writing with almost a panic hatred, but as I've said before I'm always restless when I'm not working at it. If ever I become well-known because of my writing, it may honestly be said by whatever person that chooses to tell about me: "he wrote in spite of himself." I know that what I've written so far on this book is good, but that it is far from maturity or perfection. I've noticed the maturation process taking place in me and I know I've barely started growing. I do hope to get the book finished by next summer, but I just don't know, at the rate I'm going. A man just doesn't realize, I believe, what self-doubt and despair are until he's tried to express himself in a work of art. Perhaps that is a self-conscious and adolescent statement and maybe I use the word "art" too freely, but it's the way I feel now. My moral and intellectual values are as yet far too undeveloped for me to be able to assess the worth of this novel I'm writing in terms of its conception. I hope when I'm finished with it people will read it, and I hope it's at least a good start. Beyond anything, though, I hope that the writing of it will somehow enrich my own mind in that it may teach me perseverance and calm thought and make me more of a man. Writing a novel of course involves a good deal of contemplation—most of it, it is true, false or worthless—but it is my constant hope that this pure fact of contemplation, which wise men so cherish, may lead me into sunnier and wider avenues of the spirit. I don't say that with pretension. I have somehow already felt vague intimations of the satisfaction that can come from working hard, sweating blood, indeed. If I come through it will only be at the price of a great deal of anguish, that price, I suspect, being worth the reward.

To get down to more practical matters, I would like for you to sent me $50, if you will, as soon as you can. The first of the month brought a number of bills—telephone, milk, etc—which I'm unable to pay in my present financial status. So if you'll send a check as soon as possible, I'll be greatly obliged.

In the meantime I hope everything goes well with you and that I'll get to see you sometime soon. Regards to all.

Your son
WCS jr

48. DURHAM

[August 11, 1948]
Wednesday P.M.

Dear Pop,

The chairs and shades came today and they, along with everything else, go to make the apartment quite classy and decorative. Everything that was sent has been most useful and I certainly appreciate your taking the time and effort to send them. I know it must have been a lot of trouble.

Everything here is going along on even keel. I've put the novel aside just for the moment, and am working steadily on a long short story which has, so far, turned out all right and which, I hope, will end up the best thing I've done. Each day I learn more conclusively the fact that writing is the hardest job in the world, especially if, like with me, the words come difficult. I very rarely write more than five or six hundred words a day, but I *have* discovered, finally, that the only way to get anything done is to stick to it, so I stay pretty much on a regular schedule.

I recently got an encouraging letter from Haydn, which helps. I guess a writer, being a great part child, feeds on his ego: I know I do. No one has doubted the worth of his work more than I and the temptation to throw it all up is strong, yet I keep going, knowing from experience that the sort of negative pain that results from not writing is far worse than the positive torture of writing itself.

My veteran's account hasn't been received down here from N.Y. yet, so I will be forced to ask you for $50 more to tide me over until I can get straightened out. I hate to ask you for it, but the great bulk of the expenses that moving entailed are over now, and I won't need so much so often in the future.

I hope all is well at home. I read in the N.Y. *Times* about the shipyard getting the aircraft carrier contract, which I don't suppose will hurt anybody at all.[3]

Give my regards to all and write soon.

Your son
WCS jr

3. Styron is referring to the news story "Carrier Job Given to Newport News," which he would have read in the *New York Times* for August 8, 1948, 17. The navy had announced that a new 65,000-ton aircraft carrier would be built at the Newport News Shipbuilding and Drydock Company, where Styron's father was an engineer. This was to

49. DURHAM

November 10, 1948

Dear Pop,

There's not much in the way of news down here, but I thought I'd drop you a line anyway, to let you know that I'm still in operation.

The novel is coming along all right, still very slow but more or less steady. It's quite interesting, while writing, to see just how far one departs from the preconceived idea: I write and write and it's amazing what I've written. And it's probably a commentary on my lack of discipline to note that the more I write the further the end of the book seems to be within sight. It won't be a great novel, and probably won't even be "artistic," but it'll sure have a lot of diversions within its framework. I don't have any idea when it'll be finished, but if I keep plugging, it might get published sometime late next year or in the spring of 1950.

Thanksgiving Brice and Switzer and myself, along with a few other friends, are having dinner over at his (Brice's) place. It struck me that some oysters would go well then, and if you could manage to send me a half gallon I would greatly appreciate it, and either send me the bill or pay it and tell me what the charge is. Thanksgiving is on the 26th, so if you could get them here a day or so before then, they would be fresh. You just can't get decent oysters in Durham. They taste pale and insipid.

I saw Georgia Tech beat Duke a couple of week-ends ago. It was a pretty good game, though Duke, without a star in the backfield, just couldn't get started.[4]

Tom Peyton is in Mississippi digging oil wells, and making good money, although he says the social life leaves something to be desired. My friend Mac Hyman of Cordele, Ga., and his wife are both teaching school in St. Augustine, Fla., and Bill Bowman, believe it or not, is married—out of a job, the last time I heard—and is living somewhere in Queens.

---

be a flush-deck carrier nearly twice the size of the largest vessel then in the U.S. fleet. The Newport News economy rose and fell according to the size of the defense contracts awarded to the shipyard; a big contract was always good news for residents of the city.

4. Duke lost to Georgia Tech by a score of 19–7 in a game played on October 30, 1948. The Duke football team had reached its apogee in 1942, when it was ranked second in the nation and played Oregon State in the Rose Bowl—a New Year's Day game normally played in Pasadena, California, but staged that year in Durham because of fears of a Japanese submarine attack. Duke lost the game by a score of 20–16.

That's about all worthy of note at the present. Drop me a line when you can.

Your son,

Bill jr

P.S. What does Mr. Blalock have to say about the William and Mary catastrophe over in Chapel Hill weekend last?[5]

50. DURHAM

November 23, 1948

Tuesday

Dear Pop and Eliza,

Thanks for the very fine contributions to Thanksgiving Dinner. The oysters and clams haven't arrived yet, but I have no doubt that they will arrive tomorrow. The anchovies, kippers, cheese, etc., arrived in good shape, Eliza, and I'm sure that they will be well received by all. Thanks a lot. There will be six of us, I think, for dinner, and we are getting a 15-pound turkey, and the wife of one of the English instructors is making a mince-meat pie. I shall also adjure the company to give thanks to the "Creator of Oysters and Clams." I hope that your festive board is as sumptuous and as satisfying as ours looks like it's going to be, and I shall be remembering you.

I shall be up to Newport News on the 23rd for dinner, but I'll probably leave on the 26th, instead of the 27th, since I want to go to New York for a couple of days, and it's a day's traveling time by train. I hope by that time I'll have more of the novel to take to Hiram Haydn in person, who said that he wants me to drop in on him anyway. I'm looking forward to seeing Aunt Edith, too, when I get home, and I've written her a letter.

Until then, or until you hear from me again.

Love,

Bill, jr.

P.S. I'll be coming alone, so you needn't plan for another guest.

5. The University of North Carolina football team had played to a 7–7 tie with a heavily favored William and Mary squad. The game took place in Chapel Hill on November 7, 1948.

51. DURHAM

[December 2, 1948]

Dear Pop,

Thanksgiving was very nice and afterwards, thanks to the oysters and clams, we all felt very well fed indeed. The last of the oysters we finished off Sunday, Brice and I, in a sort of stew with cream sauce, and it was very good. Brice said the oysters were the biggest ones he'd ever seen.

At the present, since it is the first of the month and the rent is due, I wish you'd send me a check for $75, so that I can pay my bills and so that I'll have enough to see me through until Christmas, and also buy what few Christmas presents I'll be able to afford this year. Please send it as soon as feasible, since the landlord starts haunting my door every day until I come through.

I'm looking forward to seeing you all Christmas; this trip to Newport News and to New York will be, I suspect, the last I'll be able to make until I finish the novel and make a million dollars (I'll *really* be disappointed if I don't make that much). Maybe I'll be able sometime to marry a tobacco heiress, though, so that my worries won't be material anymore, but just mental.

Your son,
WCS, jr

Styron visited Hiram Haydn in New York over the Christmas holiday and decided to persevere for the time being in Durham. He promised to send Haydn a substantial section of the novel in March.

52. DURHAM

January 10, 1949
Monday

Dear Pop,

I arrived here Saturday morning, after a rather grim and bumpy train ride on the sleeper, via Greensboro, but otherwise happy and refreshed after a very pleasant time in Boston, with Leon and wife and baby, and in New York. Everything after I left Newport News was uneventful but genial enough. I went to two or three very good movies in New York and the rest of the time was spent in visiting with the various friends I knew from the earlier residence. Losing my train ticket last Tuesday seemed, at the time, a real catastrophe, but everything is okay now since I learned that I can get a refund after a short waiting period.

I would appreciate it if sometime soon you would send me the War Bonds you have saved for me at the bank, and also tell me how much I have left in the bank of that $1000 that was left to me a year ago. I'd like to cash the War Bonds and open a checking account in Durham—if only a necessarily brief one—so that I'll have less trouble paying the phone, milk, and light bills. I know I don't have much of the other money left, but I would like to know how much it amounts to so that I can begin to prepare for the day of brutal reckoning.

I saw Hiram Haydn in New York and also my agent, Elizabeth McKee, who were both very encouraging and gave me hope for the New Year.[6]

Hope all is well with you in Newport News. Let me hear from you.

Your son,

Bill Jr

P.S. Everyone is quite envious of my beautiful new shoes.

53. DURHAM

[February 20, 1949]

Dear Pop,

It's been some time since I have written so I thought I'd sit down and let you know about developments—such as they are—in Durham.

The weather here, to speak of a prosaic but, this year, rather remarkable subject, is wonderful. I guess you've been having the same sort: bright, balmy days and warm nights. The nicest winter I've ever seen, and it bears out my contention that a good climate is healthy for the soul, even though I've heard that if the weather is *too* nice and free from cold and sleet, as in California, it softens the brain and produces few good poems.

The writing I'm doing I can't complain about too violently at the present. It's still very slow going and full of little agonies, the jack-pot is way over the horizon yet, but my wall of patience, though full of little cracks and fissures, still stands. I've received a number of nice, encour-

6. McKee had taken on Styron as a client in September 1948; she remained his literary agent until the late 1960s.

aging letters from Hiram Haydn and on March 1st I'm going to send him my latest installment on the novel. I'm terribly discouraged with the novel, being hypercritical enough, perhaps, to magnify its defects and to overlook its virtues, and I suspect that I'll have to consign what I've written to the fire. That's not as bad it sounds. I've reached this hypothesis: if my period of apprenticeship is to be rewarding at all it must be accompanied by the sacrifice of a writer's first and most urgent passion— the desire for recognition. I hope I skirt that pitfall. I could have written a publishable novel by now, but if it's fifty years before I see print I'm going to make certain that what I submit to the public eye is as good as I can do, and not a shoddy substitute for the best. That perhaps sounds precious, but I believe it, and I'm going my solitary, painful way about it. In the meantime I'm paying homage to the masters—Flaubert, and now Tolstoy—and all the elements of this dreary period of indenture begin to settle gradually into their places—form, technique, style—like pegs in a cribbage board.

I received a letter from Auntie Elmer in Philadelphia. Uncle Buck had a stroke, thrombosis, but apparently absorbed it all right and is now on his way to recovery. Otherwise they seem fine, and, of course, her note was very entertaining—full of curiosa about history, music, and all her endless interests.

I'm set for money for the present anyway. Prices seem to be coming down, but I might have to call upon you soon for a cheque.

Let me hear from you when you get time.

Your son,
Bill Jr.

P.S. My dog—Mr. Chips—I had to give away to a Professor of Philosophy and his wife. I'm sure Chips is becoming very profound and stoical about a dog's life, with Plato and Spinoza to sustain him.[7]

54. DURHAM

March 31, 1949

Dear Pop,

It was good to get your letter with all the fine encouragement and advice, and I would have written sooner, except for the fact that I've been giving your "proposition"—which was so generous—some serious

---

7. For the history of Mr. Chips, a cocker spaniel, see *William Styron: A Life*, 147, 158, 166.

thought. I know it isn't easy for you to do it, and that's one reason the thing troubled me, but I'll gratefully accept, provided you take to my counter-proposition: that it be in the nature of an informal sort of loan, to be repaid when I've made some money at this writing game. That, of course, is a wild sort of statement, since heaven only knows when I'll make enough to pay it back. But in this miraculous country of ours anything can happen, so it's at least worth the try. At least be assured of this: that with your backing I won't stop until I've reached the goal. This time it's all or bust, and its got to be *all*. And I'm grateful to you for your help, more than you can know.[8]

Now here's something which you may or may not take to. Between Haydn and myself we have finally—after much talking and letters back and forth—agreed that perhaps the novel I'm now engaged on is worth postponing, in favor of another project less ambiguous in conception, and perhaps less *ambitious*. This new novel I have worked out in my mind is, unlike the other, concerned with just a few characters (too many characters I fully believe, is the stumbling-block of a first novelist), is concise in its conception, and, best of all, is much shorter, viz., it can be worked out thematically in a more or less predetermined number of pages. It's actually what I should have started on a year ago.[9]

But all this only leads up to the fact that Haydn and I both think that I'd do better back in New York where, as Haydn puts it, "Uncle Hiram can keep an eye on you." For one thing my work in the last few months seems to have slacked off down here; maybe it's the atmosphere; maybe I need a change of scene. For another thing, sad but true, I guess I do need someone to throw a whip over me, someone like Haydn, until I get to the point of having enough confidence where I can wield the whip myself. At any rate, it'll be the last move for some time for me. I do know that your environment doesn't have too much to do with what you write, but I feel I've exhausted everything that Durham has to offer and that New York, with all its chaos, will be a better place to work off this first novel. The furniture I can keep in safekeeping at Brice's until I have need for it.

Enclosed is Haydn's last letter—after I had written him, agreeing that I should come back to New York as he suggested. It shows, I think,

8. Styron's father had offered to send him $100 a month—a substantial sum in 1949, approximately the equivalent of $900 in 2009. A useful Web site for making these comparisons is www.measuringworth.com/calculators/compare.

9. This was to have been a novella about the Hart's Island experience.

that he has my best interests at heart still, despite my recent defection. I'll probably leave here the last week of April.

Thanks again for your kind offer. I think it'll be best for me all around. It'll give me something added to work for and to live up to. Let me hear from you soon.

Your son,
Bill, jr.

55. DURHAM

[April 10, 1949]
Sunday

Dear Pop,

It was nice being with you last week-end. Everybody seemed to enjoy the games, and I'm only sorry that my cold prevented me from entering into the spirit of the occasion a little bit more enthusiastically. After you left I still didn't feel too hot so I stayed in bed for a few days and on Thursday I went to an ear doctor, who found some infection in my right ear and put me on sulfadiazine.[10] At the moment I'm recuperating from the dreary effects of the latter, and although I still don't feel too good, most of the cold seems to be clearing up and I imagine that in another day or two everything will be normal. Sulfa seems to do wonders but I can't say that it makes you want to celebrate anything.

So after a gap of a couple of weeks I'm about to go back into my usual routine. I haven't heard from Haydn yet concerning the latest installment I sent him, and so I'm working on that Christchurch story, the first paragraph of which I read you when you were down here.[11] I've also got about a dozen letters to write.

Paying the month's bills sort of finished me, financially, so I guess you'd better send me a check for $100 as soon as you can. I've only got enough left for a couple of days.

Hope everything is going well at 139 Chesapeake.[12] The weather here is cold, but there's a promise of spring in the air.

Your son,
Bill Jr

10. As a boy Styron had been plagued by ear infections; sometimes his eardrums had been punctured by the family physician to alleviate pain.

11. "The Enormous Window," included in appendix 3.

12. Styron's father had moved from the Hilton Village house in which he had brought up his son to Elizabeth Buxton's family home at 139 Chesapeake Avenue.

56. DURHAM

April 16, 1949

Dear Pop,

I received the two checks you sent, and am grateful for both of them. I have bought some socks and things, and I think I'm all set as far as clothes go. I think that I'll be living pretty "tightly" within the next year or so, but somehow—with your kind help—I'm confident I'll make out.

I have had what, so far, I think is a good deal of luck as far as finding a place to live in New York goes. A girl friend of mine has put me on to an apartment, owned by a woman who is a writer, in Grand Street on the lower East Side. The area is slummy, but apparently the apartment is nice, and in an isolated, by-passed section of New York where still exist a number of artists and writers. It is a fifth-story "walkup" with what I understand is a "spectacular" view of the East River, two rooms, kitchen and bath, at $40 a month. I have communicated with the woman who owns the apartment and although she sounds business-like she says she is prejudiced in favor of writers, so as far as I know the apartment's mine. The place is furnished. I'm going to take it sight unseen, because if it turns out no good I will at least have a place to camp in while hunting for better accommodations. I also expect to share it in June when Bob Loomis—the boy you met at Brice's who was editor this year of the *Archive*—graduates from Duke and comes to New York.[13] That will cut down substantially on the rent problem.

I expect to leave here within the next week or so, sometime before the 25th.

I am arming myself with confidence, realizing, as you put it, that this year will no doubt be a critical one for me. It's a case of having everything to win, so I can't afford to lose. I've quit moanin' and groanin', and I'm going to write this novel through the simple expedients of setting myself to a regular schedule and making sure that no day goes by without some tangible accomplishment, no matter how small—your three-hundred words a day goal suggestion sounds good, and although

13. Robert Loomis was about to begin his career in publishing as a reader for Appleton-Century-Crofts. He would move to an editorial position at Rinehart and, in 1957, would move again to Random House, where he became Styron's editor after Hiram Haydn left to co-found Atheneum in 1959. (Loomis remained Styron's editor for the rest of his literary career.) Styron's plan to share living quarters with Loomis fell through, causing Styron to seek lodgings in Brooklyn.

I don't know whether my snail-like pace will allow me to accomplish such every day, it's at least something to aim at.

I'm pretty healthy now, I think, drinking less beer and eating three square meals a day. Given the help of you and Hiram Haydn and God, I don't think I'll fail.

I'll let you know soon what my new address will be. Thanks again for your great help and encouragement. I won't let you down.

Your son,

Bill jr

Styron arrived in New York in late April and got in touch with Agnes de Lima, the publicity director at the New School, whose daughter, Sigrid, had been a student with him in Hiram Haydn's writing seminars. With Aggie de Lima's help, Styron found cheap lodgings in the Flatbush section of Brooklyn in a rooming house that, years later, would serve as the model for the "Pink Palace" in Sophie's Choice.

57. FLATBUSH

May 2, 1949

Monday P.M.

1506 Caton Avenue

Brooklyn 26, N.Y.

Dear Pop,

I am writing this letter from my new home in—you wouldn't believe it—Brooklyn. I arrived in New York a little over a week ago, immediately began hunting around for an apartment, but found that places to live in are still terribly difficult to get, even though I had heard beforehand that things had loosened up somewhat. The last isn't true at all. You'd think that everyone in the country had converged upon New York, and that each was making a concerted effort to get an apartment, room—even an alcove somewhere. I suppose that it all involves some terrifically complicated economic theory, but it still strikes me as being a gigantic sort of fraud—that one has to knock his brains out and pay away his soul to boot to be able to get a roof over his head and a minimum of the necessities of life. I guess it's merely the fact that I'm politically naïve, and that the way to knowledge is mainly through experience—such experience as I am going through now. I suppose, too, that 99% of the radicals, so-called liberals, and Communists are only that way, not through any *a priori,* bookish idealism, but because they were broke once, or out in the rain, and had to turn to some politico-economic father confessor. Which from *my point of view* is all the more reason for *bucking* life as you see it—artistically speaking, that is—or accepting it, or making the most of it—*writing about it faithfully,* in the long run, and not getting mixed up with the soothsayers. I suppose that if you really catch hell from life—as an untouchable, say, or a sharecropper—your artistic instincts wither, and you become political. That's natural enough. But Americans are political enough as it is. We've got nearly everything, and we still bitch about this and that at every turn.

Which is all by way of saying that though I somehow resent not being able to settle down in a cozy Greenwich Village apartment at $40 a month, I am still glad to be in Brooklyn in a clean and decent place; and although there are no doubt better places in New York I'm not going to get angry and political about it and start joining the Communist party.

Actually I hope I'm not giving the impression that I'm complaining, because this is a pretty nice place by anyone's standards. It's in an old weatherbeaten house overlooking Prospect Park. There are plenty of trees around, plenty of grass, and big windows to look at the grass through. I'm in an apartment on the ground floor—two rooms, bath, kitchen, all furnished, $70 a month—the rent being impossible were it not for the fact that I am—or will be in June—sharing the apartment with Bob Loomis of Duke, who is coming to N.Y. to get a job. Split, the rent will be $9 a week, utilities included, which isn't bad. The apartment is owned by a nice, easygoing woman who seems anxious to please. She's educated, runs a school for backward children down the block.

I've seen Haydn, and I'm ready to go; in fact, I'm more than ready. I've already started the New Novel.

For some reason, although I'm not exactly ecstatic about the world and life in general, I'm very happy. I don't know why that should be, as I've always thought of myself as an exceptionally melancholy person. Maybe the melancholy was merely adolescent, and maybe, though I can't really sense it, I'm growing up, or reaching an "adjustment," as the psychologists say. Whatever it is, it's nice.

It's not love—love of a girl, that is, because I haven't found her yet. It's not the excitement of being in New York, because I've been in New

York before and now know how to take with a grain of salt its synthetic stimuli (though I still love New York). Actually I don't know what it is. For the past four or five days I've been alone, not seeing anyone or talking to anyone I know except over the phone. Ordinarily this aloneness would have made me miserable, utterly wretched. But I haven't minded it at all. I haven't drunk hardly anything—a few beers, that's all. And yet I've been quite content, suffused with a sort of pleasant well-being that demanded really nothing strenuous of myself, or of anyone else.

Perhaps it's merely that I've gained a measure of Emerson's self-reliance. Perhaps it's just that, for some reason I can't put my finger on, I feel surer of myself than I ever have before—more confident of my worth and my ultimate success, and less fearful of failure. I used to like to drink by myself. I still do occasionally, but gradually I've found myself stopping after the third beer, because there seems to be none of that fake pleasure in it anymore.

Maybe—again for some reason I haven't quite been able to analyze— I'm finding that life excites me, appeals to me in a way I've never felt before. I still have awful moments of despair, and I guess I always will, but they don't seem to be as overpowering as in the past. I don't take so much pleasure in my despondency any more; I try to throw my bleak moods off—which again perhaps is a sign that I'm growing up.

I don't know how this novel will turn out. Naturally, I hope it's good. But best of all is the fact that I'm not afraid of its being bad, literarily speaking, provided I know I've done my best. In the meantime I'm taking great pleasure in living, and in being alone without being a recluse. At night, after I've worked through the day, I walk up Church Avenue to Flatbush and thence down Flatbush, enjoying every minute of the walk. The faces are all Jewish, all harried and metropolitan, all enormously middle-class; yet as I say it's somehow all of a sudden wonderfully exciting. Maybe it's just forgetting one's self for a minute, not trying to be smug and self-centered and aloof. And I've learned to do finally—at least with far less effort and self-consciousness—something that three or four years ago you told me was one of the touchstones of maturity: being nice to people even when they're not nice to you.

There's something hideously crass and gaudy and meretricious about modern life; not that it hasn't always existed, but that it increases proportionally with time and with Science. God seems to be at times nothing more than Someone playing a neon-colored, television-equipped pinball machine. Yet I've found that although it all revolts me horribly at times, I can take it much more in my stride than I could before. I hate the way people think, especially in America; I'll always hate the stupid and the bat-brained and the petty. But it doesn't seem nearly so important anymore to hate, as try to understand.

Now I can look at two ignorant, slack-jawed, bloodshot men in a bar talking about the horseraces at Jamaica, and I think I can understand. At least I try to understand. That's one of the things, I guess, that Christ wanted one to do. Not that I'm getting religious all of a sudden, but I think He'd approve.

It's incredible how one runs about frantically at times like a rat in a maze, not really knowing right from wrong (and often really not caring), victim of one's own passions and instincts rather than master of one's own soul. I suppose the proper thing to do is just to stop every now and then and say, Where am I heading? Actually, though I'm still much like the psychologist's rat, I find myself asking myself that question almost too often. I suppose the very fact that I realize my indulgence in too much introspection, is another sign (I hope) of maturity. Too much brooding is unhealthy and, although I still have my slumps, I've begun to realize that one of the great secrets is striking a balance between thought and action. Between the Romantic and the Classical. Just living healthily. Living, acting, thinking; not just vegetating neurotically, on one hand, or blundering about, on the other hand, like so many people do, like trapped flies. It's a hard balance to strike, but I think it can be done, and that in this exciting-sorrowful age of ours it can make great literature.

Well, I've written more than I had thought. I've got to get up early tomorrow—another innovation!—so I'll close now. I hope everything at home is going along okay, and that you'll write soon.

Your son,
Bill, Jr.

58. FLATBUSH

June 6, 1949

Dear Pop,

Well, finally summer has come to Brooklyn, after a long period during which it seemed that we'd have winter right into the middle of July.

1506 Caton Avenue
Brooklyn 26, N.Y.
June 6, 1949

Dear Pop,

Well, finally summer has come to Brooklyn, after a long period during which it seemed that we'd have winter right into the middle of July. The hotter it gets, the better this place where I'm located seems to be. It must be 10° cooler here during the day than in Manhattan. I might have told you before, but the house where I live directly overlooks Prospect Park, and often, if I imagine it hard enough, the place seems about as big-cityfied as High Point, North Carolina. The street is lined with sycamores and elms, the houses all have green lawns, and sometimes — along with the scent of mown grass and burning leaves — I seem not to have ever left Hilton Village. Especially the suburban sort of smells — grass, food cooking, smoke; these are so evocative of memory. At any rate, it's quite pleasant, if a bit far out from the City itself.

The novel proceeds apace, although at the moment it is suffering a slight interruption because of a short story I want to write. It's another Christ church story — perhaps I've told you about it. I've worked at it off and on for the past few months, and I feel that I may as well get it finished now. So far, the progress has been good, though it still grieves me

Styron to his father from Brooklyn in the summer of 1949. Courtesy Estate of William C. Styron, Jr.

The hotter it gets, the better this place where I'm located seems to be. It must be 10° cooler here during the day than in Manhattan. I might have told you before, but the house where I live directly overlooks Prospect Park, and often, if I imagine it hard enough, the place seems about as big-cityfied as High Point, North Carolina. The street is lined with sycamores and elms, the houses all have green lawns, and sometimes— along with the scent of mown grass and burning leaves—I seem not to have ever left Hilton Village. Especially the suburban sort of smells— grass, food cooking, smoke; these are so evocative of memory. At any rate, it's quite pleasant, if a bit far out from the City itself.

The novel proceeds apace, although at the moment it is suffering a slight interruption because of a short story I want to write. It's another Christchurch story—perhaps I've told you about it. I've worked at it off and on for the past few months, and I feel that I may as well get it finished now. So far, the progress has been good, though it still grieves me greatly that writing doesn't come easier to me, and that what I accomplish has to be the result of infinite and nerve-wracking trouble and toil. I sometimes think that the writing would be better if I'd try to be facile and swift, but when I do lapse into such a way of thinking I invariably find that the writing just seems plain sloppy, so I turn back to my old agonizing method of trial and error, backing and filling, searching for *le mot juste*.

I'm hunting, too, for a part-time job. So far, no results, but I understand that with the summer coming on I stand a fair chance of getting a handyman's job in some publishing house. People going on vacations leave certain vacancies. I don't want to get a full-time job—my experience at Whittlesey House taught me that if you get really involved in publishing you won't do much writing—but I've got to get something.

The check you send every month is a great thing. Without it I'd probably be working 10 hours a day in the subways.

I hope you'll be able to come to New York sometime in the near future. There are a number of fine friends I have who want very much to meet you.

Your son,
WCS jr

5 / July 1949–April 1951

VALLEY COTTAGE AND NEW YORK

Late in June, Aggie de Lima invited Styron to live rent-free at her weekend residence in the town of Valley Cottage, a short distance up the Hudson River from the city. Styron accepted and stayed there for a year with Aggie's daughter, Sigrid, to whom Lie Down in Darkness *is dedicated.*

59. VALLEY COTTAGE

July 4, 1949
c/o de Lima, Valley Cottage, N.Y.

Dear Pop,

This is a much belated letter to thank you for the check and for your birthday telegram, which reached me on the morning of June 11 and which gave me much cheer.

The main reason that I am so tardy in writing you is that for the past two weeks I have been most energetically engaged in composing literature, a thing which no doubt you will approve of. As you may note from the address above, I have moved away from Brooklyn and am now entrenched in the home of two of the finest people in the world, the de Limas, about whom I think I've told you something before. Mrs. De Lima is publicity director at the New School, and I met her daughter, Sigrid, in Haydn's class. She—Sigrid—has just had a novel accepted by Scribners.[1] They have been very kind to me, and invited me to spend

---

1. This was Sigrid de Lima's first novel, *Captain's Beach*, published by Scribner's in 1950.

the summer with them at their house in Valley Cottage, which is up the Hudson from the city, just west a few miles from Nyack.

So here I've been—writing merrily away. From my window I can see the rolling Ramapo foothills, and an ocean of trees which, despite the drought, are still wonderfully green. I write well here, away from the city, feeling that I am with fond and devoted friends. I have just finished a nice short story—the "Christchurch" one—which turned out very well, and which I've sent off to my agent. I hope it gets sold, because it's so much better than most stories I've been reading of late. Now to the novel. After I've finished a hundred or so pages I'm going to send it off to the Eugene F. Saxton Trust, which awards up to $2400 to promising novelists, no strings attached. With some luck, I think I may get it.[2]

This is a wonderful place. The de Limas are fine to talk to and be with, and there's a gorgeous radio-phonograph full of Mozart and Beethoven. What is so remarkable, though, is that these enticements don't deter me, but rather provide an excellent stimulation—for my work, I mean. Especially after my last story, I'm beginning to feel really confident that I'm going somewhere.

How are things on Hampton Roads? Is there a breeze? Please write and tell me how everything goes with you.

Your son,
WCS jr

60. VALLEY COTTAGE

[July 31, 1949]
Sunday

Dear Pop,

It's about time that I gave you a report on work in progress and also thank you for the check which, of course, is being put to good use, i.e., recompensing the de Limas in part for their hospitality, which has been considerable.

2. The Eugene F. Saxton Memorial Trust, established by Harper and Brothers in honor of one of its longtime fiction editors, provided awards for young writers. James Baldwin had won a grant from the Saxton Trust in 1944. Styron did not win the award; it is possible that he did not apply for it.

Everything goes very well up here in the Ramapos. I'm hard at work on the novel—the original one—and now that I've established a "plan of attack," as it were, it promises to go awfully well. Writing itself, as usual, is very difficult—except for those rare fine moments when it all begins to *pour*—but, inching along, I can manage now and then to see how the whole thing *will* end, and in a point of time, I hope, not too far away. Also—and this is the best thing—I think I can safely say that it's going to be an excellent book—not without many flaws, of course—but full of life and artistry, as much as I can put into it, and a good many cuts above the average first novel. Right now, of course, I'm mainly engrossed in finishing the book, but it's encouraging to hear, as I did the other day from Haydn, that if it's as good as he thinks it's going to be, he's going to promote it to the fullest. I suppose it's not "artistic" for me to think of my book in terms of publishing and sales and so forth, but I frankly hunger for recognition, even though I've heard that fame is a snare and a delusion.

This is, outside of work, a placid life I lead here. The days go by so serenely that one is hardly distinguishable from another, and I don't mark the weekends at all. There is much music here, as I have told you— something which I've come to regard almost as an essential to inspiration; right now I'm listening to a complete performance of *The Magic Flute*, over WABF, the New York FM station. I've only been into the city once or twice since I've been up here, and when I was there I found it so incredibly hot that I could hardly wait until I got back to the cool woods and clean air.

I've begun to wonder what I've done to deserve this nice way of life. I feel really *healthy* for a change—physically and mentally. I've become confident of my powers, and I'm ready to put my whole heart into the accomplishment of writing at least good fiction and, I hope, someday great fiction. Is that hoping too much?

I hope everything goes well in Newport News—I almost write "Port Warwick," for that is the name of my fictional city in the Tidewater, full of strange and wonderful people.

Thanks again for the check, Pop. Without your constant and faithful help I don't know how I could get all this done. Write soon.

Your son,
Bill, Jr.

61. VALLEY COTTAGE

September 1, 1949

Dear Pop,

The novel, I am pleased to report, is still shaping up very well. I don't know exactly how long it'll be, but I rather think that I am between a third and half finished. It's a long day, this day in "Port Warwick" that I am describing, and I still have to go pretty slow. I just completed a section that I am very pleased with. It concerns a personage whom I call "Daddy Faith," who is really, of course, none other than the renowned Bishop Grace of Jefferson Avenue fame.[3] He wears an opera hat and a diamond stickpin and he drives in a liveried Cadillac. His followers all sing "Happy Am I."

I hope I can get this book finished by next summer. For private and gratuitous reasons—rather vain, I suspect—I'd like to complete it before my twenty-fifth birthday. However, I'm not going to strain myself in that direction; if I do get it finished by then, well and good, but I'm not going to sacrifice accuracy and art for speed. If it's all as good as that which I've done up until now, and if it achieves some sort of unity, I really think you will have a son you may be proud of.

I hope that I have not taken too many liberties with the good people of Newport News. At any rate, I have certainly not set out to "expose" or vilify anyone. There are in the book probably a few faintly recognizable characters—recognizable, that is, with a stretch of the imagination—but I've treated everyone sympathetically. For some reason I find it hard not to treat people with sympathy. It'll be a good book under any circumstance, and I fondly hope that the Christmas after this one finds you with a printed, bound copy in your hands.

Everything up here goes smoothly and well. Professor Blackburn called me up from New York yesterday on his way to vacation in New Hampshire. I went down to the city and had a long talk with him. He's going to spend a night up here in the country on his way back South. He inquired about you, and sent his regards.

3. Daddy Faith in *Lie Down in Darkness* was partly based on Bishop Charles Emmanuel Grace, a charismatic African American religious leader known to his followers as Daddy Grace. His United House of Prayer comprised a chain of some twenty churches in various cities along the eastern seaboard. His church in Newport News was located on Jefferson Avenue. Styron took characteristics for Daddy Faith also from Elder Solomon Lightfoot Michaux, an early radio evangelist whose Church of God Movement drew its followers from eastern Virginia and Washington, D.C.

Thanks for the check a million times. People say, with all justification, that I'm extraordinarily lucky to have a Pop like you. The de Limas ask me to invite you up here any time you can come. I think you'd enjoy a visit as much as they would. Let me hear from you soon. How was the construction job finally?

Your son,
Bill, Jr.

62. VALLEY COTTAGE

October 29, 1949
Friday

Dear Pop,

Thanks very much for the check and the letter. Why don't you dispose of the ticket to the Carolina–Notre Dame game, so that you can be up here on that date?

Mrs. de Lima and Sigrid and, of course, I, want you to stay up here in Valley Cottage during your trip, if you have no objections to doing so. It is within easy commuting distance, and in fact if there are any morning meetings I could drive you down to New York, an hour's ride, or at least to the George Washington bridge, where you could take a subway to the Waldorf. It would also save you hotel expenses; in short, we think it would be happier all the way around.

Here is what I suggest. You say that you are arriving on Thursday, November 10th and that you have a meeting that afternoon. Unless there is important business that night, why don't you call me (this number: de Lima NYack 7-1806-W) and tell me when the afternoon session is over? Then we could arrange for you to come up here that night; I could drive down and get you, or you could easily get a bus to Nyack, or you might like to come up with Mrs. de Lima, who will be knocking off work at the New School, I imagine, just about the time your meeting is over. Then we could have a nice dinner up here, and lots of talk and music. On Friday you could go back to the city and come back up here at whatever time it suits you. On Saturday we could take a long, lovely drive through this wonderful countryside, or do anything you'd like to do. At any rate, *be sure and call me when you arrive.* I think you'll enjoy seeing this place, and you'll love the de Limas. We're all looking forward to seeing you.

I got a long letter from Eliza the other day. Please tell her that I enjoyed hearing all the news, and will reply soon.

Until the 10th!

Your son,
Bill Jr.

63. VALLEY COTTAGE

[November 15, 1949]
Tuesday

Dear Pop,

Well, I hope you had a fine birthday party. Did you get the telegram? I imagine that with the gathering of the clan a great time was enjoyed by all and also that many toasts and sköls! were drunk. I hope so.

Life up here in the North Woods goes on happily as usual, with little happening to break the routine. I'm progressing steadily on the book, and hope to be *halfway* through or thereabouts within maybe two months. The part I'm working on now interests me a lot and as a consequence goes much more easily and faster than those parts which are merely fill-ins or transitional. Sigrid and I were down in the city last Saturday night to Hiram Haydn's house, a sort of soirée. Haydn's still waiting, apparently anxiously, for the next installment. Also at the party were Aldous Huxley's son and Clifton Fadiman's nephew. Celebrities.

The weather up here is incredible. Hot days and nights almost like summer. I have a suspicion that the earth has sneaked off its orbit and is flirting with the sun; a reliable cracker-barrel source up here has it that the earth is in a periodic hot-and-dry cycle, but I wouldn't know. Incidentally, just about when are you planning to be here in November? Tom Peyton is going to be in Crozet sometime next month, on vacation, and has invited me down for a few days; I'd like to go, but I want to know first when you'll be here so there won't be any chance of my missing you. I think you'll enjoy gazing at the leaves and the lovely Ramapo hills. We have a very special drive planned for you, too—high up over the Palisades near West Point—a splendid view.

Please let me know how your party was—it sounded very nice. In the meanwhile I'm hard at work—squeezing it out, as it were. When I finish I'll be so shocked at reaching the end, I believe, that I won't even care about the publishing part.

Your son
Bill Jr

64. VALLEY COTTAGE

December 12, 1949

Dear Pop and Eliza,

I got your cards today, alerting me on the *box of comestibles* which hasn't arrived as yet, but which I'm sure will come soon and which I know will have all sorts of wonderful things to eat within. Thanks very much. I have no doubt that it will provide great cheer to all of us over the coming holidays. Also thanks, Eliza, for the letter with the news, the cigarettes that Pop brought here on his visit, and the various clippings, which were of great interest.

I have finished that part of the novel which I'm going to send to Haydn, hoping for a further monetary advance as a result. Since my last report I've amended my idea as to what percentage of the novel I have completed—one-half instead of three-fifths—but at that it seems to be a colossally thick pile of manuscript. I've started typing the thing today, hoping to finish by Christmas or thereabouts, but at the rate of speed I type it'll probably be longer than that. At any rate, I'm as satisfied as is possible with what I've done so far. I'm especially glad that I can see clearly the growth that's been taking place in my mind just during the process of composition. I've learned to write with greater ease and poise and rhythm than I did when I started out, and although writing is still difficult I find that, with all this effort and practice, I'm constantly *growing* in every way, which is the most important thing of all. The book has a lot of flaws, but I think a lot of very good things, too, and nothing whatsoever that I can be actually ashamed of.

Life up here is still slow and pleasant otherwise. Music and reading and an occasional movie in Nyack or Spring Valley. Incidentally, if "All The King's Men" comes to Newport News, which I'm sure it will eventually, I recommend it heartily. A superior picture.[4]

I hope everything is going well at home, and I imagine that Christmas, though hectic, as it manages to be everywhere, will be pleasant and cheerful. Give my best to everyone, and thanks again for the forthcoming *box*. I will give you all a full report on the reactions here.

As ever,
Bill, Jr.

4. The 1949 film version of the novel starred Broderick Crawford as Willie Stark and John Ireland as Jack Burden.

65. VALLEY COTTAGE

January 25, 1950

Dear Pop,

There's nothing much to report in the way of news this week, but I got your check a few days ago and wanted to thank you. I also have been getting the clippings that Eliza sends, and I wish you'd tell her for me that I find them very interesting and am looking forward to seeing more of them. The grounding of the *Missouri* has made great news up here and is all over the front pages. The "anti-Navy" papers, of course, have made much to-do over the incident, and have played it up for all it's worth as an example of Navy inefficiency.[5]

I've been having some trouble getting the rest of the novel rolling, but I seem to have surmounted the more dangerous obstacles and so by now I'm fairly well along into my fourth chapter (out of a probable total of six, possibly seven, chapters in all). The chapters are not really chapters in the conventional sense, but are rather "sections" in which I deal with considerable periods of time. It's still all very difficult, but, as I've told you before, I think gradually I'm developing greater fluency. By that I don't mean that I've become "facile," but rather that I'm learning how to transform thought into words in the least amount of time and with the greatest, I hope, stylistic ease. Possibly a lot of people think that writing a novel is a very simple chore, but I have found it, despite the obvious rewards, the most difficult thing in the world. I'd much rather write music although I understand that that sort of composition can involve great agony, too. At any rate, I'm happy in the thought that by degrees I'm approaching the point where I know what I want to say, and am becoming able to say it with more accuracy and grace. We live in an age of monstrous happenings and if I'm able to correct the wrongs in a small way—or merely to be able to take people's minds off events for a moment, with a laugh or two—I'll be happy.

Pop, do you think that you could put in a subscription for me to the *Sunday Daily Press*? I'd just like to read about Newport News once a week. I'd be much obliged if you would do this for me.

5. On Tuesday, January 17, 1950, the U.S. Navy battleship *Missouri* ran aground in an artificial channel dredged by army engineers in the Chesapeake Bay, not far from Norfolk and Newport News. An effort to free the vessel on January 20 was unsuccessful. See "19 Tugs Fail to Pull the Missouri Free," *New York Times,* January 21, 1950, 3.

The de Limas, and I, send best regards to all. The last of that lovely ham went yesterday—ground up in green peppers!

Your son,
Bill, Jr.

66. VALLEY COTTAGE

February 11, 1950

Dear Pop and Eliza,

As a sort of antidote to that C. V. Terry review in the *Times* Book Review of "Captain's Beach," I am enclosing a review from the daily *Times* which, as you may see, is a somewhat more accurate and sane appraisal. Everybody was rather worked up, including Hiram Haydn, over the Terry review. It's a *she*, not a *he*, apparently a frustrated old maid who has worked as hack writer for many years and who has no business writing reviews at all, since she obviously has no literary perception. Most of the other reviews were fine—*Herald-Tribune, Saturday Review, Nation*, and *Newsweek*, especially, which also ran Sigrid's picture.[6]

The cocktail party was very successful and gay. About 150 people were there, including such stellar characters as William Rose Benét, John Hall Wheelock, Ridgely Torrence, Jean Starr Untermeyer, Freda Kerchway (editor of *The Nation*), Horace Kallen, Alvin Johnson (president emeritus of the New School), and a horde of lesser luminaries.[7] Afterwards Haydn and his wife and Sigrid and I and another couple all went to a very chi-chi bistro on Waverley Place named Ricky's and had

6. For the negative review, see C. V. Terry, "Ad Lib," *New York Times Book Review*, February 5, 1950, 191; for the positive notice, see Charles Poore, "Books of the Times," *New York Times*, February 11, 1950, 22. The other reviews mentioned by Styron appeared in the *Nation*, February 11, 1950; *New York Herald-Tribune Book Review*, February 5, 1950; *Saturday Review of Literature*, February 11, 1950, and *Newsweek*, February 13, 1950.

7. These guests were visible on the New York academic and literary scene in the 1940s and 1950s. The poet William Rose Benét was one of the cofounders of the *Saturday Review of Literature* and the author of a column called "The Phoenix's Nest" for that journal. John Hall Wheelock, a published poet, was editor in chief at Scribner's in 1950. Ridgely Torrence, a poet and playwright, had been poetry editor of the *New Republic* in the 1920s and early 1930s. Jean Starr Untermeyer, then married to the poet and critic Louis Untermeyer, was a poet, translator, book reviewer, and lecturer at the New School. Horace Kallen was one of the co-founders of the New School and was a member of the faculty there from 1919 until 1952.

lamb chops and brandy, and proceeded homeward in quite a glow. As a sad sort of postscript, a friend of ours drove all the way down from Boston to the party—*the next day.*

Now everything seems to be back to normal again, and work proceeds as usual.

I was sorry to hear of the virus pneumonia but I hope that you have recovered now and that everything is proceeding normally. I have been receiving the *Daily Press,* which I appreciate very much, and I hope you don't find it too much trouble to wrap up and send me each week. It's really very interesting to read, and amazing and a bit sad to see how so much has changed in nine years since I was a permanent resident. Morrison, I notice, for instance, is now "Warwick" H.S., which is mighty fancy.[8]

About the income tax: I don't have to file a return unless I make $500 per annum, which I don't, so I imagine it's perfectly all right to list me as a dependent. I won't be a dependent long, but I suppose you know how much your help has meant to me. Actually, having taken so long to work up steam, so to speak, for this novel, it would have been almost impossible to have kept going without your aid. I'm impatient to get the thing finished (it's been a fearfully long time a-bornin') but not so impatient that I still won't work as carefully on it as I can. As I've told you before, it naturally won't be the Great American Novel (I just recently read, for the first time, Dreiser's *An American Tragedy,* which I think is the "G.A.N.," if any novel is), but you may rest assured that it will be worth all the time I've taken on it since I *do* believe that it's about as good a first novel as you're likely to see. Besides, if it were my masterpiece, what would be the use of writing any more? Steady growth, like Hawthorne's, is what I'm aiming at, and beer only on the weekends.

Love to all,
Bill Jr.

67. VALLEY COTTAGE

March 14, 1950

Dear Pop,

I got your letter with the picture of you holding forth at the SAR meet-

---

8. Styron attended Morrison High School in Newport News through his sophomore year, then entered Christchurch. He means here that his high school has been renamed.

ing, and I must say you look very imposing—far more than J. Earl Moreland, who just looks like a college president.[9]

I would have written sooner, but there hasn't seemed to be any special news to communicate. For a while I had a spell of stomach trouble but I went to a doctor in Nyack who gave me some medicine so now I'm okay again. I also had six teeth filled and I feel pretty set up about that, too, and I hope I won't have to bother with a dentist for a long time. It's good to get such things out of the way.

I'm well along into the latter half of the novel, and it seems to be going along pretty smoothly, except for the fact that once I get started on an episode I don't seem to be able to break it off short of what seems thousands of words. However, there comes a point, I'm beginning to believe, where you just have to trust to instinct and forsake the carefully-pared, precise artistic approach and hope that most of what you're writing is rich and meaningful, even if it doesn't fit into your preconceived plans.

I sometimes feel that I have been writing this novel for centuries. I write and write and it still goes so slowly and it still doesn't come even close to an ending. I probably won't know what to do with myself when I finish this one, it having been so much a part of me, but I suspect I'll just sit down and start on another one. But I do wish that this one were finished. It would take at least an immediate sort of worry off my mind, because I always seem to be perpetually fretting over the quality of certain sections, things I've done, things I've left undone. Once I commit this book to type, however, those troubles will just fly away.

There's been a lot of snow up here, and I did something I haven't done since I was 11 years old at Huntington Park.[10] I went sledding! It was a beautiful ride and I wore myself out, sliding down a long slope on a graded path through the woods—nearly a third of a mile altogether. It was so exhilarating I caught myself laughing aloud.

Tell Eliza I'm getting the newspaper she sends, also the clippings and programs, which I enjoy reading. I'm sending a copy of *Captain's Beach* as you requested, in the next mail.

9. Styron's father was a member of the Sons of the American Revolution, an organization devoted to the study of the Revolutionary War. J. Earl Moreland was president of Randolph-Macon Men's College in Ashland, Virginia.

10. A sixty-acre park near the James River Bridge in Newport News, named for Collis P. Huntington, the railway baron who chose the city as the eastern terminus for the Chesapeake and Ohio Railroad in 1880.

Best to all.

Your son,
Bill Jr.

68. VALLEY COTTAGE

April 13, 1950

Dear Pop,

Whenever I look at the calendar it always seems that it's this part of the month that I write you, and that I've been most dilatory in writing you anyway. I hope I can beg your indulgence for my neglect, this month at least, for actually what with one thing and another—forging ahead, as the phrase goes, on my novel, and finishing a short story—I look back and find that in weeks I haven't written to anyone at all. Not that that's much of an explanation.

Your advice as to my getting exercise was well taken, and the exercise itself will go into effect as soon as the weather clears. Right now, here at this late date, it's snowing in small flurries outside, though I don't think it'll stick. At any rate, I hope you weren't really concerned over the stomach upset I had, for it cleared itself up in no time at all and I feel fine once more.

The story I mentioned above I just finished a week or so ago, taking time off for a few days from my book, and I do believe it's the best short story I've done to date.[11] It concerns an "ex-" Southerner's visit to a ramshackle farm in Virginia, where he meets his old uncle, only to be driven off the place with derision and imprecations. It's not a pretentious story: by that I mean that I think I've balanced the *intention* of the story with the substance of the narrative, and all in all I believe I've managed to carry the thing off with a peculiarly, and successfully, haunting effect. The "haunting" part, I think, derives from the fact that it's based almost fully on a dreamy half-nightmare I had one night, which was so impressive that I didn't go to sleep at all but wrote the outline for the story in the hours before dawn. I've sent it off to my agent, Elizabeth McKee, who is irritatingly slow always in answering my letters to her, so I don't know whether she thinks she can sell it or not. If she can't sell this one then I doubt if she'll be able to sell any of my stories. By this time, though, I've become, if not resigned, then at

11. This story does not survive.

least accustomed to remaining in literary oblivion. I've lost most of the old frantic desire to get printed. I realize now that most of my stories of the past few years really weren't worth being printed, and it makes me happy, if not especially wild-eyed and desperate for recognition, to see how well I've progressed—as with this latest story. So I just bide my time and keep on writing with the same slow, identical painstakingness that I imagine I'll be employing forty years from now, and am more comfortable in the realization that eventually these things will not only suffer the painful *accouchement* but will get the smiles, maybe, and the approval that all good fathers' sons should receive.

I also this month completed a chapter of the novel, which leaves me, if my present plan is followed, only two more to go out of a total of six. These last chapters, however, will be somewhat longer than the first. What a baffling, splendid job writing a novel is! With all of the heartaches involved, it's the most rewarding task, in a way, that a person can set himself to. Each paragraph, each page becomes better and better—at least in my case—and it's a wonderful revelation to see how strikingly one's power of expression becomes more forceful and strengthened after the exercise of two hundred pages or so. This novel will be shot through with faults, but when it is finished I will know my own style, I will know how to write.

I have been reading Sandburg's "Lincoln: The War Years," and it's really an astonishing book.[12] It's heightened my interest in the War Between the States, which I've always had to some extent, and I think that sometime not too long from now, after reading a lot more, I'll walk over the Virginia battlefields: the road to Richmond is full of them: Seven Pines, Gaines' Mill, Malvern Hills, Chickahominy. What a splendid thing it would be to write a vast book about that war, I mean a really great book. Some say (the "intellectuals") that America has never had glory or tragedy, but, with all its stupid confusions of motive, that war was both glorious and tragic, and I daresay that it was the last war in which the Lord God of Hosts hovered over the battlefields.

The papers are still coming and I enjoy them and tell Eliza I appreciate, too, the various and interesting clippings.

Best to all.

Your son
Wm. C. Styron, Jr.

12. Carl Sandburg, *Lincoln: The War Years*, 4 vols. (New York: Harcourt, Brace, 1939). This work won the Pulitzer Prize for History in 1940.

69. VALLEY COTTAGE

May 15, 1950

Dear Pop,

Again I'm late, but not too late, I hope, to communicate my enthusiasm for your proposed trip to Haiti with Eliza. It surely sounds like a wonderful safari, and I do hope that nothing prevents your carrying the plans through. I can remember at Christchurch every day poring over the atlas maps of Haiti and the Bahamas and the Windward Islands, and wondering if I'd ever get there. Well, maybe I will someday, but until then I could get a vicarious pleasure from knowing that *you* went there. Do you remember, too, when we lived in Hilton and I was perhaps eight years old and pestered you constantly to take me big-game hunting in Haiti or Cuba? And how grimly serious I was about it, and heartbroken when you said no? I think actually it was the glamour of wearing one of those pith helmets which made it all seem, in my imagination, so exotic.

I'm now well along into what I guess is the backstretch of the novel, and have plunged into what I hope will be one of the most rousing scenes of the story—this one laid in Charlottesville. It's rather amazing when I think of it—the book has a primarily tragic theme yet each of my scenes are set against a background of carousing and gaiety. But really, how slow it all goes! Sometimes I think I'll be writing this same novel when I'm a very old, very poor man, and the others of my contemporaries have just finished spending their second million dollars.

There is little news to relate—most of it being common to practically everyone: the advent of a beautiful spring. We had a picnic last week in Bear Mountain Park and, since the park is not officially open yet, we had the park and the beautiful dogwood all to ourselves. Two other spring items: Tommy Peyton is going to get married sometime this year and Hill Massie is going to be married in Richmond on the 24th of June, and I'm his best man![13] I've met his girl, and she's really very fine. Another item, not necessarily concerned with spring: Hiram Haydn came down with the mumps, but weathered the disease without injury, and I went down to solace him and, even amid the mumps, he reaffirmed his ardent faith in me.

13. Hill Massie was a friend from Hilton Village.

Give my best to all.

Your son,

Bill Jr

P.S. Mrs. de Lima wants to know if you have any idea what the best sort of water heater is. Is one of these glass-lined, non-rust A. O. Smith heaters superior to a Rudd?[14] Have you any ideas?

In June 1950 Styron left Valley Cottage and moved back to the city, where he shared lodgings with Howard Hoffman, a painter and sculptor who was taking classes at the New School. He and Hoffman lived in a small apartment on West 88th Street. Styron finished Lie Down in Darkness *while living there.*

70. NEW YORK

June 5, 1950
314 West 88th Street
New York 24, N.Y.

Dear Pop,

I suppose you might be surprised to see the change of address above, but I moved down here a few days ago and I expect to be here all summer —a temporary stay, I hope. I think my wonderful stay at the de Limas was destined to come to an end about this time, and although the move was not effected without a certain amount of regret on all sides, it came about with as little pain as possible, and I think it was the only thing to do. I don't know whether I'll go back to Valley Cottage or not— permanently, that is—but even if I don't I'll remember my stay there as about the most pleasant, mutually rewarding time of my life. At any rate, before I left I planted corn and tomatoes in the garden up there, and so Sigrid and Mrs. de Lima and I have planned to go back most every weekend to weed and cultivate and pick the crop.

The novel still goes very well, and I have picked out a nice place, I think, to write. It's located between Riverside Drive and West End Avenue, 1½ rooms, which I share with a fellow named Howard Hoff-

14. The two leading manufacturers of water heaters and plumbing supplies in the 1940s and 1950s.

man, kitchen, bath—$8.25 a week, which is very reasonable. The guy I share the place with is a New School student—had an advertisement up on the bulletin board down there. He is a teacher and a sculptor, and seems to be both very intelligent and very nice.[15] So I think I'm all set up until I finish the novel—at which time I intend to move to Sussex County, Va., and raise peanuts, with writing as an avocation.

It has been a long hard road for me—not from a material point of view (there I've been much better set up than most, I know), but in the inner struggle and the *quest*. I'm still far from my goal, but gradually I'm beginning to see things clearer, and to learn how to relate my art to my life. I'm sure I'm writing better all the time, and that my writing is becoming stronger and more mature. I think that I am becoming more mature, too. It is certainly a manifest truth in this day that what, above all, our people need to have is maturity and strength and an illumination of that spirit which has never died, or never will die— even if it means that in order to write with truth one has to batter his head bloody against a mass of materialism, and hypocrisy, and runaway "progress." Even if it means being "reactionary" to write in the name of Christian charity and the worn-out virtues, I will show them, as powerfully as I can, if I can beat the race with time.

In regard to the money you have been sending me, all I can say is that I would have been just about completely lost without it—and you must know yourself how much it has meant to me. But I don't wish to keep taking it until my novel is written, or for any length of time, if it is more than you can spare. This is all by way of saying that I know the year is up, and more, that you offered to send me the checks, and I wouldn't feel right in accepting still others, especially in the light of the shipbuilding slump and so forth.

You have had faith in me, and it has been a wonderful feeling to know that one is not alone. Even in this day when art is frowned upon still as a not quite healthy profession, a lot of artists are lucky and I'm glad to be one of them. In the long run, despite the sneers and indifference, the artist, the real one, has always been vindicated in the end, except that it takes a *long* time and some have a more *fortunate* time than others. *Amor Vincit* . . .

15. Hoffman, an infantry veteran who had participated in the assault on southern Italy in 1944, later became a member of the faculty at Bryn Mawr. See *William Styron: A Life*, 181–83.

No other news except that everything, again, goes well on the writing front and *that*, at the risk of sounding selfish, is gradually becoming to me the only thing that matters, although the lesson is fairly hard.

Your son,
Bill Jr.

71. NEW YORK

July 8, 1950

Dear Pop,

Thanks for the clipping on Leon. As you say, he really *dood* it.[16] I wrote him a letter recently, after receiving one from him: he seems to be very happy over his achievement (naturally!) and I expect that he will make a first-rate pediatrician. I was also pleased to hear that you're coming to New York in August. I'm hoping that you'll have extra time so that we can visit before you take off for the Caribbean. Before I forget it, my telephone number is TRafalgar 7-2895, so call me as soon as you arrive.

I have some news which you might find interesting. As you may have heard, Hiram Haydn has become editor-in-chief at Bobbs-Merrill which, of course, is one of the oldest and largest publishing houses. So, through a vast amount of effort and through some private coaching from both Haydn and Mavis McIntosh, my agent, I managed to obtain a release from my contract with Crown (on a very legal level) and I will have a new contract with Bobbs-Merrill come next week.[17] It means that Bobbs will pay back to Crown the money that Crown has given me, and also means that I may get some more money from Bobbs-Merrill. Mavis, the agent, likes the novel very much and she thinks that she will be able to get part of it published in one of the magazines—Harper's Bazaar or Mademoiselle—sometime before the book comes out. Everything begins to fall nicely into place. The book itself is rolling merrily along and with luck I'll be able to finish it sometime this fall. Then I'm going to write a bunch of short stories I've had in mind for a long time; then I'd like to go to Europe before I start Opus II.

New York is fine this summer, not too hot, and except for the vague horrid threat of another war everyone seems to be carrying on with the

16. Leon Edwards had been admitted to Harvard Medical School.

17. Mavis McIntosh was the business partner of Elizabeth McKee, the literary agent who had taken on Styron as a client.

usual complement of human dignity or foolishness, depending on the person. I hope that when you come up you'll be able to see my apartment; the more I stay here the more I like it. Perhaps, too, if you have time, we can go to see the movies at the Museum of Modern Art: they have wonderful revivals—old Chaplin films, "The Birth of a Nation," and "The Great Train Robbery"! Best to all.

Your son,
Bill Jr

72. NEW YORK

September 12, 1950

Dear Pop,

It was fine seeing you both your times here in New York, and I hope that the trip left you in a fine state of health and well-being—as it did, judging by your appearance, sunburned and radiant, on the boat a week or so ago. I got the picture in the mail today and I like it fine, and I appreciate Eliza sending it to me.

There is still no word from the Marine Corps, so perhaps it means that I won't be called for a while.[18] In the meantime I'm trying to work hard on the book, which is nearing completion (or should be finished in four or five months), and maybe there's a chance I can have it done before the Marines and the war. I do, however, have to have some money if I'm to go on, and I wonder if you'd consider reinstating me for a while on the $100 a month basis. As maybe I told you, the $1000 I got from Bobbs-Merrill was on the basis of $500 (already received) now, and the other $500 when the Manuscript is accepted. This is standard procedure among publishers. Well, of the $500 I got, $250 I had to pay back to Crown Publishers for the money *they* had advanced me. Naturally I couldn't change publishers without paying Crown back what they had already given me. This left me with $250, on which I have been living since early in July. Now it's practically all gone, and frankly I just need the $100 a month from you again if I intend to finish

18. The Korean War had begun on June 25, 1950, when North Korean troops invaded South Korea. The United States sent military forces to engage the North Koreans and, anticipating a long conflict, began to move its reserve troops to active duty. Styron believed (correctly) that he would be recalled to the Marine Corps. The Korean War did not end until July 1953.

the novel. In a couple of months, when I've finished this next-to-the-last chapter I'm working on, I think I can submit the balance of what I've done on the book to Bobbs-Merrill and get, say, $250, but until then I've got to eat and pay the rent. So if you can manage it, I'll do my very best for myself, and for you, and finish this thing up in a blaze of glory.

Life up here is the same. There's war-talk all over which, to say the least, is depressing, but I guess the best thing to do is to put it out of one's mind as best as possible. I hope everything is well with you and Eliza and that you didn't find Newport News unromantic (even if cooler and cleaner) than Haiti. My best to all. I'm doing my best.

Your son,
Bill, jr

73. NEW YORK

October 30, 1950

Dear Pop,

I've owed you a letter for some time and I would have written you sooner, except for the fact that an attack of bronchitis has recently laid me low, and up until now I haven't felt like doing anything. I'm perfectly all right now, and feel very healthy once more, but for a while I felt pretty morose about things. I finally went to a doctor on the East Side who fluoroscoped me and prescribed aureomycin, which I took— 16 little pills which cost $9.00. That's the price all right, but it was worth it, I guess, because it cleared me up in no time at all, and with no side-effects. I hope it's my last for the winter. My health is fine now, and I'm taking good care of myself.

The book, after that gap, is really coming along. Last night I took a big hunk of MS to Hiram Haydn, who is going to send it out to Indianapolis for typing. I have well over the equivalent of 300 pages (printed pages, that is) and it looks as if the book will run to 125–130,000 words, which is pretty big. I've still got a couple of big chapters to go, though, so it might go over that figure and be as big as *Kristin Lavransdatter* or one of those Scandinavian epics, God forbid.[19] However, size is not

---

19. *Kristin Lavransdatter*, a long historical novel by the Norwegian author Sigrid Undset (1882–1949), was published originally in three volumes between 1920 and 1922. It appeared, in English translation, in a single-volume edition from Knopf in 1929—some 1,069 pages in length.

important; my main problem is to write the book well, which I'm doing. At least you can expect to see the thing published by sometime in 1951. Haydn would like to see it published in June, which is a good date for first novels to come out, but I think I won't get it finished until perhaps February, which will make the publication come sometime in the fall.

Did you go to Buddy Hayes's wedding? I'd like to see a clipping about the affair if you have one. I don't know why, but I visualize most everyone married except Buddy. I'll bet you there was no doubt as to who the largest man present was at that ceremony.

I write days and I'm beginning, rather compulsively, to write in the evenings, too. As someone said, writing a novel is like beating your way with your fists through a door to the outer world. It goes splinter by splinter and finally I guess there's a miraculous, unbelievable day when the whole thing comes crashing through. Best to all.

Your son,
Bill Jr.

74. NEW YORK

November 4, 1950

Dear Pop,

I was greatly disturbed to hear about your illness, but being in good hands and everything I trust that you are making a good recovery and that soon you'll be up and around and enjoying things again.[20] I hope, too, that emotionally you are taking this thing in your stride. I know how you must feel and, although I didn't get the full details from Elizabeth, I gather that it's not something which can be tossed off lightly. However, I do hope you won't let it depress you a great deal. Just by way of coincidence, I had dinner with Dr. Irving Simons in Mt. Vernon, N.Y. a few weeks ago; he is, you may remember, the father of Hank Simons, who was my best friend at Duke. He's a very prominent urologist in New York, and he had an attack much similar to yours about two years ago. He was remarking to Hank and me that in a way he was thankful for the warning: it had reminded him that he wasn't a spring chicken any more, and that he had to slow down. Since that time he's been active, but careful. By way of indicating, however, the extent to

20. The elder Styron was experiencing urinary and prostate troubles.

which he didn't allow the thing to get him down, for over a year he's done a lot of outstanding research work in soil antibiotics for Lederle Laboratories. So it seems that the prime necessity is to keep in as good a frame of mind as possible, obey all the rules, and remember that you, like others, with care, can have many more productive years.

As for myself, I'm completely cured of my little case of bronchitis, and I'm pushing my way to the finish of the book, and rapidly. I've finally learned to write swiftly without sacrificing quality, and Hiram Haydn and the others who've read the book at Bobbs-Merrill think it's just about the finest first novel they've ever read. I hope it won't be long now before you'll see it in print; it's been such a long road that I wouldn't blame you if somehow you thought the whole thing was an illusion. Take care of yourself and keep your chin up and your kilts down and let the wind blow.

Your son,

Bill

75. NEW YORK

December 6, 1950

Dear Pop,

A note to let you know that I'm thinking of you, and that I'm hoping everything goes well and you're on your way to a good recovery. Eliza has been keeping me apprised of your progress and at last reports you were doing admirably well. Keep it up and stay in good spirits and I know you'll be in prime working order very soon.

The big news up here recently has involved three things—the Long Island train wreck, the big storms and, of course, the war. The wreck was awful and most people I know out on Long Island are actually paralyzed with fright.[21] As for the storm, it really did leave havoc in its wake, as they would say in the newspapers. I was up with the de Limas in Valley Cottage that weekend and, while there was no damage to the house, all the lights were gone for three days and also the water, which is worked by an electric pump. It was an amazing journey; riding back

---

21. On Thanksgiving Eve, November 22, 1950, two trains collided on the Long Island Railroad. Seventy-five people were killed and nearly one hundred injured. See "Cars Telescoped: Hempstead Train Halts in the Path of One Going to Babylon," *New York Times*, November 23, 1950, 1.

down to the city through northern New Jersey there were whole acres in that thickly wooded area where not one tree was left standing. They were all blown down like so much kindling, looking as if a bomb had blasted away at them—an A-bomb—and it was appalling and rather pathetic.[22]

The really gruesome news here, as elsewhere, is the war.[23] I don't know what's going to happen, and I try—in order to keep my wits about me—not to think about it, and proceed about my work in an orderly fashion. The Marines (so Tommy Peyton, who is now back at Quantico, informs me) will probably not make me join up for a while yet—unless there's a real war—because reserve officers are called up by serial number, and my number is a relatively low one. So that's some temporary consolation, at least.

The book, finally, I can say, is nearing completion. I'm over the hump and the end is in sight. I've been working very hard on it lately—due to the pressure of the news and monetary considerations—and I don't know whether the book will profit or suffer by my sense of urgency. I surely hope, at least, that it doesn't suffer too much. Not that I'm writing sloppily; I'm just not taking so long to ponder and find the *bon mot*, the impeccable phrase. Right at this moment Haydn is reading for the first time the second 175 page chunk of the book, which brings me up currently to p. 365. I haven't heard from him yet, but I know he'll like it, and at any rate I'm still writing furiously, with roughly 75–100 more pages to go.

Do take care of yourself, Pop, and try not to be too depressed. Remember that you're only one of a legion of people who've had the same thing, and most of them have recovered handily and are now active and

22. An enormous winter storm with heavy rain and gale-force winds hit Manhattan and northern New Jersey on November 25, 1950. The storm caused more than twenty deaths, many injuries, widespread flooding, and much property damage. See "Floods Rout Many," *New York Times*, November 26, 1950, 1, 42. From the second paragraph of this article: "By noon the city looked as if a gigantic Halloween prankster had been on a spree in it. Store windows broke, buildings collapsed, trees toppled, cornices and roofs tore loose from buildings, and power lines snaked crazily through some streets."

23. Styron had elected to stay in the Marine Corps reserves and so was eligible for recall to serve in the Korean War. The news in early December was bleak: the U.S. Second and Twenty-fifth Infantry Divisions had been defeated by Chinese Communist forces, and the First Marine Division and Seventh Infantry Division were encircled at Chosin Reservoir.

happy. Please try to write me when you can, and give my best to Eliza and everybody.

Your son,
Bill Jr.

76. NEW YORK

January 24, 1951

Dear Pop,

I'm so glad to hear that you're up and around and chipper again, and that you're going back to build ships again. I knew that that would be the case, because, you know, you can't keep a good Styron down. You might beat him a little and rough him up and—as in certain cases I know—it might take a long while to get him in high gear, but once he's started, watch him go!

I'm sorry that you all didn't hear from me sooner. I hope you didn't think that the beautiful ties you sent me went unnoticed, because really they're extremely handsome ones, and I wear them every time I get dressed up. Also, I certainly didn't mean to give the impression that I "no longer entertained any affection" for Pop. I've thought of you every day. I'm working so steadily on the book and time passes so fast that I find that I'm neglectful of almost everything, including correspondence. Forgive me. The book is a chore and a delight. A chore because it seems that it's a weight that I'll never get off my shoulders, after having written on it so long. A delight because now, having written almost all of it, I can truthfully feel that I've not only written *a* novel but a *good* novel, perhaps even a *really fine* novel, and I hope it gives some people a pleasure in inverse proportion to the pain it's caused me in the writing. That would be a *lot* of pleasure. Haydn told me he thinks it's not only the best first novel but the best novel, barring none, that he has read in ten years, and while I think perhaps that's a pretty rash statement, I do respect his judgment in these matters. Other people who have read it have liked it, too, so maybe he's right. When you write a book you're so close to it and each sentence, comma, and semicolon is so drearily familiar, that somehow you can't help but get the feeling that it will seem as stale to the reader as it is to you. Anyway, I'm happy, I've gotten a certain command over myself and my destiny, unquote, and of course you know that you are mainly responsible for my good fortune. Thank you forever.

Everything in the worldly way goes well. I'm in fine health, at about the best weight I've ever been—162—and I even have rosy cheeks and a rosy nose, from hikes in Central Park. I have many friends and I'll send them all your regards; for all who have met you are as fond of you, almost, as I am. I'll write more soon, and perhaps it won't be more than a few months when we can have a long visit. Best to Eliza and Helen.

Your son,

Bill

77. NEW YORK

February 6, 1951

Dear Pop,

Here is the latest—and rather depressing—news. I have received a summons from the Marine Corps and am to report to Camp Lejeune on March third. It was a great shock to me and I've been walking around like a zombie for the past few days, but now, after having taken my physical and been found perfectly healthy, I am at last able to cope mentally with what seems to be inevitable. The mind takes a lot of beating but it is a wonderfully adaptable organ.

One faintly hopeful thing is the fact that I'm in a good position to get a few months deferment, in order to finish the book. From the point of view of Bobbs-Merrill—and my own point of view, too—it would be an "extreme hardship" if I were dragged into the service without finishing my work. To B-M it's an actual financial hardship (the only kind the USMC understands) and I think they can make their case out all right to the authorities. I only hope I get two months deferment, instead of thirty days or a couple of weeks. I think I can finish it easily, given the longer period of time.

Needless to say, I am about as shattered morally as it is possible to be. To work so long at something, and then to have this threat just at the end, with no hope of rest or satisfaction when the work is done: only the so well remembered and despised drudgery and discipline and authority and anxiety. What a world we live in. Of course, I'm not alone in this feeling. The eight or ten other officers who took their physicals with me at the Navy Yard yesterday all had the drugged look of men who are walking about in a nightmare. One fellow just had a new baby last week, has to close down his supply business in Jersey, and spent four years—besides all this—in the Pacific during the last war.

My right eye is now 20-70, which is half-blind. They're taking me anyway and would have taken me, I fully believe, if I had walked in there with no arms. However, there's a good chance that this eye will get me some sort of limited duty which, in this asinine war, I'm not above *trying* to get.

Please check and see if any of my officer's uniforms, both summer and winter, are around the house. If there are any there look and see if you think they can be altered to a larger size and ship them to me at once. Otherwise, I'll have to buy new ones with borrowed money. This way I can have them tailored. Also send shirts and emblems.

I'll be seeing you sometime soon, in May I hope, perhaps sooner. I've resigned myself to fate and a long season of pain, but of course I will eventually triumph.

Your son,
WCS jr.

78. NEW YORK

February 20, 1951

Dear Pop,

A note to set your mind at ease. After phone calls between Haydn and the Pentagon, I finally got the deferment. I won't have to report for duty until May 1st, so I feel that a great weight has been lifted from my shoulders. I'll be able to finish the book as a civilian. I'm on the last part right now. I expect to be finished by April 1st and the book will be published sometime in July; this is something of a record, Haydn informs me, for quick publication.

The attending hoopla I'll fortunately be spared, and perhaps, after all, the Marine Corps will be something of a refuge. I'm speaking of such things as the blurb on the book-jacket, which starts off something like "Once in 25 years does a writer like this one emerge . . . etc." The jacket incidentally is going to be designed by George Salter, who designed Mann's "Joseph in Egypt" jackets for Knopf.[24] It is really frightening the way Haydn is going overboard for the book, and as I say I'll

24. Knopf published Thomas Mann's tetralogy of historical novels (based on a section of Genesis) during the 1930s and 1940s. The volumes were *Joseph and His Brothers* (1934), *Young Joseph* (1935), *Joseph in Egypt* (1938), and *Joseph the Provider* (1944).

Dust jacket of the first edition of *Lie Down in Darkness*. Reprinted with permission of Scribner, a division of Simon & Schuster, Inc., from *Lie Down in Darkness* by William Styron. Copyright © 1951 by Bobbs-Merrill.

feel much more comfortable not having to endure the storm—if there is one—*or* the cocktail parties.

Haydn is also sending 40 or 50 galley proofs out to various critics for pre-publication comment. This sometime in May. Would you like to have one, or would you rather wait until the whole book is bound, printed, and pretty?

Hope everything still goes well with you and I'm very glad to hear that you're back at work and happy. I trust we'll be able to get together before long.

Your son,
Bill Jr.

79. VALLEY COTTAGE

April 7, 1951

Dear Pop,

I'm up in Valley Cottage this weekend with the de Limas—a beautiful spring day (the first this year up here), and listening to Beethoven's Ninth adds a touch of supernatural grandeur. The book was finished over a week ago and since then I've been resting up—as much as I can, since the rest period has involved trips to Westport with Haydn and visits to Bobbs-Merrill for touching up and revision. Fortunately, there hasn't been much of the latter, except for minor changes here and there, and I'm on my way back to regaining the 15 pounds I lost writing the final hundred pages. Now, finished, I can say I'm pretty well pleased with what I've achieved. The book has quite a few flaws but generally speaking I believe that I've accomplished what I set out to do. It's a big novel in size (620 typed pages) but I do think it's big in quality, too. I suspect that if I don't achieve fame from it I'll at least get a certain notoriety, for the last part of the book has pages that are exceedingly frank.[25] Necessary, though, to my intention. Some people, too, will no doubt think the book is filled with a sense of needless despair. I don't much care what they think; it has plenty of despair in it, but none of it, I think, needless.

25. Bobbs-Merrill insisted on expurgations in Peyton Loftis's interior monologue. See Styron's essay "'I'll Have to Ask Indianapolis—'" in *Havanas in Camelot* (New York: Random House, 2008), 65–80. A scholarly treatment is Arthur D. Casciato, "His Editor's Hand: Hiram Haydn's Changes in *Lie Down in Darkness*," in *Critical Essays on William Styron*, ed. Arthur D. Casciato and James L. W. West III (Boston: G. K. Hall, 1982), 36–46.

I've done what the true artist must do: paint life honestly according to his vision. If my vision is, to use a phrase, tragic, the tragedy is not gratuitous, but a part of our monstrously tragic times. The hope offered at the very end of the book is also not gratuitous; I think you'll agree with me when you read it. Title: *Lie Down in Darkness.*

Outside of my own reactions, the book has really gone over with the rest of the people so far. The ones, that is, including Haydn, who've read the MS. Haydn really does think I'm the best writer living and it does me no harm to hear him say it, although I'm too much the natural pessimist to let it turn my head. George Salter, the fellow who has done the jacket, has written a note to be sent out by Haydn to the booksellers. Salter is a very snooty guy, according to Haydn, and is not given to insincere tributes; Haydn will send you the note when it's printed and I think you might be pleased by it. The book, incidentally, is finally scheduled to be published on August 20th and you'll get a galley copy long before that, probably sometime in May. So far three very big literary people have promised to read the book and to give a comment, if they like it, for the jacket. They are Robert Penn Warren, Allen Tate, and Van Wyck Brooks. Haydn also expects comments from the following: Edmund Wilson, Louis Kronenberger, Budd Schulberg, Lionel Trilling, Alfred Kazin, Joseph Wood Krutch, Mark Van Doren, and John P. Marquand. Quite a list, no?[26] I might even get rich; if so, how about a new Pontiac for you?

I hope it won't disturb you, as I heard that it did, to tell you that I'm marking time, resignedly, for my re-entrance into the Marine Corps. Last time I didn't mean to give an impression of abject anything—terror or despair. I just really felt then (heightened by the sudden shock), as I do now, a sort of disgust with the whole business. One can't feel overjoyed at the prospect of being, in the prime of one's life, militarized indefinitely. Communism and its threat (acknowledged), or the fact that I've already spent three years at it before, with or without combat— these have not so much to do with my disgust as that of being faced with a civilization apparently going stark raving mad. I urge you to read a book called *1984* by George Orwell. It pictures beautifully the situation toward which we seem to be headed, and will reach unless people

---

26. The jacket for the first edition of *Lie Down in Darkness* bears no blurbs or other testimonials.

quit their mad lust for power. I despise Soviet Communism in any of its forms, but I equally believe that America is—at the moment, at least— far from guiltless and perhaps even a little criminal in its foreign policy. You understand I'm not speaking as a marine-to-be, but as a citizen. "My country right or wrong; but always my country"—these are falla- cies that should have been shattered long ago, in a nation potentially as great in its democratic ideals as this one. I realize that we face a hid- eous threat, and it's not the Marines or our foreign policy or possibility of combat which I protest so much as, again, being involved in a sort of zombie world where the only music is the sound of marching feet. *Please* don't let this personal attitude affect you. As usual we aren't tak- ing it lying down; but the young people of today who do any sort of thinking do feel, I can assure you, somehow tricked and cheated. I feel lucky. I've written a book, my words are "graven with an iron pen and lead in the rock forever."[27] But what about the ones who want to write, and won't have a chance?

You'll get a copy of the jacket and the proofs sometime in May and I hope you enjoy it—especially since you'll have the knowledge that you, mostly, made it possible. Because of more work I won't be able to see you before I go to Lejeune, but I'm sure I'll be able to see you on the weekends and furloughs thereafter.

Your son,
WCS jr

27. Job 19:23–24: "Oh that my words were now written! Oh that they were printed in a book! That they were graven with an iron pen and lead in the rock for ever!"

6 / June 1951–February 1952

CAMP LEJEUNE AND NEW YORK

Styron reported for duty at Camp Lejeune, North Carolina, in May 1951. He read the proofs of Lie Down in Darkness *while in training there. He also participated in two incidents that would make their way into* The Long March—*the short mortar rounds and the forced march that followed. On June 20, two mortar rounds fell short during a training exercise, killing nine men and wounding twenty-two. Styron drove the regimental surgeon to the area of the accident and witnessed the carnage and confusion. That night his own regiment was sent on a thirty-six-mile march back to the main base.*

80. CAMP LEJEUNE

June 1, 1951
1st Lt. W. C. Styron Jr USMCR
H & S Co., 8th Marines
2nd Marine Division
Camp Lejeune, N.C.

Dear Pop,

I heard from Eliza that you are a little under the weather now. I'm terribly sorry and know how you must feel, lying so quiescent on your back; but also knowing the old spirit, I have no doubt that you will snap back and be in good shape again soon.

If any kind of doubts or wonderings are troubling your ability to get back into shape, please don't worry about me, or let a worry about me hinder your recuperation. I am in the finest of spirits, both mentally and physically, and am making the best of my lot down here in the swamps.

I would rather, of course, be elsewhere, but I have found to my absolute surprise—after all these years of living my own life—that the new discipline agrees with me very well. I rise at 7:00, eat three big square meals a day and have a sunburn that even Johnny Weissmuller would envy.[1] We go out into the field once every two weeks for about two days and although lying on the swampy turf amid all the ticks and chiggers is not exactly my idea of the Waldorf, it nonetheless and undoubtedly gives a certain sense of physical well-being.

I'm getting the last of my proofs now, and they should be in bound pages very soon. Hiram will send you a copy as soon as they come through, which should be within the next three or four weeks. About the book, of course, now that it's over, I am wildly happy. People all over—I understand from my New York Intelligence—are already talking about it, and there's no doubt about it—and modesty has nothing to do with it—that your boy is about to become *the* sensation, at *least* of 1951. God knows, I'm not getting swell-headed over the thing—being essentially too aware of the transitoriness of fame—but I don't mind getting all this additional reward, especially after knowing that first and foremost I was honest, that the book represents hours of real sweat and pain, and that I did my level best, in every word of it.

Of course you must know what you've done for me. If it hadn't been for your faith in me, and your gentle and constant encouragement, it would never have been written. There are few enough artists who have gotten encouragement from people at large, much less their parents—toward whom the very fact that they create usually represents a tacit antipathy. But you have been faithful to the very end of my first endeavor, and I appreciate it to the bottom of my heart. We live in a troubled era, there is no doubt of that, and sometimes I wonder if we will all endure. Yet with all my complaint, often, at the times, and at life in general, I somehow know we shall endure and that all this striving is not at all in vain. The very fact that you and I have worked together, no matter with what unspoken understanding, represents a partnership of the spirit, and if that is love, it will prevail—forever and ever. I will write until my knuckles are worn and my brain bewildered, but I will write on and on, and if it can be done by a feckless soul like myself it can be done by the

1. Johnny Weissmuller (1904–1984) was the most famous actor to play Tarzan in the movies. He made twelve Tarzan movies for MGM and RKO in the 1930s and early 1940s; between 1948 and 1954 he starred in thirteen Jungle Jim movies for Columbia Pictures.

human race: this eternal creation and recreation, even in the face of the bleakest future. You have given me the chance and I'll not let you down. When you read my *second* book, or play, or whatever it is, it might not be very good, but no matter. Remember that your faith in me has given me the watchword, or something: you have believed in me, so because of that I have believed in myself, and so, having strived, I believe, ceaselessly upward (in the words of Goethe), I can be saved. And so can we all be saved.

My God, it's been a long pull, but, as I say, I'm as happy as it is possible to be. Don't mind the reviews when they come in August—they're going to raise hell with me. But I *know* that I've written a fine, true book and that it will live for a long time. And I thank you for everything you've done to make it possible.

Soon we come to Little Creek in Norfolk for amphibious training—sometime within the next month—so then I'll be able to see you. I'll give you the exact details very soon. Keep the doormat out and we'll have a fine talk together.

Your son,
Bill, Jr.

P.S. I thought the biography you sent to Duke was fine stuff, if a little embarrassing to read first-hand by the biographee.[2]

81. CAMP LEJEUNE (Marine Corps stationery)

July 9, 1951

Dear Pop,

At long last, there seems to be good news concerning me and the marine corps. It seems that they don't really want me, on account of my bad right eye, and are planning to release me to inactive duty within a few weeks. This came out during a week in which I went to the Rifle Range and found that, at 500 yards, I couldn't see a thing hardly, much less a bullseye. So I went to the hospital and they took a peek at the lens and found the old congenital cataract, no worse or no better than it ever was, and wrote out an order for me, releasing me to inactive duty.

---

2. Styron's father had prepared an eight-page biographical sketch of his son for the Duke alumni office. The sketch is published in appendix 2 of this volume.

This was a couple of weeks ago and now the order is being "processed" in some invisible place or other, but it's fairly certain that, unless some strange exigency comes up, I will be a free man soon. I'm pretty happy about it all, and there's not a reserve down here who wouldn't trade positions with me. As soon as I'm out I'll come by for a good visit with you before I go back to New York.

Right now I'm just biding my time and acting as Regimental Public Information Officer, writing press releases on reservists who are getting out, to be sent to home-town papers. It was a propitious moment, I might add, for them to discover the old eye, for lately the regiment has embarked on a series of hikes, one of which I participated in. It was 36 miles long, took all night, from 8:30 to 7:30, and left me with blisters on my feet the size of half-dollars and in a state, like the rest of the outfit, of complete exhaustion. Thirty-six miles is something of a record, even for the Corps.

Everything otherwise is fine. I'm trying to save money and am spending most of my spare time sunning at the local strand, Onslow Beach, and acquiring a deep sunburn. But it's a lethargic life now, for the most part, with morale at a pretty low ebb all over the Division, and I will be glad to get out and do something creative again.

The book is going fine, according to Haydn. The salesmen all think it's great and are going whole-hog to promote it to the limit. The bound galleys have gone out to the leading critics of the U.S.A., who will soon pass judgment on it and give it either their kudos or their condemnation. One salesman wrote Haydn that he thinks it's the finest American novel of our generation, which was a statement with no strings attached and no apple-polishing, and it pleases me.

I hope you're feeling much better now and are up and about facing life with the old Styron spirit. I may get myself married sometime soon, to someone I think wonderful, but I'll let you know more about that when I see you.[3]

Your son,
Bill

---

3. Styron had been involved in a romance with a young married woman. They discussed marriage, but she decided eventually not to pursue a divorce. The relationship ended when Styron went to Europe in the spring of 1952.

Styron was discharged from the Marine Corps in late August and was back in New York for the formal publication of Lie Down in Darkness *in September.*

82. NEW YORK (telegram)

[September 2, 1951]

WILLIAM STYRON

139 CHESAPEAKE AVE NEW PORT NEWS VIR

SATURDAY REVIEW SEPTEMBER EIGHTH QUOTE I SHOULD SAY AT ONCE THAT LIE DOWN IN DARKNESS IS A REMARKABLE AND FASCINATING NOVEL THE BEST NOVEL OF THE YEAR BY MY STANDARDS IT IS PRACTICALLY PERFECT UNQUOTE AM GLAD I AM YOUR SON[4]

BILL

83. NEW YORK

November 15, 1951

Dear Pop,

I received your letter with the note Burrelles sent you about the American Scholar review.[5] That issue won't be out until December 15th or around then, and since your subscription with Burrelles expires earlier I don't guess they'll send you a review unless you extend the subscription. I suggest that you terminate your subscription with them. I don't imagine there'll be a whole lot more newspaper copy on the book. As for the American Scholar review, you can write directly to the Scholar and I'm sure that if you tell them who you are they'll send you a single copy. The price, I think, is 75¢ and the address is The American Scholar, Phi Beta Kappa Hall, Williamsburg, Virginia. There will be, I think, scattered copy now and then about me and the book and I will try to send

4. The review, a rave, is by Maxwell Geismar, "Domestic Tragedy in Virginia," *Saturday Review of Literature*, September 15, 1951, 12–13. For an annotated listing of the notices, see Jackson Bryer and Mary Beth Hatem, *William Styron: A Reference Guide* (Boston G. K. Hall, 1978), 1–18.

5. Burrelles was a clipping agency; it was sending reviews of *Lie Down in Darkness* to Styron's father. The review that Styron mentions is Robert Gorham Davis, "A Grasp of Moral Realities," *American Scholar* 21 (Winter 1951): 114, 116; repr. in Casciato and West, eds., *Critical Essays on William Styron*, 20–21.

you what you miss. I think that both the December and January issues of *Mademoiselle* are going to have pieces on the book, so you might look out for them.[6]

Here's something you can keep under your hat: Hiram and others think I stand a much better than even chance of winning the National Book Award on January 29th, which is a more intelligent equivalent of the Pulitzer Prize and is sponsored by the American Book Publishers Council. It's quite an honor and I hope to win it, but don't count on it, though it's something nice to think about. The prize is $1500, but the cash is of course secondary to the laurels. Last year's fiction award, incidentally, went to the Collected Short Stories of William Faulkner.

I'm getting bushels of fan mail and the thing is growing, I think, all the time, though my position on the Best Seller lists has wavered erratically. I will of course send you copies of the translations and British edition, although except for the British—out next spring—they probably won't be published for a year. Since my last note there also has evolved the probability of an Italian translation, which pleases me.

Right now I've been living with a friend of mine and his wife, the John Maloneys, on 13th Street, but I intend to move out soon and get an apartment in the Village somewhere.[7] I've temporarily abandoned my plans for Europe, in favor of a winter of writing; there are certain short pieces I want to do before traveling abroad which, if I do it, will be next spring.

By the way, while I think of it, an acquaintance of a friend of mine, who knows her, reports that *Marlene Dietrich* read it and *loved* it, which proves something, I don't know what.

Last weekend I went up to Boston to see Leon and wife, and my girl, who was sojourning there for a week. Leon is fine, established in Harvard Med School, with two lovely children, and sends his best to you, whom he appropriately reveres. I got a letter from Tom Peyton; he read LDID and liked it very much. Read it in a hospital, where he was recovering from a shrapnel wound in the hand, which he got from a booby trap. It was a minor wound and fortunately, being in the engi-

6. Leo Lerman, "Something to Talk About," *Mademoiselle* 34 (January 1952): 112–13, 154. Nothing about Styron was published in the December 1951 issue of the magazine.

7. Maloney was one of Hiram Haydn's students at the New School. Haydn's recollections of him are published in his memoir *Words and Faces* (New York: Harcourt Brace Jovanovich, 1974): 38–41.

neers, he is relatively safe, but it saddens me that such a fine lad has to be in Korea and suffering.

There's not much else to report. I'm having a good time going to parties but they are beginning to pall and though I've met a lot of celebrities —John Hersey, Norman Mailer, E. E. Cummings, Bennett Cerf, etc.— they are beginning to pall, too, and I'm eager to get back to work.

Hope everything goes well with you and Eliza and that you're taking care of yourself. I hope to see you soon.

Ever your son,
Bill Jr.

84. NEW YORK

February 12, 1952
48 Greenwich Avenue
New York 11, N.Y.

Dear Pop,

After having piddled around for so long in a state of relative lassitude, I've finally made the big decision and have made plans to go to Europe for five or six months. This doesn't include the Prix de Rome, which I stand a good chance to win, since that hasn't been announced yet; I'll get it while I'm in Europe just as well as if I stay over here and so I plan to go on over anyway. I've made reservations on the Ile de France for March 5th and am due to arrive in Southampton on the 11th. It's probably sacrilege to go on a Frog boat rather than a Newport News one, but this seems to be most convenient right now. I have no idea what I'll do exactly when I get to England; there are a few people I know there, and I've learned that LDID is to be published over there in late March, which is a nice coincidence, and I expect that Hamish Hamilton, the English publisher, might arrange a little entertainment. I don't know either how long I'll stay in England but it'll probably be a couple of months, long enough for me to get some ideas for a short story or two, and then I guess I'll move on to France and Italy and come back here late next fall. I'm of course looking forward to this trip with a lot of excitement—and some trepidation, but with a lot more excitement than qualms. I've written to both the Newport News City Clerk and the Virginia Bureau of Vital Statistics for my birth certificate, which I'll need for the passport, but I haven't heard from either of them after nearly two weeks. If I don't hear soon I expect I'll have to call upon you to stir the City Clerk, at least, out of his torpor, because time is getting short.

Everything here goes on apace; I'm writing short stories and have, reluctantly, now that I look back upon it, accepted invitations to speak at two forums at the end of this week. One of them is at the P.E.N. Club, an international organization of writers which has a chapter in New York. I was asked by David Dempsey, who is a nice fellow and I suppose it was that reason that I didn't refuse. I'm to be on the panel with John P. Marquand, Mr. Wouk of "The Caine Mutiny," and a young novelist named Gore Vidal. The next night the forum is with the Columbia University English Graduate Club, and will be moderated by Malcolm Cowley, with John W. Aldridge and the aforesaid Mr. Vidal present, besides myself. I suppose these are interesting and at least in one way profitable, but I dislike them nonetheless, feeling that a writer should write rather than talk, and I'm always peeved at myself afterwards when I realize what I've let myself in for.

You might be interested to know that the contract with Signet books, the reprint house, has been signed and for the quite handsome sum of $15,000. Of this I get half, which is no small potatoes, although for income tax reasons I won't be able to start collecting on it until 1953 and 1954. So at least it looks as if, providing I husband my resources, I'll be financially solvent for the next few years and will be able to have the time to write more again of what I want to write.

I'm getting monstrous tired of cocktail parties, and I trust that in Europe I'll get shut of them, although at a recent one the scenery was graced by Messrs. Norman Mailer and James Jones, who are interesting characters and fun to talk to. Later, accompanied by some young ladies, we went uptown to a fancy cafe along with the movie actor, Montgomery Clift, and that Monty was along was a pity because he stole the show and was inundated by autograph hounds and even Jones went unnoticed. But it was fun.

If you have any advice to a prospective *voyageur*, please send it along because I'm a mighty green continental character and I'm afraid I'll be callow as an ocean traveler, and I don't spik French.

Your son,

Bill Jr.

P.S. In next week's *Saturday Review* there is to be an article on me, among others, so you might watch for it for the scrapbook.[8]

8. Eloise Perry Hazard, "Eight Fiction Finds," *Saturday Review of Literature*, February 16, 1952, 16–18.

85. NEW YORK (telegram)

[February 16, 1952]

WILLIAM C STYRON

139 CHESAPEAKE AVE NEWPORT NEWS VIR

I WON THE PRIX DE ROME AWARDED BY THE AMERICAN ACADEMY OF ARTS AND LETTERS WHICH MEANS A YEAR FREE IN ITALY STOP THE JUDGES WERE MALCOLM COWLEY, JOHN HERSEY, VANWYCK BROOKS, W H AUDEN, AND ALLEN TATE PLEASE KEEP IT SECRET FOR A WEEK STOP THE BIRTH CERTIFICATE BUSINESS HAS BEEN TAKEN CARE OF STOP BEST TO ALL

BILL

86. NEW YORK

February 22, 1952

Dear Pop,

Thanks a lot for your letter and for the letter of introduction from Mr. Fiore. I wish you would thank him for me and tell him that I will certainly look up Signor DeMarini when I'm in Genoa, which place I certainly hope to visit.

You asked me to enlighten you about the Prix de Rome, and all I can say is that I am pretty much in the dark about the exact details myself. The American Academy of Arts & Letters is apparently very well endowed and gives this prize each year—but with no apparent order or consistency—to various people who have achieved something in literature, painting, music, and architecture. I talked over the phone to the lady who is secretary of the academy and she gave me the following information: the grant is for one year, beginning in October. I am to be paid for my transportation over and back (I will be reimbursed for my passage on March 5th and the prize will in no way interfere with previous plans). Also, I get free room and board at the Academy for the year, plus $300 for travel around Italy, which one is encouraged to do, plus $150 for books, plus $1250 for spending money. There are no study requirements or schedules; it was set up—the prize—apparently to encourage American artists to absorb European culture and nothing else, in the old Goethean concept that to really create greatly one must assimilate some of the splendor of the past. I certainly hope to absorb *and* create while I'm over there. It is truly the greatest honor that a young American artist can receive and I'm grateful beyond words to the awards committee and I can assure you—as I already have myself—that it won't be wasted. The Academy, I've heard, is a beautiful place on a hill outside Rome, with about 40 people there—artists and musicians, mainly—not a bit like Greenwich Village, because none of these people are bores or phonies but all are serious and talented. It's all right to announce it now because it's being made public this week, so if you want to give Cissie Harrison or the *Times-Herald* the details including the names of the judges it's O.K. with me. Incidentally, I wish you'd congratulate Cissie and John for me.

I will try to write again before I leave, a week from Wednesday. In the meantime, if you have any more good advice please let me know.

Your son,
Bill Jr.

My address, incidentally after March 5th, will be c/o Bobbs-Merrill.

7 / March 1952–September 1952

LONDON AND PARIS

Styron's term at the Academy was scheduled to begin in October, but he sailed to England early, in March, to be in London for the publication of Lie Down in Darkness *by the British firm of Hamish Hamilton. This voyage was the beginning of his first experience with extended international travel.*

87. LONDON

March 13, 1952
Thursday
c/o Hamish Hamilton, Ltd.
90 Great Russell Street
London W.C.1.

Dear Pop and Elizabeth,

Thank you very much for your *bon voyages* telegrams and letters. The trip over on the *Ile* was very pleasant. The sea was calm, the food excellent, and the passengers all congenial—at least the ones I met. I shared a large cabin with one person, a Mr. Alexander Luoff, French citizen of Russian extraction who is a translator with the U.N. Also aboard was a New York pal of mine, Arthur Laurents (he wrote the movie scripts for "Snakepit" and "Home of the Brave") and he's an old buddy of Lena Horne and her husband, who were also aboard though in First Class.[1]

---

1. Laurents (b. 1918) was blacklisted in Hollywood during the McCarthy era and turned to Broadway as a place to deploy his talents. He wrote the book for the musicals *West Side Story* (1958) and *Gypsy!* (1960) and won a Tony Award in 1984 for directing *La Cage aux Folles.*

Anyway we had quite a few drinks together (in First Class, of course) and I must say that Lena's color soon seems to fade to white after a while. She has a white, goateed husband who's not nearly so interesting.[2]

England combines a scene of dreariness with one of melancholy beauty. I'm staying at a nice modern hotel, the Stafford, which is right in the heart of Piccadilly, is comfortable as long as it's heated, is poorly lighted by American standards, and has toilet paper which is waxed on one side, though I have no idea why. Mr. Roger Machell (a distant relative of the royal family) is my English editor and has been most nice to me, having taken me to dinner the three nights I've been here (at places where the food, although you pay New York prices, is good and plentiful, and totally unlike the average English, non-Italian or non-French restaurant, where the food is indescribably horrible) and he has generally arranged it so that I've been well-entertained.[3] I brought with me three bottles of Scotch and ten pounds of canned Hormel ham, all as gifts since both commodities are non-existent, and I don't know whether my new English friends love me for myself or for my food and drink. Anyway, this is the land of my forefathers and I admire the hell out of the people, who would still eat an old dishrag rather than have a black market. I expect I'll be here until the middle of April, making trips up to Oxford and Durham and I hope Scotland, after which I'm heading for Paris.

The book is to be published here on 21 March and I'm a little sorry, really, that I'm here at the same time because I'm pretty well fed-up with reviews and publishing in general. The reviews come gradually, I understand, over a period of 3 or 4 weeks; anyway, I'll try and send you copies. Elizabeth McKee, my agent, will send you a copy of the English edition. If she forgets, her address is 30 East 60th St., N.Y. The dust jacket is atrocious. Incidentally, the Am. Academy has not announced publicly the Prix de Rome yet, but Hiram tells me that it'll come out within the next month or so.—I hope all goes well at home and, again, thanks for the farewell greetings. God save the Queen.

Love,
Bill

2. Lena Horne (b. 1917) was married to Lennie Hayton (1908–1971), a pianist, arranger, and composer. He was the musical director at Metro-Goldwyn-Mayer from 1940 to 1953 and was nominated for an Oscar for his work on *Singin' in the Rain* (1952).

3. *Lie Down in Darkness* was being published in England by Hamish Hamilton, which would later publish the first British editions of *The Long March* and *Set This House on Fire*.

I find no Styrons in the London phonebook, but I do find one Styran, two Styrins, and one Styring. I guess they all missed the boat.

88. LONDON

[March 30, 1952]
Sunday

Dear Pop,

I'm enclosing two reviews and an ad from London papers, the reviews from the *Sunday Times* and *Times Literary Supplement,* the ad from the *Observer.* I've sent Dorothy in New York a review from the *Daily Times,* and I've asked her to send it along to you when she's read it.[4] I was a bit peeved by the reviews at first and didn't at all like the fact of being lumped in a group with other books, but I've been assured by people over here that all novels are reviewed in batches of three and four, that it's something of an honor to be reviewed first in a group, and that *these* reviews are really pretty superlative, in spite of the understatement, which is typically British, and the relative paucity of space, which is simply due to the paper shortage. Anyway, here they are, and don't be put off by Mr. J. W. Lambert who, I'm told, is about 70, and in practically every way resembles Orville Prescott except that he's even more of a spinster.[5]

Just a day or two ago I completed my tour of England. I only wish I could see more. I suppose that by now you've gotten my card from "New York." The little Austin we hired purred right along: first we went to Cambridge, where we saw King's College Chapel, a really magnificent church, and followed it up by a stop at the Cathedral in Ely, which

4. Dorothy "Didi" Parker was a friend who had worked with Styron at Whittlesey House.

5. J. W. Lambert, reviewing *Lie Down in Darkness* in "New Novels—Every Man in His Humour," *London Sunday Times* (March 30, 1952), wrote that "the frontier between true vitality and facility is ill-defined and perilous," and that Styron was "dangerously apt to slip across it" (p. 3). The British notices of *Lie Down in Darkness* were mixed: some reviewers praised the characterization and style of the novel; others criticized its overwrought emotion and the self-consciousness of the writing. For summaries of the reviews, see Bryer and Hatem, *William Styron: A Reference Guide,* 18–20. Orville Prescott's review of the novel ("Books of the Times," *New York Times,* September 10, 1951, 19) was mixed. Prescott wrote that the novel represented "such an explosive combination of blazing power and exasperating confusion of thought and narrative that it should stir up a fine controversy."

I personally think is even a greater monument to God, being tremen-
dously lofty inside, and equipped with a simply marvelous octagonal,
windowed dome. After Ely we drove up to Lincolnshire where we stayed
on a farm with some of Bryan's relatives. (Bryan is Bryan Forbes, an actor, who's temporarily over here to write a screenplay of one of Graham
Greene's novels; his wife is an Irish actress named Constance Smith
who's in Hollywood and had the starring role in "The Mudlark.")[6] They
were nice, homely country folk who put out wonderful food and hospitality, and whose house is built facing on a perfectly lovely little English river, the Witham. The surrounding countryside is the Fen Country,
which is placid and fertile and utterly flat, bordered by dikes and canals
and windmills, and seems to be a part of Holland. There's an 11th century castle nearby, Tattershall (Tattershall woolens are named after this
region, though the industry has largely died out), and we explored it
fully, climbing into dungeons and up damp draughty stone stairways
and in general behaving like American tourists. We also went to Lincoln
Cathedral, 15 miles away, but although it's of overwhelming size, it's not
nearly so perfect as Ely. After we left Lincoln we came back down to
London, where I got your nice letter, and headed southwest the same
day for Porthleven, Cornwall—near Penzance (look at a map). We arrived
after an all-night drive through absolutely empty and sleeping towns
and countryside, including a twenty-five mile trek across Dartmoor,
the bleakest part of England which is like Wyoming, past Dartmoor
prison, the Alcatraz of Britain, and past literal *herds* of wild Devon po-
nies which galloped past and across the road in the headlights. It was
all very bleak and spooky, but no Hounds of the Baskervilles assailed
us. In Porthleven we put up at a vicarage with an old friend of Bryan's,
the vicar, a Rev. Canon Gotto, his insane, bird-like little wife, and their
90-year old aunt. It was the sort of vicarage you might visualize as being a *part* of England—huge and rambling, crammed with junk, but
surrounded by chickens and lovely trees and gardens. The weather,
though a bit chilly, was sunny and vigorous and mercifully dry; we went

6. Forbes (b. 1926) became a successful screenwriter and director in the 1960s and
1970s. His Hollywood movies included *King Rat* (1965) and *The Stepford Wives* (1975).
He was married to the Irish actress Constance Smith (1928–2003) from 1951 until 1955.
She played the role of Kate Noonan in *The Mudlark* (1950), which starred Irene Dunne as
Queen Victoria and Alec Guinness as Benjamin Disraeli. Forbes published an account of
this trip with Styron in his memoir *A Divided Life* (London: Heinemann, 1992), 231–41.

to Land's End and St. Ives, which is a lovely, almost perfect seaside town with strange enclosed cobblestone streets built on the slopes of a hill and awkward-looking fishing boats in the harbor. But the most spectacular part of Cornwall for me, though, were the magnificent cliffs and the groaning, crashing sea on the rocks and the gulls which seem to perpetually wheel about in the blue, sunfilled sky. I gave the vicar a ham, some butter, and a copy of my book (which will shock him) and we came back to London, after a stopover near St. Austell to see Daphne du Maurier, who is a friend of Bryan's. She seemed very nice, gave us a wonderful lunch, and lives in a house about the size of the Chamberlin hotel, surrounded by acres and acres of rolling pasture land which slope down to the sea. She's married to a General Sir Frederick Browning, who was in command of the English army in Burma and who is now Equerry in charge of the Queen's household. Considering this, and the fact that Daphne's now #1 on the N.Y. *Times* best seller list, it's a wonder to hear her go on so much about poverty, but she does.[7]

Right now I'm spending the weekend in Surrey with a lawyer and his wife, friends of Hank Simons. Next Friday Calder Willingham ("End As a Man"), who is over here briefly, and I are taking a boat for Copenhagen, where I guess I'll be for a week or so, and then I'll go on to France.[8] I'll send you a report on the Danes.

Best to all.
Bill Jr.

I think you'd still better send all mail to Hamilton until I advise otherwise—B

Styron stayed for ten days in Denmark, then took a boat train for Paris, where he lived until October. While in Paris he wrote The Long March *and helped to found the* Paris Review.

7. At that moment Du Maurier's novel *My Cousin Rachel* was indeed in the top position on the *New York Times* best-seller list. The Chamberlain was a large hotel in Newport News.

8. Willingham (1922–1995), a native of Atlanta, had just published a collection of short stories called *The Gates of Hell*. His novel *End as a Man* had been published by Vanguard in 1947. Later in his career Willingham wrote the screenplays for several successful movies, including *The Graduate* (1967) and *Little Big Man* (1972).

89. PARIS

May 1, 1952
c/o American Express
11 Rue Scribe
Paris IX, France

Dear Pop,

May-Day in Paris is the day when *everything* is closed—buses, subways, stores, even the police, and the only people who transact business (outside of the bars) are the venders of lily-of-the-valley, which seems to have some sort of May Day symbolic significance.[9] It's a perfect day, then, to write you a letter and tell you briefly what I've been doing since Denmark. I arrived here a couple of weeks ago, after having taken the night train from Copenhagen—a twenty-two hour trip made longer than it ordinarily would have to be because of the number of island channels in Denmark that the train has to traverse—by railroad ferry. The route goes through Germany and Belgium and since most of it's at night I didn't see a whole lot, though I did get a pretty good twilight look at both Hamburg and Bremen. From where I sat both cities looked rich and thriving, but I gather that both are still pretty well smashed up behind view of the railroad tracks.

Paris is just about all they say it is, a beautiful, incomparable place, made more lovely by the springtime. I must say that the atmosphere here, however, is treacherous—so lulling and lazy that one is content to sit for hours and hours drinking a beer in a café, and to do nothing more, no work, just sit. My French is still pretty sketchy (I should have applied myself more at Davidson and Duke) but already is showing improvement, and I no longer am afraid as I was at first to go into a "Tabac" and order a pack of cigarettes. Through friends in New York and London I've met a lot of very nice and interesting people and so my days and nights are well-filled. Through one of these people, a young writer named Peter Matthiessen from Connecticut, I got a very large, sunny, comfortable hotel room in a hotel called the Liberia in

9. The French give sprigs of lily of the valley *(muguet)* to their friends on May Day. The flower is a symbol of springtime. Flower vendors and workers' organizations are allowed to sell the flowers on May Day without charging tax.

Montparnasse.[10] It costs only 10,000 francs a month (less than $40) and I've contracted to stay there until around the middle of June, after which time I think I will have had my share of Paris and will head on somewhere else. I also plan to buy this Mr. Matthiessen's 3-year old Fiat car for $500, and this will solve my transportation problems during my Rome stay, although nice as the car is, it doesn't sound nearly as jazzy as the new Pontiac you described, which indeed must be a beauty.

I've finally pretty much decided what to write next—a novel based on Nat Turner's rebellion. The subject fascinates me, and I think I could make a real character out of old Nat. It'll probably take a bit of research, though, and I've written to people in the U.S.—among them Prof. Saunders Redding (whom I saw Christmas, you remember) of Hampton Institute—asking them to pass on any reference material they might have. Perhaps you know of a book or something on Nat Turner and would be willing to get it sent to me somehow. Actually, I'd be extremely interested in anything on life around the Southside–Caroline Border country of Virginia in the 1820–1850 period. If you can get your hands on something on that order without too much trouble I'd appreciate your letting me know. I don't know but whether I'm plunging into something over my depth, but I'm fascinated anyway.[11]

I hope everything is going well. Best to all and keep your wandering boy posted.

Bill Jr.

The food here, as in Denmark, is magnificent, but I'm provincial enough to still miss Southern fried chicken.

---

10. Matthiessen (b. 1927) became one of Styron's closest friends. He would publish his first novel, *Race Rock*, with Harpers in 1954. His subsequent books include *At Play in the Fields of the Lord* (1965), *The Snow Leopard* (1978), and *Killing Mister Watson* (1990).

11. Hiram Haydn had introduced Redding, then on the faculty of Hampton Institute, to Styron. Haydn was the editor for Redding's book *On Being Negro in America,* published by Bobbs-Merrill in 1950. Redding sent Styron a packet of materials, including copies of *The Southampton Insurrection* (1900) by William S. Drewry and *A Journey in the Seaboard Slave States* (1856) by Frederick Law Olmsted. For an account of Styron's use of these two sources, see Arthur D. Casciato and James L. W. West III, "William Styron and *The Southampton Insurrection,*" *American Literature* 52 (1981): 564–77. For an overview of Redding's career, see Lawrence Jackson, "Irredeemable Promise: J. Saunders Redding and Negro New Liberalism," *American Literary History* 19 (2007): 712–44.

90. PARIS

May 20, 1952

Dear Pop,

If I don't forget, I'm enclosing a copy of the review of Lie Down in "Punch," which was sent to me from England.[12] Excellent reviews in England, I've been told, but not much in regard to sales.

Dorothy wrote me that I was runner-up in a *Saturday Review of Literature* poll concerning Who Should have Won the Pulitzer Prize. Not bad, all things considered.

Thanks for the list of books on Nat Turner. Things seem to be getting a bit out of hand, however, in my search for background material, since I've written to a couple of other people—namely my agent and Prof. J. Saunders Redding, the Negro professor of English at Hampton Institute—for material, and I'm afraid that all sorts of unnecessary duplications might result. Would it be asking too much to have you either call Mr. Redding (his number is in the Hampton phone book) or talk to him, and in any case get together and figure out just what each of you are going to send? He wrote me that he had a bunch of stuff he was going to send and I don't know just how much of that might be on the list you sent from the State Library. At any rate, I think you'd enjoy very much talking to him—a striking, forceful, but thoroughly affable gentleman whose only difference from any other human, so far as I can tell, is in the pigmentation of his skin—and I think also that he'd be in a good position to tell you which items on the list are valuable, which ones are not, and which ones, if any, he's already sent me. Pop, don't exert yourself over this thing, but if you find that it's no strain, and that you enjoy doing it—including seeing Mr. Redding, whom I think you'd like—well then that's fine. For my part, I would like to have photostats of practically all the articles on the list, if you can do it without too much trouble. #1 Redding says he's going to get for me. I think you can ignore #7, since I have no particular desire to read a fictionalized account, and #6, which I've already read and is rather slight. #10 is starred as unavailable

12. The review in the April 30, 1952, issue of *Punch*, signed "A.B.H.," was among the best of the British notices: "The writing, a rare and satisfying mixture of graphic realism and subtle impressionism, reaches a very high standard, and the story loses none of its effectiveness by starting with the dénouement and back-pedalling through numerous day-dreams and recollections. Warmly recommended" (550).

for loan, so you can forget that; but all the rest look interesting and I'd like to have them if possible. Perhaps Mr. Redding could tell you which ones of the other items are intrinsically valuable and which ones merely repeat.[13]

Pop, one thing I wish you'd do for me and that is not to bruit it about too much concerning what I'm planning to write about. I don't mind anyone knowing that I'm working, but for some reason I really prefer to be a bit secretive about the nature of the project; could you just say from now on, to people who don't already know, that I'm doing something "historical" on "Virginia in slave times," or something like that?

As for the article in the Michigan Alumni Bulletin, I enjoyed it very much; it was one of the few things Cousins ever said that made any sense.[14] This idea about "noble themes" does have some truth in it; the only catch is that a writer never must search for noble themes; he creates the noble theme himself. Nat Turner, for instance, is on the surface pretty much a bastard through and through; however, I subscribe to the theory that all people, no matter how bad—and that includes the Loftises—have a scrap of nobility in them; it's not the writer's job to particularly exalt humans or make them noble if they're not *all* noble, but the writer is shirking his duty, and is not much of a writer, if he fails to show that scrap of nobility, the scrap varying in size according to the person. I hope that when I'm through with Nat Turner (and God, I know its going to be a long, hard job) he will not be either a Great Leader of The Masses, as the stupid, vicious jackass of a Communist writer might make him out—or a perfectly satanic demagogue, as the surface historical facts present him, but a living human being of great power and great potential who somewhere, in his struggle for freedom and for immortality, lost his way. And that is the human condition and no one is even half-noble unless he deserves it and *no* one is *all* noble, even a saint. Which is where Mr. Cousins is wrong.

13. The list does not survive.

14. Styron's father had sent him a copy of a talk by Norman Cousins, entitled "In Defense of a Writing Career," that had appeared in the Autumn 1950 issue of the *Michigan Alumnus Quarterly Review* (22–28). Cousins, the editor of the *Saturday Review of Literature,* had published the talk initially in the June 17, 1950, issue of *SRL* (22–24). Styron would have responded to at least two of the points in Cousins's speech: that would-be authors who work at junior-level jobs in the publishing industry often lose the ambition to write and publish, and that a beginning writer does well to take counsel from a well-connected mentor.

As for me, I'm healthy, wealthy and happy in the Paris spring and I await your correspondence on Mr. Turner.

Your son,
Bill

91. PARIS

July 18, 1952

Dear Pop,

I received your letter today and am sorry to have been so remiss in my correspondence. For one thing, I simply haven't realized how the weeks have slipped by; for another, I have really been hard at work during the past couple of months, writing a very long story—20,000 words, now nearly finished—which, in order to get published in the place I want it, has to be completed by the deadline of August 1st. That's the main reason I haven't written; it seems that time does pass faster when one is working hard. As for the story, I've been promised space, at 3¢ a word, in a new magazine called *Discovery*, which is bringing out its first issue toward the end of this year. It's to be edited by John W. Aldridge (who, incidentally, reviewed L.D.I.D. in the *Times* Book Review) and will be printed and distributed by Pocket Books, in the Pocket Book format. Thus it will be a "little magazine" with distinguished fiction in it, but it will have a newsstand circulation of 100,000 or more. A fine idea, I think. So much for the story, which I think is going to be a good one. I'll be in the same issue with Mailer, James Jones, and Capote.[15]

As for my health, *please* don't worry about that. I am far from frail and expect to become unhealthy only when I'm 90 years old. Outside of colds, I haven't been sick since I was a kid, and I have enough sense now—whether I did or not five or six years ago—to eat regularly and not drink too much. There's not much you can get to drink over here, anyway, that's worth a damn—weak beer, foul gin, and cheap cognac. I've been sticking to the good beer imported from Denmark and Holland. So don't *worry*. I feel fine.

15. Aldridge's review of *Lie Down in Darkness* appeared as "In a Place Where Love Is a Stranger," *New York Times Book Review*, September 9, 1951, 5. *Discovery* no. 1 (February 1953) includes no writing by Jones or Capote but does have contributions from (among others) Mailer, Kenneth Fearing, Chandler Brossard, Herbert Gold, and Hortense Calisher.

I received all the books and photostats, and I appreciate them very much. I feel bad about not thanking you for them before. They look as if they'll all provide wonderful background material and I'm taking them with me to Rome, where I plan to get to work on the story. I wish, though, you'd let me know how long I can keep the library books. I haven't had a chance to read them yet, because of my work, but I hope to get a crack at them very soon—in Rome or *en route*. I know it was considerable work for you, but I do appreciate it all.

When I finish the story (in about 10 days or so) I plan to stay here for just a little while more and then go up to Salzburg for the music festival, probably around August 15th. I hope to go to Vienna, too, as a side trip and then down to Rome via Bolzano in the Italian Tyrol, where my old gal Wanda Malinowska has a villa. So most of September I guess I'll be there, with trips to Florence and Venice, and will get to Rome around October 1st in time to celebrate your birthday.[16]

I'm sorry to hear about Aunt May. I have bought her a scarf here, but I found out that the duty is very high (Aunt May would have to pay it) on articles *mailed* to the U.S. So I'm sending it along with friends of mine who are leaving early next week on the boat to New York. They will either give it to my agent, Eliz. McKee, or to Dorothy Parker in New York, who will send it to you and you can mail it to Aunt May.[17] I'll put a card in. Complicated, but the only way to avoid the duty, which is exorbitant.

My best to all, then, and I promise to be a better correspondent from now on. I'm still healthy, wealthy, but don't know if I'm getting any wiser.

Your son,

Bill jr

P.S. French translation, *Un Lit de Ténèbres,* will be out in October. "A Bed of Darkness" is the literal translation of the title, with Peyton changed to Marjorie because "Peyton," in French, read aloud, means the sound the intestines make after a large meal.[18] E. McKee will send you a couple of copies.

16. Styron had been involved in a romance with Wanda Malinowska in 1950 while he was living on West 88th Street in New York. She was the daughter of the anthropologist Bronislaw Malinowski; later she served as one of the models for Sophie Zawistowska in *Sophie's Choice*. See *William Styron: A Life,* 183–85.

17. Aunt May was one of Styron's paternal aunts in Washington, N.C., his father's home town.

18. In French slang the word *pet* means flatulence; the suffix *-on* is a common diminutive ending. Peyton's name, pronounced with the accent on the first syllable, would mean "small fart."

P.P.S. You also, along about *Sept. 1st,* might write Mr. Truman Talley at the New American Library, 501 Madison Ave., N.Y. 22, and ask him to send you a couple of advance copies of the Signet reprint edition of L.D.I.D. whenever they're available. He's an editor there, a friend of mine, and I know he'd be more than happy to oblige.

92. PARIS

September 9, 1952

Dear Pop,

The enclosed clipping is, alas, fairly inaccurate in spots—especially the business about my "recent seven months in Korea," but it wasn't my fault if the interviewer quoted me wrong; at any rate, you will note in the first paragraph that I am a "big American with clear skin, with a frank expression that becomes extremely intense while he ponders his thoughts." That's what the French girl who interviewed me thought, anyway.[19]

I'm back in Paris after a jaunt around the countryside. I hope you got my card from Carcassonne. Prior to that I spent a fine 10 days down on the sunny Côte d'Azur near St. Tropez where, among other things, I got my story, all 22,000 words of it, typed up and air-mailed to New York. There's apparently been a great hassle over it up there between my agent, Miss McKee, and Hiram about where it should be published— they both like it a lot—but God willing it should be published some- where good within the next few months. I'll let you know. As for St. Tropez, it was quite wonderful, with superb swimming in the Medi- terranean and fishing with mask and harpoon among the rocks. I stayed on a slightly rundown but still attractive 35-room estate owned by a French woman, 70 years old, named Marie-Thérèse Nénot, whose father built the estate when he was France's leading architect (among other things he designed the newer buildings of the Sorbonne and the Palace of Nations in Geneva).[20] It was great fun. I got excellently tanned and ended up being quite struck by the fact that I began to feel as healthy as Tarzan. From St. Tropez I drove cross-country through the Provence to St. Jean-de-Luz, near Biarritz, on the Atlantic, a two-day trip. I stayed there a week and got in some good surf-bathing, but the weather for

19. Annie Brierre, "William Styron," *Les Nouvelles Littéraires,* August 14, 1952, 4.

20. Mme. Nénot had been a screen actress in the early days of the French cinema. See *William Styron: A Life,* 230.

the most part was gray and gloomy, so I passed most of my time at Irwin Shaw's house talking and reading old *New Yorkers.*[21] Now I'm back in Paris after a long, leisurely drive up through Les Landres near Bordeaux (flat country that looks, with its slashed pines and marsh, exactly like the land around Jacksonville, N.C.) and up to Orléans by way of Bergerac in the Dordogne Valley, where I ate, I believe, the best meal of the many incredible meals I've eaten in France—frogs legs, *coq au vin* and a wine that was like drinking liquid velvet. Speaking of cooking, I performed a feat myself, in St. Tropez, which should keep me secure in the annals of Virginians—I single-handed cooked a fried-chicken dinner for 18 count 'em 18 discriminating Frenchmen, all gourmets, and was applauded wildly: *quel poulet! formidable!*

Night before last I went to a birthday dinner which Sam Goldwyn gave for his son, my friend Sammy, Jr. It was quite a blowout. Darryl Zanuck[22] was there, along with a slew of delectable Hollywood starlets and so I must say that in a way I was glad to return to Paris and find that all was going as usual. In a couple of weeks or so I expect to start making plans about going to Rome (I'm due around Oct. 1st) and I'm looking forward to the change. Paris is a great big wonderful city, like a beautiful woman, and I've enjoyed myself here, besides getting some writing done, but I think Rome will provide a needed change of scene. I'll let you know, of course, my address and will also tell you when I'm leaving here and when I expect to arrive there. In the meantime I hope all goes well on the Peninsula and that you are taking care of yourself. I envy your television-side seat for both the World Series and the election, which I've been following under the auspices of Henry Luce and the Paris *Herald-Tribune.*[23]

Your son,
Bill

21. Shaw, (1913–1984), then living in Europe, had befriended Styron and the other young writers who were founding the *Paris Review.*

22. The Hollywood movie producer Darryl F. Zanuck (1902–1979) was one of the founders of Twentieth Century Fox. During the 1950s he was living in Europe and producing independent films there.

23. Dwight D. Eisenhower would defeat Adlai Stevenson in the election for the U.S. presidency in November 1952. To residents of the Virginia Tidewater the "Peninsula," in the previous sentence, is the area between the York River on the north and the James on the south. Newport News and Hampton are located at the eastern tip of the Peninsula.

8 / October 1952–October 1953

ROME AND RAVELLO

Styron traveled from Paris to Rome in early October 1952 and took up residence at the American Academy, situated on the Janiculum, the highest hill in the city. Not long after he arrived, he renewed his acquaintance with Rose Burgunder, whom he had met the previous fall at Johns Hopkins University.

93. ROME

October 27, 1952
c/o American Academy in Rome
Porta San Pancrazio, Rome

Dear Pop,

Thanks for the piece by Mr. Jebb, which I liked, and for your earlier letter.[1] The reason I haven't written more promptly is because I've just recently finished a week's trip by car—along with some other members of the Academy—to Florence, Siena, Ravenna, Urbino and Assisi. It was an excellent trip, lasting about a week, and thoroughly illuminating because my companions were all either painters or, better yet, art historians who gave me first-hand scholarship and information about the Art (with a capital A) we were seeing. I think, Art-wise, I was most impressed by the Medici tombs in Florence and by the Ravenna mosaics, which date from the middle of the Dark Ages and shine today in all their glory. As far as towns go I think I was particularly struck by Urbino, which is pitched on the top of a mountain and is filled with winding,

---

1. The "piece by Mr. Jebb" is unidentified.

AMERICAN ACADEMY IN ROME

Dear Pop—

Hope you got my recent letter. In response to your last (thanks for the clipping on Discovery) I'm sending you this pic, which is the only one I could dig up in a hurry. The bldg faces toward the east, overlooking the city below. I live inside on the 2d floor on a hallway, my door being right opposite the 2d big window from the right, and my windows look out on an interior courtyard and fountain.

The American Academy in Rome, where Styron spent his fellowship year in 1952–1953. Styron's handwritten note: "Dear Pop—Hope you got my recent letter. In response to your last (thanks for the clipping on *Discovery*) I'm sending you this pic, which is the only one I could dig up in a hurry. The bldg faces toward the east, overlooking the city below. I live inside on the 2d floor on a hallway, my door being right opposite the 2d big window from the right, and *my* windows look out on an interior courtyard and fountain." Courtesy Estate of William C. Styron, Jr.

steep streets and the nicest people in all of Italy. Assisi, on the other hand, is a tourist trap, filled with knick-knacks and holy pilgrims from places like Munich and Brussels.

Back at the Academy now, I've somewhat settled down. I wish I had a photograph of the place, but I'll try and get one for you soon. It's really a lovely place, a real palace, and big enough so that no one gets in anyone else's way. The painters, sculptors, and architects all get enormous studios which would cost a four-figure sum in New York, and each of which commands a marvelous view of Rome down below. I myself, not needing so much space, have to be content with two huge connecting rooms, excellently furnished, with large ceiling-high windows and a view of the Academy courtyard below, where there is a fountain surrounded by four beautiful cedar trees. We eat in a sort of community dining hall. The food is good Italo-American style, but as in Paris I generally, except for lunch, prefer to eat down in Rome where there are of course excellent restaurants. The keynote here, somewhat like Rabelais' Abbey of Thélème, is "Do What You Will" and there is no more routine here, or regulations, than in a hotel.[2] That suits me fine. Of course I've already met some very amiable and interesting people, yet in spite of the slightly community aspects of the place, it doesn't look to me as if there will be any trouble in keeping out of each other's way, nor, on the other hand, as if there will be any lack of parties and *bon camaraderie* when the occasion demands. I have also met an absolutely beautiful girl, American, named Rose, with whom I get along right well, and who has an apartment on the other side of Rome, which will obviously necessitate my buying a car *pronto*.[3] It won't be a Fiat, but either a German Volkswagen (an excellent car) or an English Austin, either of which will cost around $1300 but which cost I can get back substantially in re-sale before I come back to the U.S.A. One thing just leads to another. A

2. The Abbey of Thélème in François Rabelais' fantasy *Gargantua and Pantagruel* is a utopia in which the normal rules of the monastery are inverted. Inhabitants of both sexes, all young and beautiful, dress and dine in luxury and play as they choose. The governing principle is "Do what thou wilt."

3. Styron had met Rose Burgunder in the fall of 1951 at Johns Hopkins. At the invitation of Louis D. Rubin, Jr. (then a Ph.D. candidate at Hopkins and later to become a prominent scholar and critic of Southern literature), Styron had come to Baltimore from New York to give a reading from *Lie Down in Darkness* and to meet some of the graduate students. One of these students was Rose, who was working on a master's degree in poetry and criticism. (Another of the students was John Barth.) Rose finished her degree and, unsure whether to pursue the Ph.D., took a year off to travel and study in Europe.

young man just must have a girl, and that always—even, or I should say *especially* in Europe—brings up the question of wheels.

The election of course is a big topic over here, too, although perhaps not so intensely emotional as in the U.S. Everyone seems to be rooting for Stevenson and I hope he gets elected, too. The only reading matter available is Time and the Herald-Tribune and it seems to me that even in those arch-Republican journals it cannot be disguised just what a prime jackass Eisenhower has made of himself. If he had come out just once and roundly condemned McCarthy he might have had a chance with the not-after-all-so-dumb voter. But by the time you get this letter I suppose all the issues will be coming to a head.

As soon as I get this car situation straightened out, I'm going to settle down for a spell of work. I have ideas for three or four more long stories, which will help me financially, and in the meantime I suppose I will have thought up something for a new novel. I suspect that my long story "Long March" will be the strongest piece in the forthcoming issue of *Discovery,* which I'll have sent to you in December or January. Meanwhile, I've gotten a proof of the jacket of the jumbo, economy-sized 50¢ Signet Double Volume, which will appear in every Walgreen drugstore in November, in which a wan, sad, half-clad Peyton is seen on the verge of climbing into bed with one of the most unsavory-looking Italians you ever saw. *Sic Transit Gloria Literati,* but it will sell 250,000 copies and my stock will soar in Peoria. Best to all. *In Italia Ego.* Yet, American to the bone, I think often of home.

Your son,
Bill

94. ROME (American Academy letterhead)

December 5, 1952

Dear Pop,

If it's not *utter* and *complete sacrilege,* I am having, of all things, a *New Jersey* ham sent to you and Elizabeth for Christmas. This I know is apt to set

---

While in Rome in the fall of 1952, she received a letter from Rubin, telling her that Styron had won the Prix de Rome and was in residence at the American Academy. She left a note in Styron's mailbox at the academy; he called her and made a date to meet her in the bar of the Hotel Excelsior, not far from the Borghese Gardens. Their romance progressed from there.

off an explosion in the heart of one who has been so gastronomically partisan, as far as Southern cooking goes, for so many years, but this ham has been recommended highly to me and I hope that it won't turn to ashes in your mouth. At any rate, let it be tender and may your Yuletide thoughts turn for a fleeting moment to Rome—or Paris, rather, where I'll be for the holidays. I've been invited up there by my friends, the Matthiessens, and so due to some weird Italian law which insists that a car such as mine of foreign make and registry (Austin, in this case, with British plates) must go out of the country once a year, I decided I might as well drive up—a three day trip which I plan to make with a young musician here, Frank Wigglesworth, and his wife, Anne—both extremely nice people, gay and entertaining, who have never been to Paris before.[4] It's supposedly an easy trip—we go by way of Genoa (I'll try to look up that friend of Mike Fiore's) and the Riviera, through Aix-en-Provence, Avignon, and straight up the Rhone valley through Lyon. It should be a fine voyage and the perfect thing to do before I come back to Rome around New Year's and settle down to some heavy work for the rest of the winter and spring.

Incidentally, it would be just as good an idea for you *not* to send me anything for Christmas this year, since I would have to pay duty probably equal to the value of whatever you send. If you've already sent something, don't worry, but perhaps it would be better to save whatever you were going to send for next year. The same laws apply *vice versa* which is the reason I'm sending you a New Jersey ham instead of some nice Florentine leather or Venetian lace.

The car is really a very commendable machine, and I'm having great fun with it. Roman traffic is really fierce, though, and it's quite a chore to drive in the city. There's a law against using the horn (once, right after the war, the ban against horns was lifted and even the Italians couldn't stand the racket) and to compensate for the silence you just *prod* the rear end of the car in front of you instead of blowing at him. It's great sport, but very nerve-wracking.

My newest project for after my return from Paris is to write three or four short stories that have been haunting me and then to gird my

4. The flutist, composer, and teacher Frank Wigglesworth (1918–1996) later chaired the Music Department at the New School. He and his wife, Anne Parker, lived on Downing Street in Greenwich Village. Wigglesworth is remembered today for his compositions *Three Portraits* (1970) and *Aurora* (1983).

loins for that famous pitfall—the Second Novel. I'm not going to rush it, though, as too many people (viz., Norman Mailer) make that mistake. *Mademoiselle* magazine wants to pay me $600 for an article on Why I Like Rome, or something on that order, and it's too good an opportunity to turn down and no doubt will be easy.[5] In the meantime, I've been having a pleasant time sightseeing—a trip to Naples and the Amalfi coast (the most beautiful stretch of green hills, blue sky and blue sea that I've ever seen) and to Pompeii with a lot of Academy art experts, where I was beguiled by the pornographic frescoes.

I hope Santa Claus brings you lots of nice things and that this Christmas season will be unexhaustingly pleasant. *Buone feste!*[6]

Your son,
Bill

95. ROME (American Academy letterhead)

[January 8, 1953]
Friday

Dear Pop,

Having arrived back here only a couple of days ago from Paris, I want to thank both you and Elizabeth for the lovely sweaters, which unfortunately did not arrive in time to shelter me from the depredations of the Alpine winter, but are serving me warmly—and handsomely, too—in the chill Roman January. They are indeed beautiful, and will make fashionable additions to my suits, which now number three. I wish you would tell Helen, too, how much I like the fine linen handkerchief, and how much I appreciate her remembering me.

We had a really wonderful time in the North. I went with the Wigglesworths (old New England name) in the Austin, and the car performed nobly, especially on the trip back—of which more in a minute. Going up we stayed the first night in Pisa, and had an eyeful the next day of the leaning tower and the baptistry, of which so much has been written that I need not amplify on their beauty. Next night, after a long, sunny and handsome drive along the rocky northern coast around Genoa, we stayed at Imperia near San Remo, after which, the next day,

5. Styron never wrote this article.
6. A common expression used by Italians to wish each other a happy holiday between Christmas and Epiphany.

we crossed over into France and thence easily on to Paris with stops at Avignon (to see the *Palais des Papes*, the early Renaissance Popes' summer house) and, at Saulieu, which Mme de Sevigny once described as the best eatingest place in all of France. It's in the heart of Burgundy and the Snail country and so we had snails, by the bucketful. Paris was grand and beautiful, but not too cold, *and* the Christmas parties were elegant and pleasant and glowing. My friend John Marquand, Jr., was there (his first novel is the Book-of-the-Month Club selection for Feb.) and so I caught up on all the goings-on which he recently left in New York.[7] Then, on Christmas night, we flew to London, leaving the Austin (which I've christened Warren C.)[8] in a Paris garage, spent three very pleasant days with a couple I met here in Rome last fall, and flew back to Paris in time to get the New Year's parties, which left me enervated and satiated with parties for some months to come. The trip back was— or would have been—uneventful, had it not been for the fact that, having decided to take a "short cut" and avoid the long Riviera journey by going *via* Grenoble, Chambry and the Modane tunnel (where we loaded the car on a train for the 15 mile trip), we ran into the worst snow storm the region has seen in 25 years. Going down the road from Bardonnecchia to Turin we were part of a caravan of 5 cars which became utterly stalled in drifts four feet high and had to be pulled out by horses. I've never seen so much snow in all my life, but five hours of pushing and shoveling, with hysterical Italians on all sides shrieking advice above the sound of the blizzard, restored color to my cheeks and tone to my muscles—and *that*, plus the fact that the Austin performed *beautifully* in spite of the snow, made us all feel warm and in high spirits when we arrived in Turin.

So now I'm back in Rome, ready for some work, which should not be too long in germinating. Upon arrival I had a letter from my agent telling me that my income tax on LDID would be *$4500*. I am the only person I know who has had an income tax of $4500 but the faint moist pride I derive from this is tempered by the basic fact that Uncle Sam is really hacking away at my bank account, and that this, if for no other

7. "Jack" Marquand, son of the novelist John P. Marquand, had published his first novel, *The Second Happiest Day*, under the nom de plum John Phillips with Harpers in 1953.

8. Styron named his automobile for Warren Austin (1877–1962), a U.S. senator from Vermont who was appointed as ambassador to the United Nations in 1946 by Harry Truman.

reason, should make me hop like a frightened kangaroo to my writing desk. So that's what I'm doing, and this winter should see some production of some sort. Incidentally, *Holiday* magazine wants me to do a whole long feature article on Virginia, but they want me to wait until I come back to the U.S. so at least it's always nice to know that I have Curtis Publishing Company finances, which I understand to be considerable, to fall back on.[9]

Thanks again, and to Elizabeth, for the fine sweaters and I hope the New Year finds you all happy and content. Write soon.

Your son,
Bill Jr.

At this point in their romance Styron and Rose learned that her mother was having him investigated by a private detective. Rose had also received a letter from Styron's stepmother telling her that Styron was a poor matrimonial prospect. This opposition from home caused them to break off their relationship for a time. Rose left Rome and stayed in Florence for several weeks; Styron resumed his efforts to write at the Academy. Eventually they reunited and decided to marry in the spring. See the foreword to this volume, pp. xiv–xv.

96. ROME (American Academy letterhead)

March 3, 1953

Dear Pop:

My story "Long March" seems to be evoking some favorable responses, although there certainly has been a paucity of reviews. Some Hollywood agent liked it enough to send it around to all the studios (though he said there's fat chance, not only being anti-war but anti-Marine, which in the U.S. is like being anti-Mom), and the editor of *Perspectives,* the magazine which the Ford Foundation distributes all over the world, called Miss McKee to say that he loved the story but it was too long to reprint. And at the moment I'm in receipt of a letter from Norman Mailer ("The Naked and the Dead") who tells me "as a modest estimate it's certainly as good an 80 pages as any American has written since the

---

9. Styron never wrote the article for *Holiday.*

war." I'm very touched by that, since Mailer of all my contemporaries is the writer I surely most admire. No need for you to think all this turns my head, as you cautioned. Along those lines Mailer added a word of criticism, implying I suppose that I should have perhaps a slightly more swollen head. "The tendency in you to invent your story, and manner your style, struck me as coming possibly from a certain covert doubt of your strengths as a writer, and you're too good to doubt yourself."

Meanwhile, I seem to have struck a slight snag in my work and have done really nothing of any value since Christmas. I'm not actually worried at this *impasse,* however, though my inactivity irritates me and seems to make much of life weary, flat, stale and unprofitable, or whatever the hell it was that Hamlet said.[10] I'm only really happy when I'm working. This I've finally realized in looking back over the periods when I was engaged in writing, those periods which seemed at the time so painful and full of drudgery and toil; actually upon a sort of Proustian type of reflection I can see that they—those hours of concentration, and slow scribbling—*they* are the moments of true delight. So, if only in a therapeutic vein, I intend to start into work again soon. The Nat Turner thing, for the moment, lies idle; Lord knows when I'll wrestle with that, perhaps not for years.

I hope you got my recent card. Since then I've been to Ravello—that town of magnificent and craggy beauty on the Amalfi coast. We drove down just for a couple of days, a young lady from Baltimore of whom I'm very fond and a sculptor named Robert White and his wife—superb people, he's the grandson of Stanford White, the architect who had a hand in building the Academy and of whom, of course, much has been written.[11] Riding in Italy, especially around Naples, is a blood curdling experience, what with the absolute unconcern the natives have for any motorized vehicle and what with the incredible procession, still, of carts and wagons. However, the highways here seem to be much safer than in the U.S., perhaps because of necessity drivers appear to be more cautious and wary. In Ravello we stayed a day and two nights in a villa of an old Countess, a friend of the Whites, and I'm afraid I could never

10. From Hamlet's soliloquy on Gertrude's marriage (act 1, scene 2): "O, that this too, too solid flesh would melt, / Thaw and resolve itself into a dew! / . . . / How weary, stale, flat and unprofitable, / Seem to me all the uses of this world!"

11. Bobby and Claire White were among Styron's best friends in Italy. The Whites served as partial models for Cass and Poppy Kinsolving in *Set This House on Fire.*

describe either the munificent, regal quality of the place or the breath-taking view of precipitous rocks and cerulean blue water over 1,000 feet straight down below. On our scouting expedition we explored half a dozen or so villas which we hope to occupy this summer, finally set-tling on one which has *nine* beds, two baths, a *view* of course, terraces, gardens, a private grove of lemon trees, and a couple of servants thrown in. All for what amounts to about $170 a month. Divided among three or four people this is peanuts. I hope to send you some pictures of it soon. Speaking of pictures, the only sour note in Ravello last weekend was the presence of Humphrey Bogart and Jennifer Jones and an en-tourage of Hollywood creatures, on location for a movie which will no doubt provide enough publicity as to spoil the place for the next 50 generations.[12] O tempore, O mores! But they won't be there this sum-mer. Hope all goes well at home, and drop me a line soon.

Your son,
Bill

97. ROME

April 8, 1953

Dear Pop,

I am enclosing two items which may be of interest to you: (a) a clip-ping from last week's Newsweek, which you may or may not have seen (I've asked E. McKee, incidentally, to send you a copy of the Paris Re-view)[13] and (b) a recent picture taken at a party. Reading from left to right the characters are Samuel Barber, the famous American composer who is visiting here; young Elliott Braxton, who came to Rome and is now gone, but with whom I had long talks about Newport News and vicinity; a young lady named Mrs. Marge Allen who with her hus-band lives here in Rome; yours truly, who somehow here looks sick and

12. The movie was *Beat the Devil* (1953), starring Bogart, Jones, Gina Lollobrigida, Pe-ter Lorre, and Robert Morley. John Huston directed the film, and Truman Capote wrote the script.

13. The first issue of the *Paris Review* had been published; Styron was sending his fa-ther a clipping from *Newsweek* announcing its appearance—a five-paragraph notice men-tioning Styron's "Letter to the Editor," in which he urges that the magazine concentrate on poetry and fiction and not publish reviews or criticism. See "Advance-Guard Advance," *Newsweek*, March 30, 1953, 94.

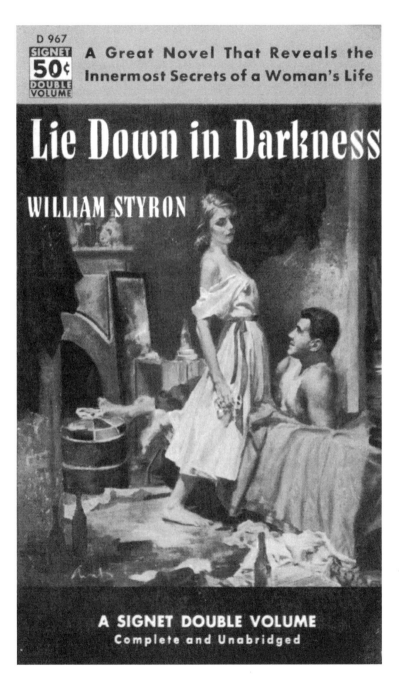

Lie Down in Darkness

WILLIAM STYRON

A SIGNET DOUBLE VOLUME
Complete and Unabridged

Cover of the first paperback edition of *Lie Down in Darkness*, published by Signet in November 1952. Courtesy Lilly Library, Indiana University, Bloomington Indiana.

disheveled, but who is actually the picture of health and whose sour appearance in the photograph can only be blamed upon the light and bad Italian gin; another composer, Alexei Haieff, who just won the N.Y. Critics' Award for the best musical composition of 1952; a young lady from Baltimore named Rose Burgunder, accent on the second syllable; and Tom Guinzburg, a good friend who is the managing editor of the *Paris Review* and whose father owns the Viking Press.[14]

I think it will probably interest you further that I am going to get myself married to the girl named Rose, second from right. I won't go into a lot of sentimental double-talk about how I think she's the most wonderful girl in the world—because I do—but suffice it to say that she's the girl from whose presence I get the greatest sense of well-being and fulfillment that I've ever had, and for whom I have the greatest affection, and I'm happy to think that you will see why, when you meet her. I imagine we will get married sometime in May, here in Rome. Incidental to this, I wonder if it would be possible for you to prevail upon Aunt Edith to send me, by registered air express, that fine engagement ring which, I gather, reposes in some safe-deposit box up in Uniontown. I remember your having often mentioned this to me, and you know of course that I would be greatly honored to be able to give it to Rose. I would appreciate it, and be greatly indebted to you, if you could arrange this as soon as possible.[15]

Needless to say, I'm delighted at the fact that you have a European trip in prospect, and am looking forward to being able to extend you and Elizabeth the hospitality of Ravello. Just let me know in advance your itinerary and all that, so that I'll be able to stock up on gas coupons and drive you both around this miraculous land. It's a trip, I'm sure, which you won't regret.

No further news. I wrote to Mrs. Ferguson and received a nice note in reply from Isobel. My writing project at the moment seems to be

14. Barber (1910–1981) was already well known in the 1950s for his *Adagio for Strings*, first performed in 1938. Young Elliott Braxton from Newport News was a descendant of Elliott M. Braxton (1823–1891), a politician, lawyer, and military man from Matthews County in eastern Virginia. The pianist and composer Alexei Haieff (1914–1994), a native of Russia and a friend of Igor Stravinsky, created the music for George Balanchine's *Divertimento* (1944).

15. This was the ring that Styron's father gave to his mother when they became engaged in 1919.

Rose Burgunder in Italy at twenty-four, early autumn 1952. Courtesy Rose Styron.

confined to an article for a symposium in *The Nation*, on "What I Believe," to appear later this spring.[16] It's a stern order, that sort of thing, to state one's philosophy in "25 words or less." Perhaps, though, it will give me the impetus for another long short story which has been slowly germinating in the back of my mind.

16. "The Prevalence of Wonders," *Nation* 176 (May 2, 1953): 370–71.

Best to all, and write soon.

Your son,

Bill

P.S. "LDID" has been accepted for translation in the German, which makes 7 languages in all.

98. ROME

April 24, 1953

Dear Pop:

Many thanks for the tie, the Wallace design of which I will of course wear with Pride, even in this country of un-Celtic Africans.

This is just a note. What I'd like to know is whether you got my letter, requesting that you send me, or have Aunt Edith send me, that sapphire engagement ring which you once told me would be mine when I got myself married, and which is presumably in a safe deposit box up in Uniontown. I wrote a letter asking for this well over ten days ago, enclosing a photograph and a clipping from Newsweek, but having not heard from you since then (except for the snapshot of the lawnmower, on the back of which you acknowledge having received another photograph at Ravello—this one, however, *not* being the important letter I sent you at the same time) makes me wonder if you received the letter at all. At any rate, in spite of the confusion, I hope this note adequately explains things. I propose to go to the altar very soon now, and if you could possibly have this ring sent to me registered air mail I would be greatly obliged. Also proud, as Rose will be to wear it.

As for your proposed trip, I went on at some length in that letter to say that I'd be happy to escort you around Italy, just let me know, etc. etc. That still goes. Let me hear from you soon.

Your son,

Bill

P.S. This might seem a strange request, but I wonder if you could have sent to me, by ordinary mail, three or four cans of black-eye peas.[17] You can't get them here and I don't know if you can in Newport News, though we got them a few years ago in Durham. I have a real craving

---

17. Served at weddings and on other occasions (e.g., New Year's Day) to bring luck, a southern custom.

for black-eye peas. But only send them, though, if they are easily obtainable and if there would be little trouble in packing them, etc.

B.

99. ROME

[late April 1953]

Dear Pop:

I hope that by now you've gotten my other letter. About the ring: I've been thinking about that and I suspect that, without certain precautions, either you or Aunt Edith or I would have to pay customs duty on the package. So here is what I suggest: Rose and I have friends here in Rome who work at the American Embassy. Packages coming to them, mailed through an APO number, are immune to customs inspection. So if the ring is mailed—*registered airmail*—to the following address, the package won't be opened: GLORIA GREEN, AMERICAN EMBASSY, A.P.O. 794, C/O POSTMASTER, NEW YORK, N.Y.[18] Two important points: (a) you can pay on this package the postage you would pay for *domestic* rather than foreign airmail (b) address the package *not* to me "care of" the above address, but to the above address directly—in the meantime we will have alerted this girl to be on the lookout for the package. You see, the regulations prohibit packages being sent "c/o" an A.P.O. address, but must be sent directly to the embassy employee.

That's about all; I hope it's not too much trouble. In the meantime, here's a choice shot of Ravello, which I hope you'll like.

Bill

100. ROME

May 6, 1953

Dear Pop:

After incredibly complicated dealings with the Italian bureaucracy, Rose and I were married on Monday afternoon (the 4th) in truly gala style, at the Campidoglio, which is Rome's city hall. It was a very nice ceremony, unlike the equivalent in an American city, I'm sure, since the

18. Gloria Green, one of Rose's roommates in Rome, worked at the American Embassy there.

little room where it was performed was covered with wonderful crimson brocade and the officiating judge (in Rome the marrying judgeship is a high civic honor and our man, Signor Marconi, is Italy's Samuel Goldwyn) was dressed in a beautiful green and red sash. On hand for the ceremony were a few Academy friends, Irwin Shaw and his wife, Jack Marquand, who came from Athens especially for the wedding, and Peter Matthiessen and Tom Guinzburg (my Paris Review friends), who flew down from Paris, also especially. Afterwards, the Shaws had a big reception for us in their apartment, with cake and champagne, and after *that* we had a big dinner in a restaurant, with *fettuccini* and chicken *alla diavolo*. It was just fine. Best man was Bob White, whom I've mentioned; and his wife wrote a poem which she sang at the reception to a special tune written by Frank Wigglesworth, who accompanied her on a recorder. This sounds extremely corny, but I assure you it couldn't have been more touching, to be surrounded by so many fine friends. No honeymoon, since it won't be long before we decamp for Ravello.

Because of my matrimonial involvements (I've also bought *four* tailored suits) I haven't had much time to write, but I did go to the American Express, as you requested, and was told very definitely that it would be far better if you arranged the travel from Havre to Italy through their New York or Washington office, rather than go through the procedure of lots of complicated air mail letters to you from Rome or Paris. I really think this would be much better. As a matter of fact, Rose's family, who do a lot of traveling, use a very good travel agent in Baltimore. The woman, whose name is Miss Ethel C. Einstein, runs the Metropolitan Tourist Agency (North Charles St.) and is a very influential person, apparently, in the travel field. She is also a personal friend of Mrs. Burgunder, Rose's mother. I suggest that you write this lady, tell her who you are, and include information on where you want to go, how long you want to stay, how much you want to pay, etc. I have a feeling that she'll fix you up much better than American Express.[19]

That's about all for now. Hope everything goes well, and I'm certainly looking forward to seeing you this summer.

Your son,
Bill

---

19. The elder Styrons decided instead to travel to South America. See letters 101 and 102.

P.S. Rose's mother's address, in case you would like to write her, is:

Mrs. B. B. Burgunder
2707 Lawina Road
Baltimore 16, Md.

101. RAVELLO

July 6, 1953
Palazzo Confalone
Ravello (Salerno), Italy

Dear Pop:

It surely must seem to be an extremely long time since I last wrote; fact of the matter is—as you must know—that I've been very busy trying to get started on this new Opus I have in mind, and, beset on every side with problems of *Plot, Atmosphere,* and *Characterization.* I've had little time to write anything else, even postcards. I trust you did get my card, however, and also the Paris literary clipping, both of which I sent around a week ago.

The place we have is marvelous—two floors of a palace which dates back to 1200. It's been completely modernized, however, and includes hot running water, bathtub, kitchen and enormous picture windows. The rent is $100 a month, which for a joint like this is nothing. We have a maid who does all the cooking and cleaning for about $25 a month, and a good cook she is, too. The Matthiessens and their baby have been staying here for the past three weeks and are leaving for the States on the "Andrea Doria" next Sunday.[20] Our routine has been close to idyllic: work in the morning, swimming off the rocks down in Amalfi from noon til mid-afternoon, tennis in the late afternoon, followed by a few conservative martinis. The "panorama," as you doubtless are aware from the postcards, couldn't be more conducive to felicitous labor, and as I gaze up from my desk I often find myself feeling that such a vista is a strange thing for a home-town boy from Virginia to be beholding every day. I'm really sorry that you won't be able to partake of our Italian hospitality, but the trip which you outlined in your letter to Rose sounds most exciting, and I don't think you'll miss Ravello when you're in the

20. The *Andrea Doria* collided with the Swedish liner *Stockholm* almost exactly three years later, on July 25, 1956, off the coast of Nantucket. Most of the passengers were rescued before the ship capsized and sank the following morning.

midst of the native delights of Chile, Argentina and Brazil. I understand that the steaks of Buenos Aires are as thick as a timber and as cheap as hash, so have one there for me. Hiram Haydn and his wife, incidentally, are flying to Europe around the end of this month and we expect to entertain them here the weekend of the 27th. It should be great fun.

Our plans at the moment for coming back to the U.S. are very vague. Since I've gotten into this new thing I'm writing on, I don't have any particular desire to break the creative flow by moving around, so we might extend our stay here from Sept. 1st—when we originally intended to move back to Rome for a while—till around the first of November, and then—when I hope to have something substantial written—set sail from Naples, or maybe go up to Paris until around Christmas and sail from Havre or London. But all that is very indefinite and we might come home sooner. To *where* I don't know, and that's the rub, for if one is not tied down to a place or a job, as I am, it's a hell of a problem to decide whether to settle in Westport, Waukesha or Woonsocket. But that problem, I have no doubt, like most problems, will settle itself. Meanwhile, I hope all goes well with you and that you're enjoying the pre-Brazil excitement. Let me hear from you when you can.

Your son,
Bill

102. RAVELLO

July 21, 1953

Dear Pop:

It was nice to get your letter and to know that you are on the verge of going south of the border; I'll bet you must be excited . . . if you're as keyed up as I was when I departed on the *Ile* last winter you will certainly need a drink, or maybe two, at embarkation time. I wish I could be on hand with the champagne. The Haydns, I'm sure, would have loved to be on hand to wish you bon voyage but unfortunately they are at this moment somewhere in Europe and in fact we are expecting them here at Ravello the day after tomorrow. They'll be here for three days and then will go back to Rome in order to catch the plane Monday for Zurich.

As the summer wears on I find that gradually I'm getting some work done, although time seems to fly by so fast that I feel that I'll be an old man before I get anything finished. This present thing looks like it will be a novelette, though it might—who knows?—turn out to be of novel length. I can't tell you much about it yet—but you might be interested to know that its first scenes are laid at old Davidson College, and that the story will have a lot of funny episodes in it, which you'll have to admit is something new in the literary approach of Styron *fils*.[21]

You mentioned something about an insurance policy in an earlier letter. I'm never too clear or astute about such things, but if you think it's good and worthwhile for me to continue it, I will. Just send it to me sometime, or send me the address of the place where I pay the premium and other details.

In the meantime, Rose and I are having a splendid summer, playing tennis most every day on the fine court they have here, and swimming often in the wonderful clear bottle-green water of the Amalfi coast. The towns hereabouts are at the moment undergoing a siege of fiestas, and they are great fun, with noise, music, processions of the saints, and truly the most fabulous fireworks to be found on this side of the ocean.

I hope you will send a lot of nice postcards from Chile, Argentina, and points south, and that both of you have a fine and relaxing time. I'm enclosing an article on *Un Lit de Ténèbres* from the Paris "L'Observateur."[22] It's as nice a review as one could imagine, and I understand that the book is making a big splash in France . . . they seem to like misery or something. How's your French? The underlined passages read: "It is one of the best novels which have come to us from America in the past few years, and one is astonished at the youth of this author who, with his first work, equals the finest of writers." And "In his book life is a question of a fight which need not end up in defeat, and of a possible hope, but of a hope not in heaven but on this earth, among other poor creatures like ourselves. Holding up to us this way of salvation, the only one there is . . . William Styron places himself among our 'liberators.' If he is not the subject of the next investigation [meaning McCarthy, no doubt], he will be condemned to the writing of more masterpieces." Very, very French way of putting things. Let me hear from you soon.

Your son,
Bill

21. This piece of writing does not survive.

22. Maurice Nadeau, "Au Plus Profond de la Nuit," *L'Observateur*, July 16, 1953, Lettres sect., 17.

103. RAVELLO

October 11, 1953

Dear Pop:

I was glad to learn from Elizabeth's letter that you arrived back in the homeland safe and sound, and that you had such a nice trip south of the border. It was too bad that you had to have a bad spell on your way home (too much high life on the high seas?) but of course I was happy to hear that you snapped back with such promptness. Take it easy. We followed your trip with great interest and I must say you all certainly seemed to do everything up brown, all right. We received, incidentally, the cards from Santiago which you were worried about us not getting. They came by Air Mail and were greatly enjoyed.

We have reservations on the Independence leaving Naples the 13th of December and stopping at Genoa, Cannes and Gibraltar. We were lucky to get 2nd class accommodations at tourist class rates, since it is the off-season. The painter Franklin Watkins and wife, who were at the Academy this year, will be on board so we won't get lonely.[23] We dock in New York on the 22nd and don't know precisely what our plans from there on are; we've got piles of baggage, for one thing, which we don't know what to do with. We'll come to Newport News some time during the holidays. Don't know precisely when yet, but will let you know well in advance.

We are certainly going to hate to leave this place, which has been a fine home for so long, but we're on such good terms with the Swiss landlord that I don't think we'll have any difficulty renting it again in future years.[24] We've had visitors off and on all summer and fall. Friends drop in for a weekend every now and then from the Academy. Then Hiram and Mary Haydn were here for three or four days; a month or so later Elizabeth McKee and husband came (he's Ted Purdy, who is chief editor at G. P. Putnam's) and this past week we were graced by the presence of none other than Professor William Blackburn, who is touring around Italy in his Austin, following a summer's research on Con-

---

23. Franklin C. Watkins (1894–1972), an American expressionist painter and portraitist, taught at the Pennsylvania Academy of Fine Arts for much of his career. He was married to Ida Quigley.

24. The *padrone* was Pasquale Vuilleumier, whose descendants continue to operate the Palazzo Confalone in Ravello. The character Windgasser in *Set This House on Fire* is based on Vuilleumier.

rad in Edinburgh. We had a fine time. I have been getting quite a bit of writing done, though. I am seven or eight thousand words along on a "novella" which I hope wistfully to have completed by Christmas.[25] I am also writing an article on the pleasures and pains of listening to the European radio, which is not finished yet, but will probably be published in *Harper's Magazine*. Then I got a letter—which you forwarded—from the Managing Editor of the *Times-Dispatch*, asking me to do a piece for their book supplement coming out November 30th. This I've done, and so you might keep an eye out for it, if you're interested.[26]

So everything is pretty serene. The only unhappy incident we've had was in Rome about a month ago, when Rose had her wallet and passport and 100,000 lire ($160) stolen, and from the sacred precincts of the American Academy. It is believed that one of the servants took it, but they didn't catch him. By great fortune, the passport was returned through the mails and we learned that $100 of the stolen $160 was insured, so it really didn't turn out too badly anyway. Italians are wonderful, but not given to any excess of rectitude.

Drop me a line and say hello to Elizabeth and Helen. Looking forward to seeing you soon!

Your son,
Bill

The Styrons sailed from Naples on December 13, 1953, and arrived in New York on December 22. After Christmas visits to their parents, they settled in a one-bedroom apartment on East 76th Street; the following October they purchased a farmhouse and fourteen acres in Roxbury, Connecticut, and lived there for the remainder of their married life.

25. Styron had completed a short story set at the Hart's Island prison (see chapter 4, n. 9). It was published as "Blankenship" in a special Styron issue of *Papers on Language and Literature* 23 (Fall 1987): 430–48. The surviving typescript of the story is among Styron's papers at the Library of Congress. "Blankenship" is included in the collection *The Suicide Run* (New York: Random House, 2009).

26. The article on European radio does not survive. The second item was published as "Novel, Far from Dead, Is Very Much Alive," *Richmond Times-Dispatch*, November 29, 1953, 14.

Three Letters from Styron's Father

The three letters below are among the few written to Styron by his father that survive. They are preserved in Styron's papers at Duke, interfiled with other correspondence from the early 1950s. These three letters are, in order, responses to letters 81, 91, and 92 in this volume.

July 10, 1951
Thursday morning

Dear Son:

I still am out of active circulation but Dr. Pierce was in to see me last Sunday and said that, if nothing happens, I can return to work about August 1. I am getting so much rest, loving care, and vitamins, that when I am released I will head for the Jungfrau—but I won't. From here out I will sing with Browning—"Grow old with me, the best is yet to come, the last for which the first was made." It is indeed a comfort to a loving parent, with the twilight of life in his eyes, to know that his child, grown to be a man, stands to justify his fondest dreams. What more does life hold than that?

I am glad to hear that you are being returned to civilian life but am sorry to hear that your eyes are the cause.[1] But even at that I am glad to hear that you feel that they are no worse than they have been for years.

It will certainly be nice to have you come to see us and I wish it could be before August 1, then we could have much time together.

I was glad to hear you say that you are saving your money for there

---

1. Styron was being discharged from the Marine Corps because of the congenital cataract in his right eye.

is nothing like having a little surplus to fall back on. Without exception the history of all successful men is that they started with a jackpot and it gave them a certain freedom of action that nothing else can give. So, son, if it develops that your book proves a financial success and if any folding money comes to your hands invest it wisely if only in life insurance or Victory Bonds.

Was surprised to hear you talking of becoming a Benedict. Who is the gal? I shall be looking forward to seeing you soon and hearing about everything.

Your devoted father,
William C. Styron

* * *

August 2, 1952
Tuesday noon

Dear Son:

Your fine letter of July 18 received and I thank you for taking time out from your creative literary labors to advise me on the state of Styron, fils. The assurance that you are healthy and wealthy is O.K. If you become too wise you will never be rich. Isn't there a distinction between wealth and riches?

I have made note of all the forthcoming literary products of William Styron and will keep an eye out for all of them.

Received a letter from Leon the other day and he is still doing well at Harvard.[2] Is anxious to get a word or two from you. He found out for me that my great uncle William Clark was the only North Carolinian at Harvard in 1840. I propose to present the old letter to the University but am having about half a dozen Photostats of it struck off before I send it to them.

I called up Washington N.C. last night and talked to your Aunt May. She is still able to get around and I am sure she will be happy to receive the scarf.

About the books from the Hampton Institute Library: Prof. Redding, as I remember, told me that you would be able to keep the books as long as you needed them.[3]

2. This was Leon Edwards, a boyhood friend from Hilton Village who was in Harvard Medical School. He is mentioned by Styron in letters 13, 14, 52, and 83.

3. These were the materials on the Nat Turner Rebellion that J. Saunders Redding had sent to Styron. See letters 89 and 90.

I am happy to hear that you will be able to take in the Salzburg Festival. I have read so much about it—it must be wonderful. I read for years about it in Musical America.

Bill, did you ever buy the little Fiat automobile from your writer friend and do you expect to tour Europe in it?

I was interested to hear that you are going to Vienna and will spend some time in Bolzano in the Italian Tyrol with your friend Wanda Malinowska. Wasn't she the girl whose father was an anthropologist at Yale and she came down with you to meet Elizabeth and me when we returned from Haiti?[4] Wasn't it at Bolzano that Mussolini and Hitler cooked up the devil's brew that brought on World War II and which led to their ultimate but well merited destruction? Watch out for their ghosts as you pass through the Brenner Pass.

Son, please keep in touch with me if only by a postcard for you know I am interested in your well being as no other person on this earth.

In the meantime I can only bestow a father's, "God bless you my son."

Your devoted father
William C. Styron

P.S. Be sure and send me your several addresses as you go from place to place.

* * *

[October 16, 1952]
Thursday noon

Dear Son:

Your first card with your permanent address was received last week and am glad to hear that you are settled at last. I am glad that you have found Academia Americana a beautiful place and that you may be able to say at the end of your twelve months, "Wonderful year" (Annis Mirabilis).

My spirits are definitely lifted up when I think of the fine things you are having handed over to you due to your literary achievements. I hope that as you walk around Rome even the humblest Roman may be able to say, "There goes a good American."

Some months ago I was talking to Mr. H. L. Ferguson after you had received the Prix de Rome and he told me that Mr. Archer Huntington

---

4. Wanda is mentioned in letter 91.

was one of the founders of the "American Academy."[5] I asked him to-day if Mr. H. also helped with the founding of the American Academy in Rome. He told me that he didn't know as he never talked of his benefactions. He said that to his knowledge Mr. Huntington is the only wealthy man who has given away $50,000,000 without having his name attached to any of his benefactions.

Mr. Ferguson asked me how you are getting along and I told him that the last time I heard from you, you had just climbed to the top of St. Peter's dome and you were pooped out. He asked me how you are getting along. I told him as far as I could tell you are doing O.K. He said more power to you as "he is a grand boy." A prophet is not without honor . . .

I guess you are keeping up with the political doings in these U.S.A. I guess I am still a boy emotionally because I get all het up over the charges and countercharges and it is not good for me at my age but son, I know what is considered right in God's sight. I have seen so much history made in this country. We are now paying for the selfishness of our earlier generations. If our cathedral falls it will be because we have not had the architects and the artists of the grade of those who put their lives in the building of St. Peters. I know St. Peters is good for a thousand years but I have my doubts about our American Institutions lasting that long unless there is a definite change of heart here.

I know you are having to do a lot of clerical work but again I suggest that you make notes of what you see for there is "no impression without expression."

Keep well my son and may God bless you.

Your devoted father
William C. Styron

P.S. Son, don't eat so much Italian food that you will grow gross and heavy like Thomas Wolfe. Extra weight certainly shortens our lives.[6]

---

5. Archer M. Huntington was the stepson of Collis P. Huntington, the railroad magnate who, in the late 1870s, chose Newport News as the eastern terminus of the Chesapeake and Ohio Railroad. The city became a major port as a consequence. Archer Huntington devoted his career to philanthropy.

6. Styron's father had sent him a photograph of a young, slim Wolfe taken during Wolfe's student days at the University of North Carolina.

Appendix 2

The Genesis of William Styron

WILLIAM C. STYRON, SR.

No biography of a man, not even a literary one, would be complete without a backward look to his forebears, not "for such boastings as the Gentiles use," but that we might thereby discover the wellspring of a talent.

It could be said that William Styron was fortunate in the choice of ancestors, for his family lines on every side stem from good European stocks: Scotch, Scotch-Irish, Welsh, Swiss and English. To do justice to his family connections in the United States would require a very large volume.

His ancestors first settled on the Atlantic seaboard, in Pennsylvania, Maryland, Virginia and in North Carolina, and some of them later moved west and south—the traditional routes of the settlement of the United States.

Among the Conrad Weiser papers in the Pennsylvania Historical Society there is a list of settlers killed on the Lehigh River during the years 1755 and 1756. The list is signed by one Captain Jacob Arndt, and includes a statement that John Waterson, his wife, and a small son were killed by the Indians. William Styron's great-grandmother, Susannah Waterson Showalter, a small child at the time, escaped. One day when

This account of Styron's life was written by his father in 1951 at the request of the Duke University alumni office. The document, previously unpublished, reveals the father's fondness for genealogical research. It also contains much information about William Styron's boyhood that is recorded nowhere else. A draft of the account is among Styron's papers at Duke; a finished version, from which the text here is taken, is in the Bobbs-Merrill collection at the Lilly Library, Indiana University.

her mother and father were at the barn, two Indians came to the house and then later went to the barn. One of the Indians came back to the house and told Susannah that the other Indian was killing her mother and father and she had better run or he would kill her too. So she took the baby and ran to a neighbor's house, but the son was left behind and was also killed by the Indians.

The Ulrich Showalter whom Susannah Waterson married was brought from Switzerland as a child by his parents who landed at Philadelphia about 1750 and settled near Allentown before going to the Shenandoah Valley of Virginia. He later moved to Fayette County, Pennsylvania.

According to Marquis James the forebears of Andrew Jackson first settled in Pennsylvania and came down the valleys of that State and Virginia before they settled on the North Carolina–South Carolina border. Although William Styron's Jackson forebears in Pennsylvania were stalwart Unionists and fought for the North during the Civil War, his great-grandmother Eliza Jackson always claimed kinship with the redoubtable "Stonewall." Her home in Smithfield, Pennsylvania, was less than fifty miles as the crow flies from Clarksburg, West Virginia, where he was born.

The first North Carolina ancestor on the Styron side was a George Styring who came from the West Riding in Yorkshire, England, in 1719, and settled in Carteret County. The first representatives of the family in the New World were a George Stiring who was living in Barbados in the West Indies by 1638 and a John Stioring who was living in Virginia by 1650. In the early days there were about a dozen spellings of the name. Most of the Styrons were sea-faring men, therefore perhaps too busy trying to gain a subsistence along the inhospitable coasts of Carolina and Virginia to care much about how the name was spelled.

His father's mother was born Marianna Clark on her father's plantation in lower Beaufort County. The first Clark ancestor to settle in North Carolina was Captain John Clark, who came to Beaufort County in the last quarter of the seventeenth century and settled near Bath. He was a vestryman in St. Thomas' Church during the time of Edward Teach, or Blackbeard, the pirate. About one hundred years later there was another ancestor, Rev. John Clark, a minister of the Primitive Baptist faith who, being a contemporary of Alexander Campbell and approving of his aim, "the restoration of primitive Christianity," joined the religious body known as the Disciples of Christ. Leaving North Carolina he moved south establishing churches as he went and was instrumental in founding over fifty churches of his adopted faith. He was a man of great eloquence, and it is said that his congregation in North Carolina wept when he left them.

William Styron's great-grandmother, Frances Selby Clark, remained a Primitive Baptist. She was a woman of great piety and intelligence and was very liberal-minded for her day. She joined in many of the religious discussions and contributed learned papers on doctrine to the contemporary religious publications.

William Styron's grandfather on his mother's side was Enoch Hamilton Abraham, a pioneer coal and coke operator in Western Pennsylvania. He was closely associated with Henry Clay Frick and before becoming an independent operator was at one time superintendent of the first Frick mine at Mount Pleasant, Pa. At the turn of the present century an executive position in the coal and coke industry was no sinecure, particularly during those turbulent periods characterized by bloody strife between capital and labor. In addition to being a good financier and executive, this grandfather was possessed of considerable mechanical inventiveness. As a young man his grandfather Abraham had been a school teacher.

William Styron's grandfather on his father's side, Alpheus Whitehurst Styron, was a pioneer in the operation of steamboats between eastern Carolina towns on the Pamlico River and Norfolk, Baltimore, and Philadelphia from the period shortly after the Civil War until the railroads came. He was instrumental in building and operating over twenty river steamers. After the railroads came and he could not compete with them, he engaged in the mercantile business in Washington, North Carolina. Although he was a self-educated man he possessed much native writing ability, a vivid imagination, and was a persuasive talker. As a boy of fourteen he enlisted in the Confederate army and served on General Hoke's staff as a courier. He had a good singing voice and was a ready raconteur as he had lived through the tragic Reconstruction period and had much to tell. He was never quite so successful in business as was William Styron's grandfather Abraham. But often it is the son or grandson of the dreamer who is the creative artist. His grandfather Styron had a genius for friendships and most of the public figures of his time in North Carolina, from Zebulon Baird Vance to Josephus Daniels, were his friends. However, he remained until his death a man of Christian humility.

If William Styron has any pride or conceit in his make-up it comes from his Clark ancestors as they were a proud stiff-necked people. They were once numerous but are now depleted and few. They possessed broad acres and for generations sent their sons to the colleges and universities of North Carolina and the North for their education. Two of his Clark relatives, a great uncle and a cousin, were attending Trinity College, then in Randolph County, during the Civil War, and left there to enlist in the Confederate Army.

William Clark Styron, Junior (William Styron), was born in Newport News, Virginia, on June 11, 1925, the son of William Clark Styron, a native of Washington, Beaufort County, North Carolina, and his wife, born Pauline Margaret Abraham in Uniontown, Fayette County, Pennsylvania.

William Styron's father graduated from North Carolina State College when it was known as "A&M." One of his favorite teachers while there was Dr. Thomas P. Harrison, a cousin of Sidney Lanier, and a purist in English. Dr. Harrison always held before his young pupils the beauties of the English language. The elder Styron adjured his son to spend as much time as possible with his dictionary in order that he too might discover the wonderful nuances of sound and meaning in our native language. Practically all of his father's adult life has been spent as a member of the engineering staff of the Newport News Shipbuilding and Dry Dock Company.

Several incidents in the early life of William Styron confirm the old cliché—that the child is father to the man. In his case they at least indicated a trend which, coupled with certain native talent, good preparation, and fixture of purpose, enabled him to produce a novel of literary excellence before his twenty-sixth birthday.

The apartment in which the Styrons lived in Newport News, Virginia, adjoined a large athletic field with bleachers and which was surrounded by a high board fence. When about three or four years of age "Billy" Styron would never go to bed without saying goodnight to his friend Scubishay. Each night he would stand on tip-toe before an open rear window and yell at the top of his little voice, "Goodnight, Scubishay!" For weeks his parents were unable to learn from him the identity of his friend. It finally dawned on them that his friend was only the echo of his voice, and the name Scubishay was a product of his childish imagination.

Before he was old enough to attend school he evinced such a keen desire to spell and read that a good friend and neighbor, the late Sally Cox Hayes, volunteered to help him. Mrs. Hayes had been reared just off the campus of what is now Longwood College, Farmville, Virginia, as her father had been bursar of the college for many years. After graduating from Longwood she specialized in the teaching of beginners and for some years taught in the public schools of Newport News. She instructed her young pupil so thoroughly and well that he "could read like a house afire," as someone said, long before he entered school.

One day when he was about five years old he accompanied his father to a local barbershop and while the elder Styron was being barbered he, childlike, wandered around the shop to "see what he could see." There was an empty barber's chair in the shop, and he espied a strange new word cast in its footrest. "Billy" kneeled down and with his chubby forefinger traced out each individual letter—H-E-R-C-U-L-E-S, then loudly pronounced the word HERCULES. The customers in the barbershop were astounded, the barbers guffawed and almost jumped through the ceiling—they too were surprised that such a little fellow could spell at sight such an unusual word.

His interest in words was almost an obsession. One of his teachers tells that one day she was seated at her desk during his first year at school when he walked in. Seeing a bottle on a shelf over her head he said, "Miss Jarman, I can spell the word on that bottle"—the new word happened to be formaldehyde.

His childhood passed quietly and apparently like that of any other child in the average cultured American home. There were the usual children's diseases, communicable and otherwise. No winter ever passed without his having infected ears. This infection finally developed into mastoiditis when he was nine years old, and an operation became necessary. He now played the harmonica quite well, and while he was in the hospital recuperating from the operation he entertained the nurses with his mouth organ. His showpiece was "Roll out the Barrel" which at that time was enjoying quite a vogue.

Although his father and mother were quite musical, the harmonica was the only musical instrument he ever attempted to master, and even this seems to have been a passing fancy as he soon lost interest and gave it up.

His mother was a person of unusual intelligence, personal charm, and strength of character. She was educated privately in her home state of Pennsylvania and when still in her teens was sent abroad by her parents to study voice, German, and French in Vienna, Austria, then one of the great cultural centers of the world. On returning home she entered the University of Pittsburgh where she majored in public school music and studied under Will Earhart, who is known as the father of public school music in the United States. For several years she was music supervisor in the school systems of Pittsburgh and Pueblo, Colorado. She was also a letter-writer par excellence.

Shortly after William Styron's birth his mother developed a malignancy from which she never recovered. Her life from then on was a series of operations, which she endured with Christian fortitude until her son's fourteenth year when she was compelled to give up the struggle and died. The great love for her one and only child seems to have sustained her through the many years of invalidism, and as long as she had the strength she never ceased to make his welfare the major concern of her life. Being very musical and a voracious reader she contributed much to his cultural development. His world was one of good books and the best in music.

The year after his mother's death he entered Christchurch School for boys near Urbanna, Virginia. This school is one of seven small schools operated under the auspices of the Episcopal Diocese of Virginia. He remained at Christchurch for two years. The years at this school were spent without his displaying any special gifts for literature, although he did some writing while there. He always excelled in reading and on graduation received a prize for excellence in reading. The two years spent at Christchurch with sixty boys varying in ages from ten to eighteen seem to have affected him deeply, as some years after leaving he wrote to a friend, "I have the fondest and gentlest memories of Christchurch, and believe me when I say that there I spent the happiest days of my life." Each evening at vespers in the little chapel at Christchurch big boys, little boys, and motherless boys gathered to learn and sing of Jesus and his love.

In the summer of 1942, shortly after his seventeenth birthday, he entered Davidson College. It was just a few months after Pearl Harbor, and the accredited colleges and universities of the country were on an accelerated basis. He never entered much into college athletics, except as a spectator, but became interested in writing. He was a "feature" writer on the newspaper The Davidsonian, and was on the editorial board and contributed articles to the monthly magazine Scripts 'n Pranks.

Just before he celebrated his eighteenth birthday and still at Davidson he enlisted in the U.S. Marine Corps. The Marines had just started their slow march, beginning at Guadalcanal a few months before, to drive the Japs from the South Pacific. On July 1, 1943, he entered Duke University under Navy V-12. He continued at Duke until October of 1944 when he was transferred to Parris Island, S.C., where he spent the winter of 1944–1945. It was at Duke that he was permitted to take Dr. William Blackburn's course in creative writing. Here he learned the age-old truth that "Art is not for art's sake; art is not for teaching's sake; but art is for life's sake." Although he had a keen desire even from grammar school days to write, it was under William Blackburn's guidance that he discovered he was in his artistic environment. One day he typed a story as a class assignment which he titled "Where the Spirit Is—a Short Story" and at the bottom of its cover page was the notation: "Dubiously submitted—Bill Styron." This story was his first really superior work. It was returned with a notation in William Blackburn's handwriting: "A sincere and beautiful story. You have got to the inwardness of your subject and that is poetry." This story was suggested by his school days at Christchurch, and it, with many others, was later published in *The Archive*. Two of his short stories were also included in One and Twenty, an anthology of Duke University stories published in 1945.

It was through this teacher-pupil relationship that was formed one of the great friendships of his life. As William Lyon Phelps at Yale was to Sinclair Lewis, so William Blackburn became to William Styron at Duke: literary mentor and friend.

After some months at Camp Lejeune and Quantico, having been admitted to Officers' Candidate School, he received his commission as Second Lieutenant, U.S. Marine Corps, at the latter post, and was ordered to duty at the Disciplinary Barracks on Hart's Island in New York

Harbor. He only served there a few months as the Japs had surrendered in the meantime and he returned to civilian life.

The winter of 1945–1946 was spent at his home in Newport News, Virginia.

In March 1946 he returned to Duke University to complete his education. During vacation of 1946 he made a trip to Trieste on a cattle boat. This experience inspired a sketch, "A Moment in Trieste," which appeared in an anthology of short stories, "The American Vanguard" published by the Cornell University Press under the auspices of the New School for Social Research.

In August 1946 and just after returning from Trieste, he attended the Bread Loaf Writers' Conference at Middlebury College in Vermont and there met several of the leading poets, writers, and publishers of the United States, including Robert Frost. He had very little to report on this conference. It may be assumed that he saw these celebrities at too close range to be overawed by their greatness.

In the autumn of 1946 it was suggested that he try for a Rhodes Scholarship to Oxford, which scholarships were being revived after World War II. He approached this project with much uneasiness as he knew that the competition was stiff, that he was not particularly scholarly and would be pitted against boys, most of whom were Phi Beta Kappas and "exceedingly well on the ball." However, he was selected as one of three boys from North Carolina to go to Atlanta for the Southeastern divisional competition. The choice finally came down to himself or a candidate from Florida. The Florida boy was finally awarded the scholarship as one of the committee members later informed Styron that the black F's he had received in physics were held against him. Again he was submitting to the dictates of destiny. In composition, history, and the humanities he excelled, but in science he failed. Angelo Patri once said that if you have a boy who does fine work in certain studies but fails miserably in others, don't be discouraged for you may have a potential genius under your roof.

Failing to receive a Rhodes Scholarship to Oxford he continued at Duke for a short while hoping that if he made up his failures in physics he might be more successful the next time the tests were held. He tired of college life and finally left Duke and found employment as associate editor at Whittlesey House, then the non-textbook department of the McGraw-Hill Book Company. After about six months in this work there was a change in editors when a Mr. Aswell came over from Harper's and fired him for being too young and inexperienced. Aswell never realized what a contribution he made to William Styron's future by firing him from this job.

Upon leaving Whittlesey House he wrote to his father, "I am glad that you see eye to eye with me about my present attitude towards writing and the loss of my job. I realize that I've finally come to grips with myself and that the job was a delaying action. Writing for me is the hardest thing in the world but also a thing which, once completed, is the most satisfying. But someone, I think it was Henry James, said that only through monstrous travail and agonizing effort can great art be brought forth from those like himself (James) who are not prodigies or like Shelley or Mozart, spontaneous fonts of genius. Anything less than unceasing toil will produce nothing or at best, facility. I am no prodigy but Fate willing I think I can produce art. For me it takes much girding of loins and an almost imbecile faith in my potentials, but I suppose that is part of the satisfaction."[1]

At this time Dr. Hiram Haydn, then editor of Crown Publishers, was conducting a workshop on the novel at the New School for Social Research in the Greenwich Village section of New York City. Dr. Haydn had taught creative writing at the Women's College of the University of North Carolina and welcomed William Styron to his classes. It was on Dr. Haydn's advice that he started his first novel, which has just been completed after nearly five years of effort.

During one year of the time while he was writing on the novel he lived in Durham, just off the Duke Campus, but returned to New York and there finished the manuscript.

Thirty years ago Willa Cather said: "A book is made with one's own flesh and blood of years—it is cremated youth. It is all yours—no one gave it to you. The unanimous testimony of a host of witnesses is that art, regardless of its form, is a jealous mistress demanding everything from those who would live with her."

---

1. The senior Styron is quoting here (with a few alterations) from his son's October 28, 1947, letter, number 42 in this volume.

Apprentice Writing

Reprinted in this appendix, with bylines intact, are six prose pieces published by Styron during his years at Duke and the New School. For a full listing of Styron's apprentice work, see James L. W. West III, William Styron: A Descriptive Bibliography *(Boston: G. K. Hall, 1977): 188–91.*

THE LONG DARK ROAD
William Styron

Dewey Lassiter walked along the road slowly, the dust rising in little vaporous clouds around his bare feet. He stopped at intervals to roll up the wet ends of his overalls, which slipped down to his ankles every few steps. In the distance, not more than half a mile across the broad, flat Delta country, he could see the lights of the store glowing faintly. Dewey increased his pace, still pausing occasionally to adjust his pants leg.

It was getting darker now, the boy thought to himself. He'd better be getting home, or he'd catch it plenty from his mother.

"Maw's gonna whup me," he thought aloud. He was surprised at the sound of his voice.

"Maw's gonna whup me," he said again, louder. From a heavily clumped pine grove off to the right beyond the cotton he heard the echo, "—whup me!" He laughed.

He shouted, "Maw's gonna whup me!" And the echo came back as before—"gonna whup me!" Then he was silent. He had better hurry, he thought, or he really would catch it.

From somewhere there came the harsh, long call of a bluejay. The boy walked on.

Lassiter's General Merchandise was typical of the many small country stores which one sees in the South. Its clapboard front, begrimed with the dust of many storms, was partly shielded by a flimsy roof, which was supported by two splintered and blackened posts. Between the posts were two old-style gas pumps and a pump for kerosene. And beside the door was a battered bench, hollowed through use and stained gray with time, above which was the fly-specked window and the chipped lettering: "A.J. Lassiter, Gen'l M'd'se."

The bench was the focal point for all local social activity. Worn into its grain, impressed into its gray and solid planking, were the imprints of many an overalled rump, and in its splintered fibre were the memories of numberless afternoons devoted to talking and spitting and thinking.

A.J. himself was an immense, ruddy-faced man of about forty with flaming red hair. He had a coarse and broad face, full of robust good humor; and his monstrous, balloon-like body, which seemed to overflow his shirt and pants with a fleshy and Gargantuan enormousness, gave him an appearance of stout and amiable heartiness. But A.J.'s most startling characteristic was his laugh.

It was no ordinary laugh. It was something akin to an explosion. When A.J. was amused, his massive face would seem to widen perceptibly, and his mouth would break out into an enormous grin. For a brief moment there would be a suspenseful silence; then it would begin. From somewhere in the depths of his voluminous bulk would emanate a sort of wheezing groan which built up gradually until his whole ruddy face and the entire immensity of his frame was convulsed by latent tremblings and rumblings. And then, his head thrown back, mouth agape, and face constricted with mirth, he would eructate in an ear-splitting paroxysm of exuberant, uninhibited laughter. And minutes would pass before he had, with countless wheezes and renewed outbursts of jollity, regained his composure.

A.J. had a family. His wife, Mamie, had borne him two sons and a daughter. The girl, Louesta, was now nineteen and studying to be a nurse in Memphis. The boys were Roy, who was twenty, and Dewey, who was just going on fifteen.

Roy worked in a garage in Clarksdale, twenty miles up the river. A.J.

had wanted him to stay home and help on the farm, but Roy had told the old man he would rather "get out on his own." Roy was big and heavy like his father, and rather stupid. His new-found independence in Clarksdale consisted mainly of fierce gin bouts with his friends and parties on the weekends with the whores in Memphis, and more gin.

Dewey opened the screen door and went into the store. It was eight o'clock. He could tell by the big clock with the Agrico sign on it. It said eight fifteen, but always ran a little fast. No one was in but the old man, who was cutting some cheese in the back.

"Hi, Paw," he said.

A.J. looked up. "Hello, son," he said, smiling his broad smile. "C'mon back."

The boy went back to the big square wooden table. It had always sort of excited him, that huge heavy piece of wood with its countless cleaver marks and its warm mixed smell of strong cheese and raw, bloody meat. It was a savage sort of feeling that the block aroused in him, a feeling faintly bringing to mind pictures of blood, gore, and guts, like the sacrificial altar of the Aztecs he had seen in a history book. But it reminded him, too, of good food, of thick steaks, tender chops, and of Sunday dinners.

The old man was cutting through a big waxed block of yellow cheese, cutting it in long, easy strokes so that uniformly shaped wedges fell at the edge of the knife.

"Where you been to, Dewey?" he asked.

"Been fishin' down to the branch."

"Ketch anything?"

"Naw, dad-dratted catfish pulled my line in. Los' my bait an' my hook, an' I slipped in too."

A.J. looked up and saw the boy's wet overalls. He chuckled. "That'll learn you. Can't ketch no catfish with pork rind. Holts on too hard. Gotta use 'hoppers or red-worms." He laughed silently, his great body heaving. "Fell in! That'll learn you. Who'd you go with?"

"Lynwood Huckins."

"Why, that's George Huckins's young'un, ain't it?"

"Yep."

"Did he tell you 'bout his paw ketchin' that nigger?"

"Yep."

"Reckon he's might proud."

"Yep. Lynwood said they're goin' to lynch that nigger."

"Now, son, don't say that." His father's face had lost its usual smile. "That nigger's gonna git a fair and square trial."

"Where's Maw?" the boy asked.

"She's up to the house. She's waitin' supper on you now. You better git up there or she'll whup you." He laughed. "You don't want to get whupped."

And he thought about his mother, how she hardly ever said anything when she was mad like that, except to say, "Fetch me a cane, Dewey." But then, it never hurt very much, and besides, the old man had told her that he thought Dewey was getting too old to be whipped. The old man was like that—easy-going—wouldn't even cuss a nigger. Anyhow, it wasn't how it hurt his tail; but it hurt his feelings more. She was getting easier on him now. Maybe he *was* getting old.

"Yer brother Roy called up," A.J. said. "Said he'd be here around nine o'clock."

The son of a bitch, Dewey thought, the son of a bitch. The boy had nothing but hate and loathing for his brother, and he'd admit it to anyone. His own flesh and blood, but he detested the very sight of him. And he'd be here tonight, his fat, pasty yellow face, and his bleary eyes, his smelly breath and dirty nails, and he'd talk about himself.

And he'd be mean and nasty, and probably drunk, and he'd cuss Dewey and make him miserable like he'd been doing ever since he could remember. His own flesh and blood.

And the old man was just crazy about him. It was "Roy this" and "Roy that" and "He's goin' to be a success in this gosh-dern world, mark me!" And all the time the son of a bitch was in Clarksdale drinking and laying out in the gutter all the time, and he'd come back to the store about once a month, and all you'd hear was talk about how drunk he was last Saturday in Memphis and how much tail he got that night. Then he'd make Dewey run up to the bootleggers at Injun Mound and get him some whiskey and wouldn't give him anything except maybe a dime. The son of a bitch.

His mother hadn't whipped him, so Dewey felt relieved after supper. It was dark when he went back down to the store, which was connected with the house by a narrow path some eighty yards through the cotton field. From the back of the store he could see Nate Smith's battered old Ford under the dusty glare of the lights, and he knew that Nate and the old man would be out front on the bench talking.

He heard them as he rounded the corner of the store.

". . . an if'n I had my way, A.J., I'd take that black bastard and rope 'im to the highest tree in Mississippi!"

Dewey sat down on the strip of concrete near the pump and across from the two men. He listened, feeling the sand cool and brittle between his toes.

"Well, I wouldn't be saying anything as rash as that, Nate." His father's voice was low and steady and rich. "As I sees it," he said, with a trace of a smile playing around the corners of his wide mouth, "as I sees it, the State is the decidin' thing in all such matters of justice. When the prosecutor and the judge is elected by the people, the people is supposed to back up their decisions, and as I sees it, after they says their decisions, the people should let well enough alone."

But Nate was vehement in his convictions. "I know, I know, but goddamit—" His face was dead set, earnest. "All right, let's look at it like this. Suppose you was ol' man Hooker. He was crippled up, almost helpless, A.J.; you know that yourself. All right. You're sleepin' over your store one night peaceful-like. Suddenly you wake up and hear somethin' creepin' around. You're helpless now, A.J., and you're all alone. You holler, 'Who's there?' and then you see somethin' like an ape over your bed, and he's stranglin' you with his big, black, common nigger hands! Why, goddamit, A.J., John Hooker didn't have no more strength than a baby. How can you sit there—" He stopped, breathing hard, and his lean, wrinkled face was a mixed study of anger and overworked imagination.

A.J. was calm and reassuring. He placed his fat hands on Nate's knee comfortingly.

"I know, I know," he said softly; "calm yourself now, Nate; there ain't no use gittin' so riled. The way it looks to me is that nigger is safe behind the bars up to Injun Mound, and there ain't nothin' me and you can do but let justice go its way and—"

"Yes, but goddamit, he was a nigger, a black, common, dirty son of a bitch of a nigger, and—"

"Sure, sure, it was a pretty terrible thing to do, I'll admit, even for a white man, let alone a nigger; but there just ain't one thing we can do. Let's just forget about it an' have a drink."

He looked at Dewey, and the boy knew what to do. Dewey went into the store and got three coca-colas out of the drink case and brought them out and gave one to the old man and one to Nate. Then he went over and sat down again on the concrete steps.

He took a swallow of the coca-cola, and it tasted good. And then he suddenly became aware of something. It was something he could not place exactly; but there was a certain feeling that made him uneasy. It was not a feeling that something was wrong; but he was conscious of the fact that there should be something there that wasn't. Something vital in the atmosphere was missing. He couldn't place it.

The air was hot and sultry, and he could smell the loamy, heavy odor of the Delta soil. He heard the steady drone of the flies and there was still the distant piping song of the frogs. A grasshopper spanked up against the screen and clung there momentarily, then buzzed away. From across the field he could hear the sudden, haunting, echoed call of a whippoorwill. A car passed on the road.

They were all there. But something was the matter.

"Yes, A.J.," he heard Nate say in his halting, cracked voice, "I ain't as spry as I used to be. Ol' Doc Barham up in Memphis says its dia-bee-tees. Cain't travel much. Like to come up here and talk with the boys, though."

The boys, the boys. That was it. Where were they? Monroe Davis and Charley Cutchin and Dexter Capps and all the rest. It wasn't right. Something was missing.

And then the horrible thought struck him, smote him with the jolt of a two-ton tractor. It was a lynching party. That's what Lynwood Huckins had said, had said that all those friends of his old man and old Huck himself were going up to Injun Mound and break that jail and get that nigger out of there and string him up; it was a secret. It was a secret. They were going to take him and string him up.

And then a strange feeling of unutterable terror came over the boy. He was afraid, but he could not comprehend his fear. He was conscious of strange, benumbing reality, knowing that somewhere not far away something inhuman and terrible and brutal was happening. It was fierce, unbelievable, untrue. But the incredible thing was there; and time passed slowly as he sat there, dazed, listening blankly to the drone of the two men's voices and the steady thrumming of the flies and the slow, interminable ticking of the clock.

Then suddenly he heard the faint sound of a car horn far down the road. It shocked him suddenly and hard. For the sound, as slight and noiseless as it really was, like the soft rustling of a mouse in the moldering antiquity of a forgotten attic, was to him as enormous and as frightening as the report of a cannon.

And now, above the sound of a horn, which was blowing continuously, he could hear the staccato clacking of a cut-out on a high-powered engine. It was Roy. Dewey looked at the clock. Nine-thirty.

The car, wheeling and lurching off the dusty road, came to a jarring halt in front of the store. The men, who until then had been obliviously lost in the meanderings of their conversation, looked up in gaped-mouth astonishment at the car. Then the old man recognized his son and got up heavily and rose to greet him.

"Ho, Roy. Where you been?"

The youth did not answer his father, but leaned a drunken, leering face out of the window and began to laugh. It was startling to Dewey, and there was something hideous and obscene in the laughter. It was a ghastly and fiendish travesty on the laughter of his father, which, coming now with no apparent cause or reason and lacking any of the good-natured robustness of his father's laugh, seemed to echo a sound of loathsome and sickening bastardy in its foul coarseness.

Then he stopped suddenly and turned his drowned eyes on the startled people.

"They're bringin' that nigger up here."

The old man stared at his son, and then, as if the full but yet incomprehensible horror had dawned upon him, he leaped to the window.

"What you talkin' about, Roy? What nigger?" His words were almost savage, but they were the words of a man who has just been stricken by some nameless fear and, instead of planning escape, attempts to cover his terror with disbelief. "What's the matter with you?" he cried, his huge body trembling with each gasping breath. "What nigger you talkin' about?"

"You know what nigger I'm talkin' 'bout," Roy said drunkenly. "They done sprung that nigger from jail. Dexter Capps and Charley Cutchin and a big bunch of them. They're bringin' him up here!" And then, with a sodden leer, he said, slowly and thickly, "They're goin' to burn him."

The old man stood there clutching the side of the door so that the backs of his hands were white. His voice was a whisper as he spoke to Roy.

"It ain't goin' to happen. So help me God! It ain't goin' to happen."

Just then Nate, who had been listening intently to all that had taken place, gave a sudden yell. "Listen! Listen! They're comin'!"

And they turned their eyes to the south, down the dark road. Dewey could see, not far away, a white glare of headlights; and he heard the jumbled noise of many cars, going fast, as they sped in a whirl of dust down the road.

The cars, drawn up in caravan fashion and numbering perhaps ten, stopped on the opposite side of the road. Each one was packed with five or six farmers. The men got out of the cars and walked over in front of the store and stood there, muttering in little angry groups and smoking and spitting and waiting.

Dewey heard his father talking. "What you all come out here for? I don't want any . . ."

"Look, A.J." It was Jim Bickford's voice. "We had to bring him out here to git away from town. Anyhow," he said meaningfully, "there's kerosene out here."

"But hang it all, Jim, I don't want . . ."

Then Dewey heard his brother. "Here comes the truck! Here comes the truck! Hot damn!" He had staggered out of the car and was standing in the middle of the road, reeling and shouting and laughing like an idiot.

The son of a bitch, Dewey thought, the son of a bitch.

The truck, a huge hay wagon with slatted sides, stopped noisily in front of the store. The crowd of men gathered around it.

"Bring the bastard out of there!" someone shouted.

"Get that rope!"

Two men moved toward the store.

The old man lumbered over to the door. "Stop it now," he panted. "It's wrong!" His huge face was contorted and red. "Stop it—"

The men brushed him aside. "Git out of the way, A.J.," they said.

The two beefy farmers who had been in the truck got out. Between them, almost slumped to the ground, was the nigger. He was thin and short, so small that he looked like a dwarf beside his captors. Dewey could not see his face, but he could hear him. He was moaning. It was like nothing the boy had ever heard. It was something like the thin, piteous cry of a dog that has been caught in a steel trap; and yet it was something like the stricken wail of a woman, something mournful, terrible, and lost.

The two farmers pushed their way through the crowd, dragging the nigger between them. "This'll be all right," one of them said.

They pushed the nigger down on the steps, and he slumped life-lessly against the screen door, sweating, his eyes closed, still moaning.

Then Charley Cutchin stepped up beside the nigger and, grasping his collar, jerked him up. Charley was a tall and skinny man, thin almost to the point of emaciation. He wore steel-rimmed glasses and his eyes were bloodshot.

"Listen, nigger, you know what we're goin' to do?"

The nigger opened his eyes and looked at the cadaverous figure swaying before him. The white-shirted men had crowded around the door and were gathered there in a sweating mass beneath the lights, muttering and shuffling nervously.

"I tell you what we're goin' to do," he said, in a low voice; "we're goin' to hang you by your goddam black nigger neck. And then," he whispered, pointing to the gas pump, "we're goin' to burn you."

The nigger slumped back against the door, his hands in front of his face. And then he began to speak for the first time. He was sobbing now; the words came hoarsely.

"Don' burn me, suh; don' burn me."

Roy pushed through the crowd and lurched toward Charley.

"Let's get started, Cutchin; the police might be comin'."

"Yeah," said Charley, "let's get started."

The men moved back again toward the road, and six of the farmers grabbed the nigger. The nigger had now collapsed, and he shuddered as they dragged him over beneath the rafters. Roy, who had been hold-ing the rope, threw the looped end around the nigger's neck and jerked it roughly. A little grazed, bloody patch showed where the fiber of the rope had scraped the skin.

Charley grasped Roy's arm.

"Take it easy, goddamit; we don't want to do it too soon!" He turned to Jim Bickford. "Get the truck."

Dewey saw them bring the truck up and back it up to within a few feet of the nigger, who had now fainted away completely and was being held up by Charley. A young boy had climbed a ladder and was tying the free end of the rope to a rafter which supported the roof.

And Dewey saw the crowd of men, perspiring, red-faced, and silent, who now stood as a mass, motionless, at the edge of the road. Hardly a word was spoken. They watched and remained silent. Dewey could hear only the steady thrum of the night flies, and the low muttering of the little group of men who stood around the nigger, intent, nervous, quiet. The old man was sitting on the bench alone with his head in his hands, rocking back and forth, and saying: "Oh, Jesus, oh, my sweet Jesus."

Charley, with Nate and Bickford, picked up the nigger, the rope still tied around his neck, and put him in the back of the truck. There was a dull thump as they dropped him in a lifeless heap on the planking.

Jim kicked him, kicked him hard, so that he sprawled out on the floor of the truck.

"Wake up, nigger," he said.

But the nigger would not move.

Roy shouted to the three men on the truck. "Throw some kerosene on the son of a bitch. That'll fix him!"

Someone handed a can of kerosene to Charley. Charley unscrewed the top and threw the contents into the nigger's face. The kerosene soaked into his clothes and dripped down on the floor of the truck. The nigger woke up and began to scream, awfully, hoarsely, and like a woman. The kerosene glistened on his black face.

"Don' burn me!" he screamed. "Oh Lord, don' burn me!"

Charley knocked him down with the kerosene can. The nigger, stunned, lay on the floor, sobbing and moaning.

Someone shouted from the road. "Let's get it over with, Cutchin!"

Dewey saw the three men jump down from the truck. Roy reeled into the driver's seat and started the motor. There was a tremendous roar, and a blue burst of flame exploded from the exhaust. Over all there was the heavy odor of kerosene, and the terrible moaning of the small black figure in the back of the truck. The nigger got up and began to hold onto the slatted sides of the truck. He was screaming again, screaming in a high-pitched wail that echoed above the sound of the motor into the stillness of the night.

"Let 'er go, Roy," Charley shouted.

Dewey saw the truck lurch forward. There was a grinding of rubber against the gravel. The nigger's hands were torn loose from the palings as the rope drew tight around his neck and stifled his screams. He skidded sideways across the floor of the truck as the machine tore from beneath him. There was a heavy jolt, and a crack of loosening timbers. The body swung gently beneath the rafters.

Dewey was running, running across the cotton fields, and he could feel the clumps of earth between his toes and there was a smell of kerosene still in his nostrils . . . running, running, running. . . .

Running. And the great forest loomed far and away. For there was somewhere the smell of kerosene and sweat and burning flesh. Far and away. And beyond the fields of cotton there was a great forest. Far and away, Dewey, far and away. The tears stung his eyes, his eyes, Dewey, far and away. And running through the fields where the brambles are and the sound of a lark, Dewey, far and away. And running from death and burning niggers and Roy Roy Roy son of a bitch sooo-o-o far and away. The old man's laugh sitting with head in hands and the smell of kerosene, Dewey, Dewey, Dewey, Dewey, it is me me me, Dewey, me doan' burn *me* suh like a woman. Late late in the evening and the hounds are calling; somewhere the river flows far and away. Oh my Jesus my sweet Jesus and murmuring voices far and away.

In the distance a train whistle blew, wailing up through the valley. All was quiet.

Archive 57 (March 1944): 2–4. Reprinted in *One and Twenty: Duke Narrative and Verse, 1924–1945,* selected by William Blackburn (Durham: Duke University Press, 1945), 266–80.

SUN ON THE RIVER
Bill Styron

"Pretty soon they'll be bringing her out," Tom said.

The three boys, none of them over twelve years old, stood straddling their bicycles on the sidewalk across from the house. It was a cold, windy Sunday afternoon in the middle of March. The sun shone down with a cold brilliance on the village street, and the sycamore leaves rattled in a scraping flurry of dust in the gutter.

"How long they been in there?"

"Almost an hour now," said Tom.

In front of the house across the street was a long, polished hearse. A man in a black suit stood with one foot on the running board smoking a cigarette. For a block on both sides of the narrow street stretched a long line of automobiles, and on the door of the house hung a plain white wreath. Over all the street, even above the frenzied, tossed roar of the wind in the row of sycamores, there was an immense, almost startling, quiet.

Chris, a short, thin little boy of about eleven, stood with the two other boys as they talked in low, half-excited, nervous voices. He stood on the sidewalk, one foot on the pedal of his bicycle, looking with intense, absorbed curiosity at the darkened house across the street.

"Did you see her face?" he asked Tom.

"No, I didn't want to."

"I wouldn't want to, either."

But then, Chris thought, wouldn't he want to see her after all? He hadn't known Jenny very well, but he had spoken to her a lot of times. She had been a grade ahead of him in school—he was in the sixth—but he had seen her almost every day. And then on Friday morning she wasn't at school, because she had been riding up at Mrs. Scott's stables and the horse had thrown her and she died a few minutes later. She broke her neck, they said.

It was the first time that anyone he had ever known had died, except Buddy Atkins who was drowned up at Yorktown a long time ago. But he didn't remember that very well. And now Jenny Pattison was dead. Gone. Just like that. He couldn't describe how he felt to anyone. Even if he didn't know her very well, he had seen her, and one time when he was working on Thompson's truck on Saturday he delivered some groceries to her mother and Jenny was in the kitchen washing dishes.

"Hey there," she had said.

He told her hello. He looked at her and for the first time he saw how pretty she was. That was all. He just saw her a lot of times and spoke to her.

Now she was gone and couldn't come back. He couldn't describe to anyone how he felt. He wasn't exactly sad. No, it wasn't sadness. He felt more a sense of loss, like the time he woke up on a stormy September morning, dark and bleak, with the gray and windy clouds scudding across a dreary sky. He had looked out of the window and had seen that the huge old oak tree at the end of the back yard had blown down. He remembered how he felt then as he looked out with his nose pressed against the screen, feeling the hot September storm wind fanning his face and blowing into the room early in the morning.

He had seen the oak tree which had been there all his life, all uprooted and twisted, and the green branches pressed flat against the ground and the carrot-colored roots sticking nakedly out from the huge yellow clod of earth. At that time, he remembered, he had a terrible feeling of loss, as if something intense and close and personal had left him.

And now it was the same as he stood here on the sidewalk watching the sun cast its moving shadow patterns on the ground, and listening to the whispering of the branches as they moved and tossed in the wind.

Tom said: "They'll be bringing her out in a minute. Here comes old man Hook."

A tall gray-haired man, dressed in black, appeared in the doorway and, extending a black gloved hand, beckoned to the man at the curb.

Chris stirred uneasily. People began to come from the house. Friends of the family. They blinked in the sudden brilliance of the March sunlight. Quickly, with soft murmurings, they moved toward the cars. Then came Mr. and Mrs. Pattison. He was a huge ruddy-faced man who owned a coal-yard, but now as he stepped down to the sidewalk, supporting his frail wife, all of the fire was gone from his face. He was a great blank ghost who stared with inarticulate grief into the windy street.

"I'm sorry for Mr. Pattison," Tom said. "Pop went to see him and Mr. Pattison couldn't say anything except, 'my little girl, my only little girl.'"

The winter breeze fanned the branches. April shall never come again.

Slowly the procession moved into the cars. The little casket was placed into the hearse. The motors started, the policeman gave the signal, and the caravan began to move. A line of cars passed the corner, turned, and was gone.

Chris turned to the other two boys. "I'll see you later," he said.

The boy got on his bicycle and rode down the street toward the river. The wind blew strongly, and he pulled the cap down around his ears. He wasn't thinking of anything much now. It was so strange, so new, this day. He turned the corner into the little street which ended on the river bank and the pier. He passed the three homes that the new people had built on the waterfront. As yet there were no trees planted, and the earth was a yellow, raw ugliness, furrowed and wet after the recent snow. But people lived there, he could tell. The windows were closed and shaded, the houses were closeted in warmth, and as the sun beat down in its wintry brilliance, and as the wind blew its cold salt blast from the river, he had a feeling of emptiness and of Sunday afternoon.

He pedaled hard. The road ran off the asphalt and into a muddy path which ran through the pine woods above the river bank. He rode down the path which dipped into a little gully and then onto the narrow pier.

The rough pine boards made a rubbery clacking sound against the tires.

At the end of the pier Chris got off the bike and leaned it against the railing. He was by himself. Across the three miles of river the white caps foamed and lapped themselves against the blueness of the waves. The sun blasted the cold wind against the shore. Chris looked down the river, toward the broad river mouth which met with the sheer blue wall of sky, slightly hazy now, to form the bay.

"This day is so strange," he thought. "Where is she now, and the oak tree? Are all of these gone now, and will they ever return? This is Sunday afternoon. This thing, and all my thoughts now, are here—and they will go and never return. The gulched earth is yellow and raw in March, and the wind wrestles with the sycamores along the streets. This is Sunday afternoon, the days are changing, and they will never come back."

Far up the river bank the pines roared in the wind, and on the beach the broken bottles, stogged in the sand, lay glistening in the sun.

(The winter wind fanned the branches. April shall never come back again.)

"The oak and Jenny are gone," he said.

As the sun shone down in all its glorious radiance, and as the wind whispered its March sadness in the pines, the boy clenched one small fist by his side and whispered to the sky in a voice that was a sob: "Good-bye! Good-bye!"

Archive 58 (September 1944): 12–13.

AUTUMN
William Styron

Weatherby stood at the edge of the grassy bank which sloped down from the school to the river. The October breeze fanned the wisps of gray hair on his head. He was a short little man with a round paunch, like an unripe melon, which no one could deny, of course, to a man of his years. At one time, when he was young, his waist had been as straight and hard as a cedar plank; but, after all, one does grow old. His eyes, though, even after years of grading English themes, were as strong as any man of fifty-eight could claim, and as he stood there he could pick out the tiniest houses across the river.

Weatherby always liked these early morning walks, and this one was especially pleasing. Unless it was raining, he would arise at six, an hour before the colored boy rang the bell to wake up the boys. Then he would take a quick shower in the bathroom, which he shared with the upper-form boys. Afterwards he would dress, sometimes in the gray tweed suit which the headmaster's wife had said was so becoming to him, and walk briskly down the stairs and out onto the campus. This walk was a daily ritual with him, and his path would invariably follow through the woods which stretched eastward down the river. Now and then, near some venerable oak or at a quiet little spot beside the lake, cool and shadowy in the dawn, he would hold reverent communion with himself. During moments like these, when he felt especially humble in the glow of God's morning, he would almost imagine himself in Wordsworth's shoes, and he would try to imagine what *he* would say at such a time. Then he would recite out loud, thrilling somewhat to the sound of his slow, measured voice, lines from Wordsworth or Matthew Arnold, both of whom, like himself, were disciples of Nature.

At the end of his walk he stood for a while and gazed at the river, the river which in its blue calmness never ceased to be a source of beauty for him. He would put all of that in his book, he thought. That would add a depth, a resonance, to the lyrical passages. "The great Rappahannock, the American Oxus, gulching the clay-ribbed land with its slow blue course, flowing silently, ever onward and downward to the sea." His heart now gave a sudden jump as he thought of the great bottomless well of emotion within him, the *bigness* of it all, and with that he recited aloud, a little choked, the entire middle part of *Tintern Abbey*.

He heard Richard, the colored boy, whistling as he came across the yard to wake up the boys.

"Good morning, Richard," he said, full of vigor. "Nice day, eh?"

Richard smiled, tugging on the rope of the heavy bell.

"Mawnin,' suh! Yassuh!"

Weatherby rubbed his hands briskly, staring at the sky with his neck craned in mock concentration.

"Ah-h, let's see, Thursday morning, ah-h, could it be that we have, ah-h . . . scrambled eggs today?"

Richard laughed a throaty Negro laugh.

"Yas-*suh!* You always guesses it right!"

As he walked toward the dormitory he thought a bit unpleasantly about the watery scrambled eggs, which usually put him in an uncomfortable mood for breakfast. But strangely enough the food at St. Stephen's was much better than at the other schools. Littlefields, for instance, which was so heavily endowed that it could have afforded roast pheasant every day. Dear God, how many meals had he eaten at those schools? First there was Benton, ten years mastership there, just after he graduated, then Beaumont, then Weldon, Crendall, St. Mark's (he would have been department head if that infernal Westcott hadn't swaggered his way into the Board's attention), Compton, then that miserable year at Littlefields, and now here. Perhaps now he was settled for good.

Weatherby could smell the warm fragrance of coffee and toast coming from the dining room in the basement. Above him, from the second floor, came the sound of boys' voices and splashing water. Mrs. Pettiway, the hostess, passed him on the walk. She was a pleasant, middle-aged woman with a calm, quiet manner.

"Good morning, Mr. Weatherby," she said. "Enjoy your walk this morning?"

"Ah-h yes, Mrs. Pettiway," he beamed, "a gorgeous morning. Why, I walked almost half the way to Urbanna, basking in this *most* radiant sunshine; and do you know, I almost completely forgot to come back!"

She smiled, and they talked about the weather as they walked down into the dining room. He liked her very much. She was a widow and had been at St. Stephen's for eight years, ever since Mr. Jones had become headmaster. She had a charming apartment over the infirmary, and now and then she invited him up for coffee and to listen to Delius and Beethoven on her phonograph. Weatherby was especially fond of the *Pastoral Symphony,* and they played it nearly every Sunday night.

In the dining room he greeted the four other masters with a brisk and hearty "good-morning," reserving, of course, a more dignified greeting for Mr. Jones, who stood with his wife and daughter at the big round table in the middle of the room. As Weatherby passed him, the headmaster bent slightly from the waist, made a little wry but agreeable smile, and murmured, "Good morning, sir." He was only about forty-eight, at least nine or ten years younger than Weatherby, a tall thin man with gray, steely hair; gray, piercing eyes; and a lean, stolid, gray face. Indeed, thought Weatherby, everything about the man, even down to his suit and woolen socks, was gray. This grayness gave an air of coldness and impenetrability to the man, something that made him impersonally cordial, but rather unapproachable.

The buzzer sounded, and the boys stumbled noisily down the creaking stairs and into the dining room. There were five boys assigned to his table, and as each took his place he mumbled a respectful but sleepy "good-morning" to the master, which Weatherby acknowledged with a reserved nod of his head and a small trace of a smile.

After Mr. Jones had asked the blessing and Weatherby had begun ladling the smoking oatmeal into the white bowls, he noticed an empty seat at the table. He looked around him.

"Where is Calloway?" he asked.

There was no answer. The two upper-form boys, Randolph and Trimble, stared intently at their plates.

"I asked you," he repeated, "where Calloway is."

Randolph looked up at him with a strained face.

"I—I, well—"

"Go on, boy. Where is he?"

"He's sleeping, sir." The boy stared nervously back at his plate.

"Sleeping, eh? Well, you run up and tell him to get down here right away, hear? Immediately!"

Weatherby nearly choked in indignation. This was not the first time that this Calloway had caused him trouble. Imagine the little upstart sleeping through breakfast! He had given the boy fair warning the time he caught him out of his bunk at night, and now such an act of complete disregard for authority warranted an immediate report to Mr. Jones. It was enough to drive a man mad, playing nurse to such a brood of spoiled youngsters. Of course, not all of them were like Calloway; some were splendid, quiet boys, not too obviously impressed with their self-importance, but Calloway had now grown entirely out of hand. He was sixteen, an above-average student—excelled in composition— but ever since he had arrived he had borne some sort of hidden resentment against Weatherby. Perhaps it was because he had scolded the boy sharply that first night when he had caught him sneaking down the hall. At any rate, Weatherby had tried to be nice to the boy (that is, as nice as the bounds of convention between master and student could permit), but there was always a latent feeling of antagonism on Calloway's part that even at times bordered on the insolent.

In the first place, Weatherby knew that he did not have that certain knack of handling boys. He did not have a "way" with them, that gentle, soothing, soft persuasion and indomitable heartiness which turned schoolmasters from pedagogues into doddering, plum-ripe old fools. Although he himself was not too strict a disciplinarian, he rested assured in the fact that he would never approach that idealized, picturesque state he had seen so often, that of a master, bristling with tireless energy, waddling about the campus and quoting platitudes to his charges with the amiable nonchalance of Falstaff. In the second place, Weatherby was fundamentally a scholar. He would never, no, never, let himself fall into the degenerate role of certain masters he had known who complacently smiled down at their boys with dew-rimmed eyes, declaiming from Cicero in a quavering, honeyed voice, and generally acting the part of a wise and kind old walrus. No, Weatherby had found that, although he was never too popular with his students, he would always be essentially the scholar, dispensing knowledge with a firm and just hand, completely free from any drooling, extra-curricular sophistry . . . all of which made him very, very happy.

Weatherby mused reflectively over his oatmeal, listening idly to the murmured breakfast conversation. His eyes wandered over to Ridley's table. The boys at the table were laughing uproariously, probably at one of Ridley's jokes. He was a tall, handsome young man with a lean, athletic body and a tanned face. He coached football and taught biology and lower-form arithmetic. Weatherby noticed that the boys adored him. On the football field Ridley swore at them with a soft, Deep-South enunciation, which seemed to endear him that much more to the boys. Weatherby thought it rather disgusting. As he took his walk through the fields in the afternoon, or stood above the wind-swept playing field, he often could hear the young man's voice clear and frosty in the autumn air:

"God damn it, McLeod, over tackle, over tackle!"

Yes, it *was* disgusting!

Randolph and Calloway came into the dining room, Calloway sneaking in through the side door so as to be unnoticed by Mr. Jones.

The infernal cheek of the little rascal!

As Calloway took his place, Weatherby spoke to him.

"Well, sir," he demanded, "what does this mean? What do you mean by being late to breakfast?"

The boy gave a little grimace, somewhat resembling a nasty scowl.

"I—I, well, I was sleepy, sir."

"Here, here," he spluttered, "do you think that's any excuse? Do you? Do you?"

The boy muttered something beneath his breath. Probably an oath, Weatherby thought.

"What's that you said?"

The smaller boys at the table were nudging each other in delight.

"I said, sir, that I studied late last night, and I was sleepy."

"It makes no difference whether you were studying or not—" he was almost shouting—"you must, *must* be punctual!" Then, in a lower voice, with a sigh of finality, he said: "It shall be my duty to report the matter to Mr. Jones." The breakfast proceeded in silence.

Weatherby held English class at nine o'clock. It was the upper-form class in literature, and he had scheduled a test for the day. He bustled into the class with the papers under his arm.

"Well, well," he said, erasing the board in broad, vigorous strokes, "a little examination today, eh, gentlemen?"

The boys groaned in pained resignation.

"Come, come, gentlemen," he chuckled, "it's not as bad as all that!"

As he passed out the papers, he noticed that all of them, except Tidewell, were seething at his affected good humor. Calloway glared at him, then turned away. Tidewell, on the other hand, faithful, studious, brilliant Tidewell, smiled at him with a broad, gleaming mouthful of orthodontic braces.

"Thank you, sir," he said.

As he turned, someone hit the back of Tidewell's head with a piece of chalk.

Now they were all at work, bent over their desks. For a minute he watched them closely. He must keep a lookout for wandering eyes. The windows were open, and a gentle breeze, warmed by the bright October sun, fanned his face. He became drowsy, and looked out of the window. An immense green fly droned lazily above the window sill and settled on the screen next to him. His gaze traveled from the fly out onto the green campus, past the two gnarled cedars and the little chapel, its stained-glass windows glistening in the sun. Beyond the chapel and the clay road the blackened meadow stretched its charred stubble to the border of the woods. Even from where he sat he could see the brown oak leaves falling and fluttering through the burnished foliage.

The gaunt green pines stood out against the other trees, drenched in the red of fall. He could name the trees from the color of their leaves. A wispy wreath of blue smoke curled from the bottomlands upward to meet the lighter blue of the sky, now splotched with little puffy clouds drifting sleepily to the west.

Weatherby nearly fell asleep, but was awakened by the deep humming of the fly, which renewed its lethargic activity on the window screen. He heard the soft rustling of the papers and the steady scratching of thirteen pencils. Through the window drifted the heavy autumnal smell of burning leaves, the familiar odor that made him think of rotting stumps smoldering in the distant, loamy bottomlands.

The buzzer rang at last, and Weatherby nodded upward with a start. The boys were still working on their tests, trying to struggle through the last, impossible question.

"Come, come, gentlemen," he said; "time is up. Turn in your papers."

Calloway bit his pencil and scowled. The boys handed in their papers sullenly and trooped out of the room. Weatherby heard one of them sigh an agonized "Jesus Christ." Perhaps the test was a bit intensive, but he prided himself on stimulating the boys to effort.

After lunch Weatherby had coffee with Mr. Jones at the headmaster's table.

"Mr. Jones," he said, "I think I should inform you of some—er—misconduct on the part of Calloway."

The headmaster rapped on the table with a cigarette, arched his gray eyebrows, and leaned back in his chair.

"Frankly, sir, I think the boy is a misfit. Why, only this morning he came to breakfast five minutes late. And he has taken a peculiar aversion to me, which at times borders on rank insolence. Now I don't want to appear overbearing, but—"

"I see, I see, Mr. Weatherby. The boy has me stumped too. Something definitely will have to be done."

Then somehow the headmaster changed the subject.

Later Weatherby went up to his room on the second floor of the dormitory. His door opened out onto the hall where the boys slept. The dormitory, with the classrooms beneath, was built in the shape of a T. Instead of rooms the boys slept in small cubicles which lined both sides of the hallway. The master's room was well situated, for from his room at night he could keep an ear cocked for any disturbance coming from the corridor. Whenever Weatherby heard the sound of stealthy creakings, he would creep softly to the door, flashlight in hand, then suddenly fling it open and trap the culprit in the beam of light. Old as he was, he could still pride himself on a certain amount of speed and agility.

He went in, seated himself at his desk, and began to mark the day's test papers. After a few papers he began to get sleepy, and, shoving the tests aside, he reached for the sheaf of manuscript beneath the desk. Thumbing through the last pages, he noted an error and corrected it in a small, neat hand. The manuscript, written at long intervals over a period of ten years, was a collection of formal essays—mostly fragmentary, since Weatherby wrote at his utmost leisure—consisting mainly of critiques, in a philosophical vein, of most of the major poems of Arnold and Wordsworth, with a word or two here and there on Sophocles and the Stoics. Although it was impossible for him to believe that he had been writing so long, he was not nearly finished. Only when he was aroused by the heat of inspiration, stimulated by some grand solemnity of Nature—an oak, or a great river—could he push himself to the agonizing torture of forming the twenty-six symbols of the alphabet into their mystic combinations. Someday his essays would be published. Someday. And he was comforted by the thought that the intolerable boredom of school-mastering could be relieved in some measure by his contact with Nature, the quietness of the sparse but unspoiled countryside, the sacred communication between himself and the earth which he held close-locked within him—but which could finally be released in a flooding glory of prose. *The Earth Is Mine: A Collection of Formal Essays on Nature,* by George Weatherby. He sighed deeply.

As he checked back over the manuscript, he heard Calloway's voice coming from below on the campus. He winced sharply and was suddenly surprised at the gesture. Now, why on earth had he done that? he wondered. This situation with the boy was beginning to irritate him. Although many times before there had been boys who had given him trouble, he had never had a case quite like this. The boy must have been utterly spoiled. Weatherby had seen him when he first arrived at school at the beginning of the term, with his father, a rich, hearty-looking businessman from Richmond. The father, so it was said, was a staunch and loyal churchman and had contributed not a little in support of the school. Perhaps that was the reason Mr. Jones was so hesitant in disciplining the boy with any degree of strictness.

But there was no doubting it: the boy disliked him fiercely. He could see the look behind Calloway's sullen eyes. The boy was a leader; he got along well with the others, but the master was quick to notice that there was an element of—well, sneakiness in him, and a rejection of authority. Of course he would, like the other boys, respond readily to the mandates of that young boor, Ridley, but when Weatherby himself attempted any measure of control, there was quick and immediate repulsion. Perhaps it was because Weatherby was of the "old school" of teaching. His habit of aloofness and reserve (which, after long years, he had conceded to be the best approach, in the long run, to master-student relations) had evidently rebuffed Calloway from the beginning. All of which was extremely unfortunate, but he would certainly not discard his theory for the benefit of one recalcitrant boy. True, he had been a bit harsh with the boy that night when he caught him out of his bunk. . . .

Then suddenly a wave of indignation came over him, partly because of Calloway's loud voice beneath the window—the harsh crow-sound of a boy whose voice is changing; but he was irritated more for letting the thought of the whole matter, a completely silly, trivial thing, goad him into such a state of nervousness. He slammed down the window angrily, scattering the pages of his manuscript over the desk. Tonight, he thought, he would drive over to Urbanna for a few beers. They would do him good. He had found a place when he first came to St. Stephen's the year before where he could have a few drinks without attracting the attention of either the students or the faculty. Although he well knew that what he did with his spare time was his own business, he had thought it best to keep such activity to himself. It was harmless enough an enjoyment—a beer or two at Bristow's (dear God, he had no other occasion for recreation, except for the chats with Mrs. Pettiway on Sunday nights)—but being at a church school and all that, well, one could never tell what nasty rumors might spring up.

Weatherby worked for nearly two hours, grading themes and checking the test papers. Calloway, he noticed, had written an extraordinarily good theme on sailing. He gave him a B-plus and then went to dinner.

After dinner Weatherby walked across the campus to the garage, backed his Chevrolet around the dusty driveway, and drove the four miles to Urbanna. The shadowed, orange glow of October dusk had already fallen over the little town when he parked his car behind Bristow's

Café. From where he stood he could see a flock of seagulls squawking noisily over the marshy river shore, paling now in the twilight. He went in and sat down in one of the booths near the back, where he could look out of the window toward the river.

The boy behind the counter brought him a beer, and he began to drink. It tasted good. Almost immediately he started to feel better. The feeling of depression which had come over him during the afternoon fell off quickly after two beers, and soon the slight sense of exhilaration wore into a sort of pleasant meditation. He gazed out of the window toward the darkening river, lying calm and wide, like a misty shadow, in the last fading gold of the sun. Far over on the shore, dotted with tiny white farmhouses, a pale rind of moon was rising behind a hazy pall of autumnal smoke. As he gazed at the river, once more he was impressed with its flowing, somnolent beauty, its weary, ever-lasting strength, running out like a man's life to the sea.

Weatherby turned away from the window and ordered another beer. This was his third bottle. He knew that he shouldn't drink too much, but he ordered another anyway. The record player was playing a Western song, sung by a man with a guitar and a sad voice.

> I've drifted all alone, no one to call my own;
> Don't leave me now to face the lonely years . . .

For some reason the song, the sad, vibrant, far-away sound of the guitar affected him deeply. It made him think of old, forgotten time, of autumn twilight, of hearing the song in some imaginary place in the West, of the lonely guitar echoing back from the bare and vacant hills. It was a music strange and foreign to him, a lover of Beethoven, but there was something about it, a forlorn sadness that was inescapable. It was a melody of lost love, and barren years; and the mournful wail of the distant guitar summoned thoughts, bell-like, from the past.

> You said we'd never part; don't leave and break my heart,
> I love you, dear; don't let your sweet love die . . .

There was a voice which came like a shaft of sunlight from his childhood:

"George! George Weatherby!"

Then there was the dreamlike awakening, the cool October breeze from beneath the window crack, and the morning light on his pillow.

And his mother's voice again:

"George! Wake up, George!"

And there were other voices that came to him suddenly, mistily: the voices of children calling to him from beneath the sycamores, dropping like bird-notes from the past.

"Georgie is a scairty-cat . . . a scairty-cat . . . a scairty-cat. . . ."

Then the voices grew more insistent and loud, a whole multitude of voices that marched through his mind, whispering and clamoring for attention. They came and faded and came again, like the tinkling of spinet music in a drowsy flow of dreams. As he heard them and the sound of the distant guitar, Weatherby knew that he was like any other man who grew old, who sat in little cafés at twilight listening to faraway music, and who mused in a hazy, sorrowful dream over the fallen years.

I've drifted all alone, no one to call my own . . .

He sat for a time listening to the music and drinking beer. Then, after paying his bill, he walked, a bit unsteadily, out to his car and drove back to school. It was not a long trip, but he took his time going by the river road. When he got to school it was almost bedtime. As he climbed the stairs, he noticed that one of the other masters had turned the light off in the hall. Twice he stumbled going up the steps. That beer, he thought, had certainly taken its toll on his perceptual faculties. Never before had he allowed it to affect him so.

He was very sleepy. The beer had made his mind hazy and thick. Without even brushing his teeth—he was usually meticulous about his toilet—he turned out the light on his desk and got into bed. Before he had turned over beneath the covers more than twice, he began to hear soft noises in the corridor. There was nothing more than the creaking of a loose board, the sound of stifled laughter, which crept half-heard through the opaque shadow in his mind. Then, when he was about to drowse off, he was abruptly wakened by a tumbling, crashing sound at the far end of the hall, and the sound of hoarse, choked laughter which was suspiciously like Calloway's. Weatherby climbed out of bed, threw on his bathrobe, and fumbled in the dark for his flashlight. As he stood erect, the room lurched in the pale glow of the moon from the window. The commotion was louder now, and he could plainly hear the sound of boys' voices. He flung open the door and flashed the light down the hall. As he did, he caught sight of pajama-clad figures scurrying into their cubicles. Walking down the hall, he half-stumbled against the radiators and heard excited, whispered warnings coming from the direction of Calloway's bunk. He would put a stop to that! He flashed his light into the cubicle. Inside, on the bed, Calloway and Marks sat, the remnants of a cake between them. They stared back at the light without blinking.

"What is the meaning of this?" His voice was blurred, and he could hear himself shouting.

There was no answer from either of the boys. They gazed straight at him, and Weatherby thought he could detect a trace of a smile on Calloway's lips. His head was pounding, and the boys' faces wavered in a fog before his eyes. It was all very strange, the silence and Calloway's unwavering gaze. To cover his nervousness he played the light around in the corner of the cubicle. Then in a voice which was stern, but which he thought was more tempered, he said:

"All right. Which one of you was responsible for all the noise down here?"

There was still no answer. Then suddenly, from an adjoining bunk there came words which shocked him. They were horrible, coming from the mouth of a boy; but what jolted him more was the manner in which the words were delivered:

"You drunk old bastard!"

Sneering, muffled, mocking words. And then the whole hall burst into an uproar of laughter. Weatherby was unable to say a word. He was stunned, while the laughter came back, wave on wave, through his confused mind. He spluttered feebly, trying to recover his authority and dignity.

"Who—what—who was that that said that?"

It was unbelievable, untrue, but it was happening, and through all the turmoil in his brain he could feel his self-confidence toppling. Calloway and Marks broke out into broad grins, but a certain solemnity, born out of respect for the master, caused their faces to become drawn and serious.

"You—you," he muttered, pointing a finger at Calloway, on whom he laid unaccountably all of the blame. "I—I shall feel it my duty to. . . . You report to Mr. Jones in the morning! Hear me? Hear me?"

Then he fumbled his way, almost stupefied with shame and humiliation, up the hall and into his room. As he slowly closed the door, he could still hear the boys' laughter. How had they known? Was it his breath, or had they heard him as he stumbled up the stairs? Maybe someone had seen him in Urbanna. He didn't know, but the whole thing had confused him so that he had to sit down and think. His cheeks were still flushed with anger and shame, and a quick, sharp feeling of self-repugnance came over him. Imagine, after all these years, to be unable to cope with such a situation! It was frightful. How would he face them in the morning? Should he go out now and make a stern rebuttal, let the little mongrels feel the full lash of his wrath? Or should he demand a full apology in the morning and promise to report them, especially Calloway, to Mr. Jones?

What bothered him most, though, was the way in which he had failed to master the situation. Of course, he had been drinking, but never before had he so lost control of himself. It was weakness, pure and simple, or merely his age . . . his age.

Then suddenly, as if blown in through the window by the smoke-laden autumn breeze, a rending pain of loneliness came over him. From the river came the sound of a distant whistle, and his years swept down upon him like fallen leaves.

Archive 58 (February 1945): 6–7ff. Reprinted in *One and Twenty*, 36–53.

THE DUCKS
William Styron

Frank Thornton, bundled thickly in a light brown hunting jacket, squatted with his gun in hand and gazed upward into the gray light of early morning. At his side in the duckblind his dog lay half-covered by the decoy bag, shivering in his sleep. As Thornton gazed out over the water, he could see the first pale light of the dawn slanting up over the wide reach where the river met the bay. A few feet from the blind, the decoys bobbed softly in the lapping waves which crept in little eddies against the shore.

Thornton cautiously peered through the dried reeds out across the river. As he did, the cold breeze whistling inshore blew flush against his red and puffy face. With a slow motion he wiped away the tears which came to his eyes at each chilly gust of wind. He mumbled silently under his breath, grunting at the cold and the discomfort, and again carefully parted the reeds. The middle of the river, a mile away, was empty and misty. A low-lying blanket of haze was gently rising from the channel, revealing the shadows of the fish stakes and, farther out, the tiny black specks which were flocks of widgeon and mallard.

"Why don't they rise?" he thought. Were they going to sit out there and feed until the sun came up?

The river was silent. As he crouched there, Thornton could hear only the sound of the crows squawking in the cornfield behind him, and occasionally the far-off report of a shotgun in the farmland to the north.

Thornton had been there shivering for nearly forty-five minutes, huddled in the wretched cold. Whatever prompted him to come here every winter was beyond reason. It was always this constant waiting in the chilly mornings, squatting in the damp sand, forever shivering. And now, during the past few years, these solitary hunting trips had ceased to be a pastime, and were more and more an habitual contest with the weather and his own patience. The ducks were getting more scarce, that was true. And the Fisheries Commission wouldn't allow river blinds, so you had to sit in the confounded sand on shore and shiver and curse and wait for the ducks to fly over the beach—which was seldom. Next winter he'd rent a blind on the Chesapeake, perhaps buy a small boat with an outboard. He smiled and ran a gloved hand over his chapped lips as he envisioned a sturdy blind on the Bay, with perhaps a lodge on shore (but that would cost money), and great flights of mallard flying over the blind, wings down, and plummeting with a splash into the water as he released two well-aimed barrels. He clenched his gun and strained his eye upward into the faintly silvered sky.

Then Thornton relaxed and sat back down onto the sand, one hand resting lightly on the head of the dog that shivered and snuffled painfully as he slept. Thornton's eyes wandered back to the little rise of ground above the beach where his old car was parked beneath a scrubby tree. It was strange, he thought, how he kept coming back to this same place year after year. Of course, that new young doctor— whom he did not trust too much, anyway—had told him that his heart would not take this sort of weather anymore. A man of Thornton's age, he had said, was not expected to sit in the sand like this, to wade in leaky boots in the icy water, and to withstand the excitement, mild as it might be, of hunting. Especially with Thornton's blood pressure being the erratic torrent that it was.

"Well," Thornton mused, "you're only young once." But young? No, he couldn't say that. A man's not young when he's a more-than-flabby specimen of fifty-five. But a person must be philosophical about such things. Thornton, although he was a man of practicality, and a good fellow to boot, was given to musings, strange thoughts which came to him at odd moments, moments such as this, even in this cold morning air. They came usually when he was alone, away from the noise of the city, in the quietness along the river shore. He had never told anyone his thoughts, not even Marie; they would sound rather silly if he spoke them aloud. But though he was perturbed and even exalted by these thoughts, he suspected that the law of chance should have it that others thought in the same manner. Everyone has a philosophy, he reflected. What did this Omar say? "Eat, drink, and be merry. . . ." That was a good philosophy, he had concluded, even though it wasn't accepted by the Methodists. He chuckled to himself as he thought of Marie's reaction if he should reveal his contemplations. She'd probably pack up and leave, what with her church circles and prayers every night. But it was funny, all right. Time and space, for instance. Try and define time. You could measure it; it was there. But what was it? Oh, well. . . . The world was too full of troubles, what with the strikes and Harry Truman and the poor starving Poles, to worry about such generalities.

A sharp, piping sound, a rippling whistle came through the clear air above the river. Thornton pushed himself up to a half-standing position and thrust aside a bunch of reeds. Just outside of gunshot range, a lone pintail soared downward and lit on the gray water. He bobbed there for a moment, ducking his head for food. Thornton watched tensely, and released the safety catch on the gun.

"Come in, come in," he muttered to himself. "Come on in."

The pintail turned his black crowned head toward the shore. He seemed to be gazing at the decoys. Then, as if he suspected at that moment something queer about the nodding cork ducks near the beach, he wheeled about quickly in the water and took off with a scudding splash down the river. Thornton watched the pintail until it disappeared, a black dot on the horizon.

Thornton cursed quietly, and jammed the safety back in irritation.

"Blasted pintail," he thought. "Blasted Fisheries Commission." If they would just let a person build a blind a hundred yards out, it would be easy. But the ducks wouldn't fly over the shore, unless there was a strong onshore breeze. The blasted ducks were always out of range.

He sat down again in the sand. The dog woke up and stared at Thornton with sleepy eyes.

"That's all right, old boy," he murmured. "You just wait. We'll get 'em. You'll see."

Thornton crossly broke open the breech end of the gun and checked his shells. Then he snapped the stock and barrel together with a sharp crack. By God, he'd get some ducks today if it was the last thing he did. He'd walk into the house with the ducks held high, tied together by their feet, and the clotted blood on their wings. What would Marie say then? Yes, what would she say? Well, as usual she would not say much of anything—merely walk up to him in that weary manner and kiss him on the cheek and say, "How nice," in her tired, listless voice. It seemed of late that she was always tired, not saying much of anything, simply look-ing at him with her sleepy eyes, smiling now and then, not saying much at all. What got into a woman at that age? What made them act like that? By God, he bet that Helen Chappell. . . . Well now, what made him think of Helen Chappell? But that wasn't too strange. He had thought of her often—not incessantly, of course, but often enough—since he and Marie had been married.

But she was a peach, though, wasn't she? He remembered her sit-ting at the table in Cole's that night. How long ago? Twenty-eight years? No, twenty-nine, because it was in that year that . . . Oh, well: twenty-eight. It didn't matter. But he remembered the way she looked down at the table, her blonde hair falling at the sides of her face, and the way she ran her finger slowly down the crack in the slate-top of the table as she listened to him talk. And then she looked up and he thought she was going to answer him.

But all she said was: "We'd better go, Frank."

So they left that evening, and that was the way it was. And a week later, Thornton learned that she had become engaged to Harry Snider. But that was the way it was. A man had to be philosophical about such things, even in those days.

So what did he do then? Well, he met Marie and courted her like the young fellows did in those days—very quietly and soberly, and at the same time full of small laughter. Then they got married. She wasn't too much to look at, but she had what he supposed was a "sweet" face, and a sort of gentle, quiet laugh which she still had, even to this day. By God, though, he didn't know what happened to Helen. That night she just walked away and never came back. He was never given a chance to ask why or how, and he could only guess that he had said something that offended or hurt her. It took him a while to get over it, even after he was married. There were those first hot, passionate nights when he kept saying: "Oh, Marie honey, Marie honey," and when he really was trying to think of Helen Chappell, of Helen lying there in his arms. But after a while he forgot about her, except for the times when her brief image would come to his mind for a moment or two and then disappear.

Well, he had no cause to complain. Marie was a good wife. She knew how to take care of a person. Of course, after young Frank died, she said that she would have no more children. It was quite a shock to her. She had wanted a kid so bad. You could hardly blame her, though, not wanting to go through that trouble all over again, being afraid that the same thing might happen. But they had managed. Children weren't everything, although Thornton had begun to wonder lately if a young boy might not be pretty fine to have around for company on one of these trips, or when Marie went into one of those mopey spells.

The sun was coming up over the Bay, and the gray sky began to brighten with streaks of orange. The leaves on the small trees at the edge of the cornfield had stopped their rustling and trembling. It was getting warmer. Thornton took off his gloves, carefully stuck them in the decoy bag, and peered out from the side of the blind. Out on the river the mist had lifted. He could see the woodland on the other shore; and outlined against it in the channel the ducks bobbed like pinheads far out beyond the rickety fish stakes. Two seagulls lifted up from the water near the beach with a short splash and winged slowly over the blind. It occurred to Thornton that seagulls were very smart. They knew a duck hunter when they saw one. They knew he was not after gulls. Or were they just stupid? Perhaps the fact that no one ever shot at them made them dull-witted about such matters. With a sigh he sat down again behind the blind and lit a cigar, taking care to blow the smoke downward toward the sand.

Thornton's eyes wandered back toward his car. It was certainly nothing much more than a junk heap, but it managed to get him down to the river each year. The cylinders were acting up again, though, and the inside was a mess. When the prices came down on the new cars, he would have to get one, or even a good used car. By God, though, wasn't money a pain in the neck? Ed Miles had said to him a few days ago that money wasn't everything; but that was the way it was with people who were well set up in business. The ones who had all the money seemed to forget its value. Yes, and he remembered how Ed had managed to get all that money. He shouldn't say "all that money," for Ed was no millionaire, but by all rights (although Thornton disliked admitting it to anyone) he himself should be in Ed's place instead of out on the route in the truck and reporting to Ed in his office three times a week. By God, sometimes he almost hated Ed Miles; but then, being sort of philosophical, he counted it up to bad luck, and tried to be as friendly to the fellow as possible.

He remembered how it was that day when Mr. Simmons came down to Richmond to appoint a new District Sales Manager; how he and Ed stood out on the steps smoking while Mr. Simmons sat in the office looking over their references and credentials; how Ed kept saying sort of wistfully: "Hell, Frank, you'll get it. You had a year of college," and how all along, right up to that time, Thornton was confident that he'd get the job.

But Ed got the position, and afterwards, when Thornton went in, bewildered and angry, Mr. Simmons had looked up at him through his thick glasses and said in the clipped, brusque voice:

"I'm sorry, Thornton, but Miles seems to have a more satisfying sales record. Martha Washington Coffee appoints its district managers on the basis of sales alone. There's nothing I can do, really, you should know that."

Then Thornton turned and went out, not daring to speak, for fear that he'd get so mad that he'd throw something at Mr. Simmons' bald head. Anger was a funny thing. He didn't often get mad, but when he did he felt as if he would burst if he didn't do something, tear up things— anything. But getting angry never helped. After that he was cooler toward Ed, but friendly enough. It was silly to hold a grudge against a person. Just forget about it and be philosophical was the best policy.

Thornton heard a dull chugging coming from the Bay. He peeped through the reeds and saw a line of oyster boats far down the river, heading upstream in the channel. That would be fine, he thought. The boats would stir up the ducks and chase them toward the shore. He eased back down in the sand and softly stroked the dog's head, listening with pleasure to the distant puttering of the engines. He'd just sit it out and wait and then, by God, the ducks were certain to come in.

He relit the cigar and gazed up into the sky where the crows were still gliding over the cornfield in the early morning sun. It was strange, he thought, how everything seemed always out of reach. Every time he got a chance at something big, he muffed it. But it was a good thing he always had his philosophy to settle back on. He had begun to wonder during the past years if perhaps the Methodists weren't all wrong. How did they know? How can a man base his faith in anything sure, when everything is so uncertain? Even certainty was uncertain. The Lodge, for instance. Why, that was all that he had heard the brothers talk about. All of them had told him that he was a sure thing for Grand Exalted Emir, and what had happened? The night of the election, they had made Jim Alderson Emir, and he had come out a poor third with Most Worthy Rajah. Of course he had been disappointed; who wouldn't? And it was going to be a big year for the Lodge, too. But that was the way it went.

When you had a bad heart, though, you couldn't merely forget about it and be merry. You had to put your faith in something. But what? Every time you thought you had something sure—whango!—there it went. Maybe that young doctor was wrong, anyhow. It was natural for a man Thornton's age to have high blood pressure, wasn't it? That was the trouble with modern medicine. By God, every little ache and pain meant that you had cancer or thrombosis or prostate trouble. A man might as well have a good time while he can.

"Ain't that right, boy?" he said, scratching the dog's long ears. "Huh? How about it, boy?"

Suddenly Thornton heard a fluttering sound above and behind him. Six ducks came over, wings down and flat, necks strained forward, and were gone before he had a chance to raise and throw the gun to his shoulder. Thornton was trembling with excitement. He looked out over the water. A flock of ducks—nearly ten or twelve—were headed in low across the water toward the decoys. He nervously fingered the stock of the gun, and spoke softly to the dog.

"Ho, boy," he whispered. "Steady. We'll get 'em now."

Thornton crouched tensely behind the reeds, hardly breathing.

The blood rushed to his brain, and he could feel his cheeks becoming flushed with a thrill of anticipation. The ducks were coming in fast, skimming over the surface of the waves to the bobbing decoys. When they were about twice gunshot range, he softly pressed against the safety catch. His whole body was quivering in fascination as he watched the ducks scud past the fish stakes and into range. "Hold it," he thought, "hold it 'til they're on the decoys." They were so close now that he could tell what kind they were. All mallards. "Don't get up too soon," he cautioned himself. Suddenly, they were on top of the decoys. Thornton stood up quickly and took a sight on a fat drake that was flying at the head of the flock. His left hand shook so that he could hardly keep the gun steady. He pulled the right trigger with a sharp jerk. A miss. Trembling, he lined up on another drake who was swiftly heading down river. His eyes began to blur. He cursed himself silently. Blindly he pulled the trigger. Another miss. Thornton took the gun from his shoulder and jammed the butt in the sand in bitter disgust.

"Damn!" he said. "Damn!"

The dog was out among the decoys, splashing about excitedly for the ducks which were not there. Suddenly Thornton saw two stray mallards winging in toward the decoys from the fish stakes. He called frantically to the dog.

"Come here, come here! Get out of there!"

The damned dog would scare them away! He fumbled wildly in his pocket for two shells, and popped them into the barrels.

"Get out of there!" he yelled. "Come in here!" The dog, unheeding, continued to paddle around in the shallow water. Thornton crouched rigidly behind the blind. He saw the two ducks come within range and then, seeing the dog, they swerved in a wide arc to the left down the river. Thornton ran madly out onto the beach, stumbling in the sand and driftwood. He was breathing in deep gasps as he came to a halt by the water and raised the gun to his shoulder. Taking a sight on the swiftly disappearing ducks, he released both barrels at once. Both misses! Out of range. His heart was pounding, and his brain ached and throbbed. As he stood there, his whole body became weak and limp, as if made of water. A sharp pain surged up from his chest and then to his neck. Then the river and the sunlight faded quickly and vanished. He fell forward and collapsed in the sand.

The dog swam to the beach, padded softly up to the prone figure, and sniffed at a limp hand. Then he sat down, trembling. After a moment he got up, shook off the water, and trotted back to the shelter of the blind.

Archive 60 (October 1946): 8–10ff.

A MOMENT IN TRIESTE
A sketch by William C. Styron, Jr.

"This was worth the trip," Doc said.

"Yes," Nick said. "This is the life." And he looked at the girl he was with—she was a large cheerful girl named Maria—and he squeezed her plump hand happily, gazing up at the sky.

There were four of them sitting in the twilight on the *terrazza* behind the wine shop, where they had come that evening after wandering all over Trieste searching for an open-air place with a garden and a view. After their third bottle of chianti that afternoon in a damp and rancid saloon in the center of town, where the wine tasted like alum and the sunlight, sifting in through barred cellar windows, perished as quickly as it fell, Doc had declared loudly that the air of Italy could only be savored properly at twilight, in a garden, and that it was criminal to waste time in a Capuchin tomb. So they had stumbled up into the violent sunlight and had spent an hour walking aimlessly down the swarming and dusty summer streets, past the shop windows with their hopeful displays of costly, unsalable bric-a-brac, and the deserted restaurants where yawning waiters flicked mechanically at the tablecloths. Then Nina said she remembered a place on the edge of town, near the Yugoslav border, where there was a view and—if the place was the same as before the war—the best wine to be had anywhere.

And they had ridden on the ancient neglected trolley for miles, it had seemed, across the tired city, around the blue rim of the harbor where in the glitter of the afternoon sun they could see the ship that Doc and Nick had come over on, riding high at anchor, the cattle all unloaded now, and beyond the ship the low bristling outlines of the English destroyers, leashed and straining at their moorings. Then the trolley dipped rattling past the gutted docks with their bright ruin of concrete and steel lying tangled and gleaming under the Adriatic sun, and finally out beyond sight of the harbor itself, where they could see only the row of crumbling warehouses on a bare acre of clay, among which scavenger children darted like sandpipers.

Finally the trolley labored up a steep hill for more than a mile, and the sultry air and dust seeped into the car and the heat was thick and stifling and full of the sour vegetable smell of Italian streets. The city, both in external design and in atmosphere, was changed now, for the houses and buildings which in the older part of town were a neat and happy mixture of Latin and gingerbread Austrian became here dingy and bleakly austere. At the same time the whole air of the section—in contrast to the war-weary but affecting sense of laughter and diversion along the Via Paduina and the Piazza Garibaldi—seemed lugubriously Slavic. Most of the windows were boarded up along the route, and the houses which in the other section of town all had been graced with flowers or greenery—if only a few bright red *garofani* in the window boxes—were here weather-beaten, gray, and rather menacing. On the brow of the hill near the border they could see trios of armed British soldiers on patrol, and on some of the stone walls of the houses were painted legends such as TITO and VIVA TITO and glaring crimson words in Serbian that none of them except Maria, who was born in Fiume, could understand.

"The Soviet will triumph," she translated, and Nina wrinkled her lovely face in scorn, and repeated the phrase in Italian, and muttered: "Tito! *Cane bisunto!*"

Then Doc, who had drunk too much chianti, and half a bottle of cognac besides, was sick out of the window and Nina, giggling, held his head while the people in the car stared and mumbled to each other and laughed.

II

Later, however, as they sat on the *terrazza* in the cool air of twilight and watched the sun fade behind the mountains over Yugoslavia and saw the gray barren faces of the hills grow dusky with the coming of night, they all felt better and even Doc ordered another bottle of wine. Below them the hill upon which the terrace was situated swept down into a rocky valley and through the valley snaked a water-filled gorge. On the heights above the gorge there was a single narrow-gauge railroad track which wound out of the city past the wrecked piles of masonry which had once been tanneries and rendering plants, and then disappeared, miles away beyond the sparse vineyards of the foothills, into the mountains.

They watched and drank alone for a while, since there were few people besides themselves on the terrace. The men who composed the dance band had just arrived and walked about perfunctorily, setting up their music and tuning their instruments.

"Maria," Nick said. "I love you, *bella mia, bella donna, fortissimo.*"

"Ah," Maria cried, her big breasts heaving, as she placed one arm on Nick's shoulder and laughed. "I love you too. But you are drunk already."

"No, Maria," Nick said. "Not drunk, just happy. Americans don't get drunk."

"Yes," Maria said. "That is what I hear always, but you lie."

"That is right, Maria," Doc said. "Tell him so. He is the biggest sot in the world."

"Sot?"

"Yes. Sot. You know." Doc lolled his head forward and goggled his eyes in a pantomime of drunkenness and Nina's dark eyes glowed and she raised her glass triumphantly and laughed. "*Umbriago!* Yes? Sot is *umbriago.*"

Then Doc called the waiter, who brought them a silver platter covered with thin slices of bologna and salami and warm strips of brown-crusted fragrant bread, dark ripe olives as big as plums, and more wine, and they sat and talked in buoyant broken English as they watched the wavering last light fade behind the mountains.

III

The terrace was becoming dark and the pavilion and the tables at its edge were beginning to fill up with customers. The people who came in were for the most part wide-faced Slavs who sat down inertly at the tables and ordered "*vino!*" in heavy voices. A few feet away two men with their girls took a table. The men were in shirt sleeves and wore red suspenders and the girls, both of whom were very young, chattered with childish poutings and plucked at the sleeves of their men, who smiled briefly and returned to their wine with darkly stolid faces.

Now the lights were turned on all around the terrace, illuminating the swarthy faces of the men seated near them and sending down unshaded beams of light on the dance floor and on the ubiquitous faded terra-cotta frieze above Nick's head of Dante lurking at the Ponte Vecchio. Doc was teaching Nina a song and carefully in the shadows beneath the table Nick stroked Maria's fleshy knee.

"Maria," he said loudly, "come with me to America."

Maria closed her eyes and gently nodded her head to the first bars of the music. The band—a five-piece affair—was playing "Honeysuckle Rose" very loudly and in mincing ragtime, and the people at the other tables began to dance while Nick, whispering half-hearted words of tenderness to Maria, stared through a translucent winey haze at the people on the floor, at the blunt surly men and at the fatuous lovely faces of the girls, and thought that this was indeed the life.

The two couples at the next table were not dancing, and Maria pulled Nick by the hand toward the dance floor, and he, lurching cheerfully through the crowd, looked back at the two tables and saw, at one, Doc smiling, whispering intently into Nina's ear and, at the other, the two men staring with sullen resentment at Doc's back and then into his own abruptly startled eyes, the two childlike girls prattling and frowning petulantly at the men, and saw one of the men—a tall, scornful fellow with grim lips and a muscular neck—suddenly lean back and give a wild bellow of a laugh and grasp his girl roughly by the wrist and half-stagger onto the floor.

Above the shuffle and slap of the dance and the dissonant music Nick could hear Maria's voice saying "Niccolò, you dance well," and for some reason incongruously at that moment he remembered that Joyce wrote *Ulysses* in Trieste, a thought which was lost amid the swirl of thick guttural voices and the feel of broad hips jostling his and the sudden glimpse of the man who had been at the table now dancing a yard or two away from him, his lips twisted in sarcastic contempt, his little button blue eyes staring at him full of outrage and scorn.

IV

Now the orchestra began to play "Begin the Beguine." The throng on the floor took up the amazing rhythm, which was no more Latin in its mood than a Norwegian folk tune, impelling the people into a shuffling travesty of a dance, their elbows wildly gyrating and their feet stomping the floor in lumpy precision. And Nick, maneuvering awkwardly with Maria, felt himself being forced gradually toward the broad heavy back of the man who had been staring at him, and, though unable to see his face, knew that the man's eyes wore the same look of cold fury and derision, and sensed somehow, without looking, that the other man at the table had now joined the dance.

Then Nick turned his head, hardly feeling Maria's plump arm around him, and saw Doc's lips moving gaily as he talked with Nina in the corner and heard Maria's voice once more, saying "Nicky, what is the matter?" and turned back again, seeing the sudden alarm in Maria's eyes as they both heard the two men's voices singing—high, harmonious, and derisive above the noise of the dance—a parody of "Begin the Beguine" in guttural and mucous syllables which ended with the contemptuous word: "*Americani!*" And Nick, listening to the words rising high and taunting over the music, suddenly felt the entire dance floor become tense and nervous with the contagion of the song and heard a restless tremor of excitement run through the crowd until, hemmed in with Maria between four couples and watching a few feet away the faces of the two men—their wide mouths agape, eyes insulting and cruel—he felt the electric flow of anger rising around him and the mounting turbulence of indignant voices, and finally the music stopped and an oppressive buzz hung over the room, and he saw the ridiculous arm of the bandleader hovering cataleptic over the murmuring crowd. Somewhere a glass shattered and the air was full of the thick odor of wine.

Then a curious thing happened. As Nick stood in the center of the floor, feeling the hostile pressure of the bodies against him, he heard a shrill woman's voice shout something unintelligible, and saw the crowd turn away from him and surge past and around him toward the edge of the *terrazza.*

Nick looked down at Maria who clutched his arm tightly and whispered, "*Fuochi di gioia,*" and then he gazed past the people gathered at the rim of the pavilion and saw, high in the starless dark above the valley,

the flaming letters TITO burning on the mountain and two huge blazing red stars at either side. It was a black night and the outlines of the
mountains were hidden and it seemed from the *terrazza* as if the symbols were flickering in mid-air.

"They put petrol on the ground and burn it," Maria said. "This is the
first time in months."

"Let's get out of here," Nick said.

Doc and Nina had moved around from the crowd and stood closely
together at one side of the pavilion. Doc was holding Nina tightly and
her eyes were wide with fright.

"They are beasts, all of them," Maria said. "We should not have come
here."

"Let's go," Nick said. He motioned to Doc and the four of them
edged out of the pavilion. Nick, passing through the door, looked back
at the people intently watching the fires, and saw for an instant the
frieze above the heads of the people, and Dante, stooped and pensive,
regarding the faded impassive face of Beatrice with timeless despair.

American Vanguard (1948): 241–47.

THE ENORMOUS WINDOW
William Styron

Mr. Jones walked along the flagstone path which ran between the headmaster's house and the school. It was a bright May morning. Around
him the cedar trees, rustling in the breeze from the river, cast trembling shapes of light upon the ground. The sky was cloudless and deep
blue. A faint chill lingered on the air, although in the woods beyond
the school a locust's fretful scraping gave promise, later on, of heat and
dampness. As he approached the main building he smelled breakfast
cooking and at the porch the sudden sweet odor of flowers in bloom.
He looked down at Miss Dabney's garden. There was a row of nodding
petunias, roses, yellow daisies, and a plant he took to be phlox, though
he could not be sure. He picked a daisy, inserted it in the lapel of his
gray flannel suit, and entered the door, conscious of his smile: spring
mellows the heart of man, he thought.

In the basement dining-room the five young masters, his subordinates, were standing at their separate tables waiting for his arrival, and as he passed briskly to his own table in the center of the room he nodded to each, smiling agreeably, and said, "Good morning." For a moment he stood behind the chair at his table talking to Miss Dabney, the pleasant-faced, eager woman who was the school dietitian. The weather, they agreed, was lovely. "I'll bet that's one of my daisies," Miss Dabney was saying, but his eyes strayed to an empty table nearby: where, he wondered, was Margaret? Suddenly the bell upstairs rang; muffled by the walls came the sound of the boys' voices, a tumble of rowdy feet down the creaking stairs, and then grave and subdued and sleepy-eyed the boys trooped in, as quietly as they could manage, to their various tables.

The room was quiet. He said grace aloud, repeating the simple prayer in a distinct, nasal voice—the voice to which he had imparted, through many years' habit, a tone that was neither pious nor indifferent. Then they all sat down to their corn flakes, muffins, and scrambled eggs. Two boys, Cabell and Tidewell, both honor students, were allowed the privilege of sitting at the headmaster's table. As breakfast proceeded Jones divided his conversation between the two students and Miss Dabney: today would be a fine day for sailing; yes, they could stay out late on the night of the graduation dance, provided they behaved themselves; yes, the examination schedule would be posted tomorrow. Once with light familiarity he paused to tease Cabell gently about his girl. Cabell was a bashful, warm-hearted boy with ungainly arms and legs and, as all the school knew, he was in love.

"You'd better watch out for these Richmond girls," Jones said. "I know. One got me." And everyone laughed except Cabell, who only grinned miserably as the embarrassment reddened his cheeks like fire.

"By the way," Miss Dabney said, "where is Mrs. Jones this morning?"

"Amy? She had a little headache," he replied, "but she said she'd be in later for coffee."

"Oh dear, that's a shame," said Miss Dabney, buttering a muffin.

Over the conversation at his table—Miss Dabney was talking now in her busy, anxious voice about the price of gardenias—he was aware of a jumble of sounds. From one end of the tables, above the hum of voices, came hoarse adolescent laughter—hushed abruptly by a reproving master—while all through the room fifty spoons tapped against fifty cereal bowls with bright tinkling sounds, like a chorus of tiny bells. Blue morning shadows filled the room, pierced by slanting beams of light. Through the light, motes of dust rose in a little storm and he thought—suddenly feeling unaccountably drowsy—that he should tell Richard, the janitor, to wax the floor.

Miss Dabney was still talking about gardenias. "Awful, awful," she was saying, "what they charge." He nodded softly in agreement but his gaze, wandering about the shadowed room, again sought the table with the empty chair. She was not there. For a moment he felt a violent tug at his heart: was she sick? But no, he would have been told. Perhaps, like Amy, she would come in later for coffee. The noise in the room subsided, murmurous and indistinct, and he allowed his thoughts to stray. No doubt she was having breakfast in her room. In his mind he pictured the room, sunlight streaming in the window. He had never seen the room in the light of morning but there had been so many times that he had contrived to visit her—always upon some shameless pretext—that every detail of her room was as sharply printed on his memory as if he lived there himself. There was a tasseled lamp standing in a certain corner, antimacassars on the sofa, three washed-out prints from *Harper's Weekly* of solemn ladies with parasols. She had a damaged little radio, made of counterfeit ivory and bandaged with adhesive tape. Always at night when he visited her he stood fearfully at the door until she answered his knock. He trembled with love and fright. He knew by the sweat on his forehead and by his quivering hands that he would betray himself. But when she appeared he somehow managed to say with a certain calmness: "I hate to bother you again, Mrs. Temple . . . a rather important matter." She had come to the school that fall as business manager. She was a widow. He didn't know her age, but she was no longer young.

He had fallen in love with her. He loved all those things he would have fallen in love with thirty years ago. He loved her warm, modest laughter, her hair, her disarming gaze, full of questions—even the particular, indefinable way she smoked a cigarette. To her he had never spoken her name, but the word "Margaret," which he repeated over and over to himself like a lovesick boy, inflamed his senses and filled him with anguish and desire.

Once one sunny morning while taking a walk he had seen her as he passed her window. She had worn a shabby housecoat, blooming sadly with faded flowers, and her black hair was twisted at the back of her head in a coil. She stood at the window, not looking out, with one finger pressed against her cheek as if in thought. He could smell the odor of boiling coffee. In the room a plaintive tenor was singing "Only a Rose." She hadn't seen him. He had turned his head quickly, feeling a tender thrill of joy. He had wanted to stay, to somehow become invisible, so that he might watch while, unconscious of his gaze, she went about her small affairs. But burning with shame, despairing of all forgiveness, he had walked swiftly away, muttering, "My God, my God."

Giddy patterns of dust swarmed in the sunlight. He felt very tired, as if he had had no sleep at all. He looked away from her chair, groaning inwardly—"My God," and gazing down, he saw that his eggs were growing cold. Miss Dabney turned to him with sudden, disheartening intensity. "Don't you think so, Mr. Jones?" she said.

"Pardon, what's that?" A sudden hot rush of blood fired his cheeks—could they tell?—and he said with a nervous little chuckle: "My mind's wandering. Getting old, I guess."

"Don't you think that florist should give special prices to the boys? After all—the dance. They can't be expected. . . ."

"Yes—" he began, but just then his wife and step-daughter, Julia, entered the room. Rising with his napkin in hand he seated his wife at the table while Cabell, with flustered gallantry, pulled back Julia's chair.

"And are you feeling better, Amy dear?" Miss Dabney asked. She reached out and patted his wife's hand in the quick, impulsive gesture that women use.

"I took an aspirin," Amy said, and then to Moss, the colored waiter, hovering at her shoulder: "Just coffee, please." She was a small, pretty woman, plainly dressed, with aimless, sorrowing eyes and graying hair. Now and then while talking to Miss Dabney she smiled, but it was a remote and distracted smile, as if her mind lingered pleasantly upon something else, in another time.

"I wouldn't be surprised," Miss Dabney said, "if they weren't caused by some allergy. I've read how in the spring a certain pollen might cause headaches. Does your nose run, too?" Jones felt a sudden, weary impatience. He looked about the room. Most of the boys had finished breakfast. Some of them drew random patterns on the tablecloths with their knives or, leaning back recklessly in their chairs, chattered to friends at other tables. Slowly, with a deliberate motion of his arm, he reached forward and tapped the little brass bell in the center of the table. Chairs scuttled back noisily. The boys escaped from the room with a show of hurried composure, whispering together in groups of two or three, brazenly groping in their pockets for forbidden cigarettes. He should give them a lecture, he thought.

Miss Dabney and the two boys left, and he was alone in the room with Amy and Julia, except for Moss who lingered nearby rattling dishes as he hummed a mournful, wordless tune. Amy had brought the *Times-Dispatch*. He sipped lukewarm coffee, scanning the headlines—something about a heat-wave, ominous moves in Berlin—but the words rambled on senselessly and he found himself thinking: perhaps now standing at the window she is thinking of me, perhaps in the sunlight. . . .

"Mama, *why* can't we go to Richmond? Why, Mama?"

"Now Julia, I told you. . . ."

"But Mama." She was spreading jam on a piece of muffin with messy concentration, tossing the hair back from her eyes. She was a brash, haughty child of eleven with a spoiled mouth and a grown-up air of pained boredom.

"I told you we'd have to wait."

"But *Ma*ma!" She tapped at her plate with a spoon, her mouth stuffed with muffin.

"Julia!" he said sternly. "You stop that right now. Right now. Hear me?" He wagged a finger at her angrily. "You just *hush!*" He rose abruptly from the table, sensing their startled wonder—for he rarely so lost his temper—but the anger suddenly fled from him, leaving him ashamed and faintly distressed. He patted Julia's hand. "That's all right, honey. Mama's going to take you to Richmond soon." She sulked, tugging her hand away. For a moment a somber cloud of suspicion seemed to have fallen around him. Could they guess anything? But no. As he stood there he looked at Amy. Her eyes were sad and wilted, but a faint pale echo of a smile hovered around her lips. She moved one hand slowly toward her throat.

"Willis, your tie is all crooked," she said.

He patted her hand, too, with a murmur: "I'll see you at lunch, my dears," and left the room hurriedly, hot with confusion, thinking that the day wasn't going well at all. Amy's look—grave, sad, somehow hurt—haunted him as he went up the noisy stairs—her asthma seemed so bad these days—but suddenly she was forgotten, for he felt his heart beating cruelly from the climb. He was getting old and this thought, as it always did, caused him a vague resentful fear. Pausing on the landing now as he gazed out at the sunny lawn, he sensed hot blood pounding at his temple. There was a cool moustache of perspiration on his lip, and on his brow a dozen beads of sweat clustered like tiny blisters. Once in his seminary days in Alexandria he had raced three classmates to the top of the Washington Monument. He had set some sort of unofficial record, had been able to run a mile. . . . He began to dab at his face with a handkerchief, while from above him, harshly, a boy's wild voice floated down, and a sloppy tumble of feet on the stairs.

> *Sticks and stones will break my bones,*
> *Bricks and sticks and Old Man Jones . . .*

He drew back, oddly embarrassed, into the alcove beneath the stairs, listening uneasily to the hoarse sing-song verses, broken by snickers, vaguely indecent. It was a familiar song; faintly, and always, it seemed, from a distance, the words had followed him during his years at St. Stephen's. He had never known the words except to sense that they were somehow unflattering, and that they applied to him. In the morning as he strolled near the dormitory he had often heard them singing the tune, made faint by water splashing in the showers, or at night before bedtime, in rollicking solos and quartets. He had been able to pick out words like "groans," "bones," and of course "Jones," and he had always smiled, secure in the reasonable knowledge that it was only sly fun and that boys, after all, will be boys. But now the words seemed to have an insolent, personal ring, full of the nastiest scorn.

The song was foolish and mocking and not funny at all. Once more a hot anger surged up in his chest and when the boys, three of them, galloped by on the landing bleating madly, he stepped forward and said, "Stop right there!"

They halted abruptly, their eyes, rolling back in unison, exposing wild alarm. One of the boys, Jeffries, a skinny lad with uncombed blond hair, had a cigarette drooping from the corner of his mouth. Somehow —perhaps now it was just his callow, gangling look—Jones felt that Jeffries was the most to blame. Wasn't it Jeffries he had heard singing the song?

"Jeffries," he said furiously, "your mouth's too big and you use it too much!"

The boy wriggled miserably, throwing stricken glances at the walls.

"Yes, sir," he said weakly. The cigarette, forgotten in his peril, bobbled up and down between his lips.

"Take that thing out of your mouth," Jones commanded. He turned to the others. "You know the rule about noise in the hallways. All of you are restricted to campus. Understand? Now get along!" They fled, banging the screen-door behind them, but Jones called angrily after Jeffries. He'd put a stop to this thing once and for all, give the boy a good talking to. Besides, he thought quickly, there was that other business. Mr. Hollister had told him last night—something about postcards, dirty pictures. . . . Jeffries turned slowly on the porch, eyes clouded with despair.

"You report to my office at eleven-thirty. Understand?"

"Yessir," he said sulkily, and was gone.

For a moment he stood at the doorway, looking out over the lawn as the anger settled within him like a dying fire. The grass was green and placid; the morning dew had already melted. Nothing stirred on the lawn. He was utterly alone. He trembled a little, weak and chill with shame. Two times in the same number of minutes he had committed the terrible sin of anger. Those boys, helpless and trusting, children really—what a thing to say: "Your mouth's too big!" There had been no reason for such an insulting outburst. Never, never before had he let himself go like that. He felt defiled, empty, as if he had yielded to some gross and unspeakable lust. He was going astray. A spiteful presence, hovering nearby, seemed ready to lure him into even more hateful wrongs and as always, in such deserted moments, his mind instinctively echoed an urgent prayer. But as he stood there, eyes half-shut against the dazzling sun, he saw Margaret on her porch across the lawn and the prayer faded on his lips.

She walked slowly to the railing of the porch, holding something bundled against her breast. It was a checkered red tablecloth. One, two, three—he could hear the flapping sound as she shook the cloth, blooming once, twice, and again like a gaudy sail against the sky. Crumbs scattered earthward, reflecting sunlight. When it was done, the cloth folded neatly, she stood quietly for a while and gazed out across the river, shielding the light from her eyes. She was dressed in blue, although it might have been a shade of green, for a scrawny hedge grew around the porch, casting about her a confusion of blue and trembling shadows that obscured his view. He followed her gaze obediently to the river—saw a mile of water, murky green, whitecaps, oyster-boats at their moorings—but in an instant he was staring at the porch again. He felt hot and sweaty. He knew he should turn away, for his heart began to pound frightfully and a thin voice tapping at his mind insisted, "you must stop this," but as he watched her a gentle wave of happiness coursed through his veins, as warm as sunshine, and there was nothing he could do.

For what seemed minutes he watched her, his eyes narrowed against the morning light, and then, drifting back into the shadows, she was gone. Helplessly, he felt a bitter, childish disappointment. A wishful, greedy desire seized him: to rush across the lawn, throw open the door without warning, say . . . ah, what *would* he say? Voices drifted up from below, footsteps on the stairs: Amy and Julia. He hurried down the hall to his office where, fumbling at the lock, he thought of sudden flight: anything, a fishing trip, a drive to Richmond—anything to get away.

II

The morning had become soggy with heat. Even the mocking-bird, which all morning had kept up a facetious chatter, had given up and flown away. Outside the office window Miss Dabney's flowers nodded in the sunlight, sending up a swollen fragrance. The light seeped into the office through half-drawn blinds, printing the walls in pale damp patterns as, one by one, it defined objects in the room: two corncob pipes, a crucifix, a photograph of the bishop in a leather frame.

Jones, drowsing over a chapter in Hebrews—part of the evening's lesson—tried hard to concentrate, but from time to time he found his mind wandering. *Work*, he thought wearily; he hadn't realized how tired he was. The end of the year brought so much to do.

He turned toward the lawn, gazing at a patch of green where tiny insects darted fitfully in the sunlight. From around the corner of the chapel his old hound dog, Lady, ambled feebly into the shade of a cedar tree and flopped out in instant sleep. He could smell the coarse hot scent of new-mown grass and this odor, mingled with that of the flowers, desperately sweet, helped send his thoughts drifting gently away from God. A cold drop of sweat oozed down his cheek, making him drowsily conscious of his flesh. For an instant as he yielded himself up to the day he felt languid, drained of strength, like some pale jelly that floats in the sea; indolent, unfamiliar shivers ran down his arms and legs and he thought . . . but, Lord, what was he doing! He snapped erect in the chair, turning quickly back to the Testament.

> *Now faith is the substance of things hoped for, the evidence of things not seen . . .*

A knock came at the door. It was Jeffries. The boy stood quietly in the doorway for a moment, blinking calmly. Then, when Jones motioned to him, he sat down beside the desk in a small straight-backed chair. For a while neither of them spoke. Jeffries' eyes, pale blue, gazed down at his folded hands with grave, almost tender, concentration. Jones glanced at the boy: what should he say to him, how to begin?

He settled back in the chair, pressing tobacco in his pipe as he thoughtfully composed himself for the ordeal. In many ways he dreaded this sort of thing. He respected truth so much, yet it was a simple matter to make snap judgments, give ill-considered answers. Then, too, he seemed to have become so fidgety today. . . . *Margaret*. It gave him a painful start, for momentarily he had forgotten her. Margaret. Oh, dear God. Desperately his mind went back to the boy and almost without thought, so naturally did they appear, two familiar words formed themselves in his consciousness, offered up as if in supplication: *Guide me.* But the heat in the room, enfolding him suddenly, seemed almost palpable—an ominous thing, heavy with the odor of flowers.

"Jeffries," he began hesitantly, "I've been getting reports about you. Rumors—not very nice rumors—have been going around the school. About you, I mean. What's the matter, boy?"

Jeffries made no answer but Jones, avoiding the boy's gaze, heard his calm breathing, a thin faint whisper in the quietness.

"Jeffries," he went on, "you see, you have a lot to your credit, so much—" he searched for a phrase—"'on the ball,' you know. You make good grades and I know from watching you that you play a fine game of basketball. But you see that's not the point so much. There are other things." He paused. "You see," he said, tapping lightly at his chest, "it's what's *inside* the man that really counts. Discipline. Self-discipline. That's what we all have to have. Do you understand me?"

Still the boy said nothing and Jones had the abrupt curious sense—surely, he thought, a foolish thing to imagine—that Jeffries had not been paying attention, but instead was mocking him silently, perhaps even muttering things beneath his breath. It was a disquieting thought and certainly not true (no boy, not even Jeffries, could have *that* much cheek), but the heat in the room had become unbearable so he swung around in his chair, away from the boy, and began to fan himself with a blotter. What now? he wondered, remembering from Ephesians: "neither filthiness, nor foolish talking, nor jesting"—but no, that would never do. This was no time for the scriptures, but for manly common sense. Carefully pondering his words, softening his voice—for he felt that up until now he had been a trifle direct—he said slowly: "Someday walking down the road of life you'll meet a man. That man, Jeffries, will be you. Ask yourself now: what sort of person do I want that man to be? And if you're afraid, afraid that that man will be a weakling, a slacker, someone you wouldn't want for a friend, then remember this: you yourself are the only person that can make this man fine and good and true. Understand, Jeffries?"

No answer.

"This man will be a good man only because of you. Only because you had the guts—this discipline I'm talking about—only because you had the strength as you walked down the road of life to say *no* to yourself. Do you see what I mean?"

The boy still remained silent and Jones wanted to burst out, "Answer me, boy!" Instead, he continued to gaze out of the window, puffing nervously on his pipe. He felt certain now that Jeffries, secretly, was jeering at him, certain, too, that if he turned to confront the boy there would still be no reply: only those two pale-blue sullen eyes peering upward derisively, without protest and without innocence. Oily blue coils of smoke filled the air. The boy coughed. Far off in the woods a locust commenced a fretful, staccato scraping. *Sticks and stones.* . . . "Insufferable insolence," he said to himself, remembering almost in the same instant young Hollister, saying so earnestly: "Oh Mr. Jones, I can't show them to you. . . . I destroyed them all. . . . Obscene, really sir, obscene." The pictures—that one of *his* students should possess them—all this filled him with sudden loathing and anger, and he turned about and thumped his fist upon the desk.

"Sex," he said sharply, "sex isn't something low and dirty, boy. You don't snicker at it. Sex—"

But the boy, his face flushed with outrage, had half-risen from the chair, saying in a hurt, choked voice, "*No* sir, I—"

"None of your back-talk," Jones replied furiously. "I won't have it. I won't have it, do you hear me? I won't have this filth around school. I'll see you expelled first! Understand me, boy? Answer!"

"*No* sir, I don't know what you mean," the boy said defiantly.

At that moment, horribly, Jones knew that he hated the boy. In his confusion he groped for something to say. Brutal, damning words trembled on his lips but he said nothing, for just then someone tapped at the screen.

"Mr. Jones," Margaret said, standing outside, her face hidden by shadow. "Excuse me," she said gently, "but can I see you for a moment? It's pretty important."

Oh God, had she heard him?

"What—oh yes, yes, Mrs. Temple. Come in." And then in a fierce whisper to Jeffries, whose face now was streaked with angry tears: "Leave, boy, leave! I'll see you later!"

The boy fled, blurting out something stifled and incoherent, and Jones slumped back into the chair, waiting for Margaret. Heat filled the room like an oven. Confused, trembling, nearly sick, he fumbled at the Testament, but it was no use. He heard her footsteps on the porch outside, saw her hair for just a moment, glowing beautifully in the sunlight. Oh my darling. Shape, form, shadow swam before his eyes, but he rose and went to the door, waiting.

III

The afternoon brought rainclouds, hovering above the distant bay like piles of dingy fleece. With the clouds a breeze came, blowing up small whitecaps offshore, making it a fine day for sailing. Some of the boys went out in the boats; others canvassed about the school until there were enough for a baseball game. From where he sat on the grassy hill behind the school, Jones could see both—sailors and ball players. Between his knees he held a hickory walking stick. He wore a light tan nylon jacket, and around his neck there was suspended a pair of binoculars. These—stick, jacket, binoculars—were uniform equipment. He never took a walk without them.

Every so often he would look through the glasses toward the river, picking out one by one the boats heeling recklessly away from the wind, decks awash; or, hearing the distant wooden plunk of a baseball bat, he would abruptly turn and train the glasses on the playing field. Still more often he would merely peer at the woods beyond, trying to distinguish among the rustling weeds those birds whose various calls, ringing out on the quiet air, he knew so well.

After an hour had passed and the four o'clock bell had rung he lay back against the grass and closed his eyes—because he was sleepy and because he was tired now of everything but thinking. An ant crept across his hand. Distantly he could hear boys' voices, a rustle of wind in the woods. Thoughts like bright shapes came and went in his mind, populating the edge of sleep: Margaret, then Julia—"No, Daddy," she seemed to say; an infinity of white sails like soaring clouds— unalterable, timeless, a pillar of smoke trembled on some remote horizon, dissolving instantly into light: he had awakened to the sharp sound of a baseball bat. Only a few seconds had passed.

Now he was hungry. After he had seen Margaret he had not gone to lunch, afraid to face anyone because he had become so unnerved. Iced tea and a handful of Julia's soggy animal crackers had given him some strength, composed him a bit, and it had been then, sitting on a stool in his kitchen, that he had said to himself wearily: *I mustn't see her again, not even to say good-bye.*

She had told him she would have to leave. A telegram had come, her father out in—Ohio, was it?—had had a stroke. She would have to leave. "Does that mean—" he had said, repeating stupidly, betraying himself, "Does that mean—" For good?

If he didn't mind—

"This week?"

The books were in order. Papa was getting so old now. Since the term was almost over, she thought . . . oh, she hated to leave.

"I know. I know. I'm sorry," he had said futilely. Then, in that sudden moment of desolation, he had looked at her steadily, tenderly, and without shame, saying, "I'll miss you very much, you know."

"Yes," she had said gently, evading his gaze. "I know that."

Without another word she had left. She understood. Most likely she had known about it all the time. That was the thing which now caused him the greatest distress. But she was a woman; how could he have expected otherwise? She knew what would have been unavoidable, and so without question took the only course she could, not even trusting a long and solitary summer, away from her, to ease his passion.

"Oh God," he said with his lips, addressing the blue sky, "there is such a little bit of time left. Don't let me go astray." Above him, just within his line of vision, a vagrant seagull flapped in slow-motion, soared upward and out of sight.

A vast, intemperate hunger had seized him, a feeling he had never in his life known before. He felt old, empty. His body ached. He was tired. But the hunger remained; it seemed to assume dimensions, form—an absolute craving to embrace everything about him: meadow, woods, enormous sky and all. Vaguely this feeling frightened him, but it was pleasant, too, and so he closed his eyes once more, listening to the birds and the faint fitful stitching noise of insects among the weeds. Strength ebbed away from him like water draining from a vessel. He drowsed.

Sunlight warmed his face and hands. Sleep came, then receded like waves washing at a shore. Submarine shapes of light, sea-glimmering and fathomless, glowed warm and tender and aching on lost drowned shoals of memory as, dreaming now, he saw a rabbit with agate eyes crouching in the weeds beside him. He called to it softly, but the rabbit vanished. Music followed him in the darkness—"Only a Rose"—and an enormous window loomed around him, a masked woman, too; she was naked, he could tell, but for the life of him he couldn't see her, even with these huge binoculars—only a tangle of smoky hair floating like seaweed against the window. Frantically he tried to pull the shutters aside so he could see her, touch her, but a boy's face, also masked, leaned out colossally, shouting something obscene. He struggled wildly: love, desire, like hot gusts of wind, swept through him. *Oh darling,* he was crying softly when he awoke, lying in the weeds on his side, his arm pinched beneath him.

Long shadows lay across the grass. The playing field was empty; the boys had gone. He sat up slowly and looked around him, brushing the hair back from his brow. His spectacles had fallen off and he fumbled about in the weeds for a moment until he found them. For long minutes he sat there expectantly, propped up on one elbow, gazing into the weeds. Funny, but he felt that some creature was waiting there, hidden in the grass. At any instant he expected something soft, furry, and harmless to come bounding past him out of the weeds: a cat, perhaps—a dog?

Nothing happened. He looked around him, wondering what time it was. Playing-field, lawn, buildings—all were deserted. The sun, descending in the west behind iron-red clouds, cast an immense and somber light against the sky, reflecting against the river, where he now gazed, a faint weird glow the color of rust. The sailboats had disappeared as if swallowed up by the waves.

Now, unaware of the fever burning at his face and brow, he stretched out on his belly, inching forward methodically, pressing closely against the earth so that he could not be seen. At the edge of the hill he halted and looked through the binoculars, fumbling for a moment with the knob that focused the thing. Porch and window came into view, trumpet-vines and hollyhocks and roses softly trembling in the wind, casting long twilit shadows against the house. Nothing stirred within. Dimly he could see rustling curtains, a table, and what looked like a lamp.

"Come," he whispered aloud. "Come on." But she, like all the rest, seemed to have disappeared. *So very strange*, he thought vaguely.

It was a long time, as he lay there silently watching, before he became aware of the music floating upward to him across the meadow; an organ was playing, boys were singing—a remote sorrowful sound, faintly out of tune. Why of course, he thought drowsily, they were all in chapel, gathered there—it must be very late—for evening prayers—she, too—and the hymn, it was: "Awake My Soul, Stretch Every Nerve. . . ." That's where they were, in chapel. For a moment he pondered this thought, vaguely troubled. He was supposed to be there leading the service, becassocked in the chancel as he had been every evening for years: "Let my prayer be set forth in thy sight like incense," he would be saying, "let the lifting up of my hands be an evening sacrifice." And the lesson—something from Hebrews.

Wonderful, incomparable thought: she would be there, too, up front in the third row, rapt lovely eyes gazing upward, adoring him—had she thought he couldn't tell? Oh, what a beautiful thought! He would gaze back at her and of course she would turn away, but then, at some stolen moment when all heads were bowed, their glances would meet—hers finally confessing all, regretful, desiring him. . . .

A tender thrill of joy surged through him, warming him like a flame. The day, the night, the future all seemed to open up before him with a glow of infinite promise.

IV

Beneath the window a row of steps, open to the sky though enclosed by concrete walls, led darkly down to the cellar, and it was here that he had hidden himself at a little past nine o'clock. The night was moonless and still, much cooler now. A million stars crowded the sky, arching over the cedars around him, but Jones was aware of neither trees nor stars, intent as he was upon the window above. Crouching on the steps, he was careful not to rub against the cobwebs or the grimy walls, for he had dressed up in his new sport jacket and yellow tie. Toilet water—his wife's Yardley's—he had also added, just a touch here and there, and this odor he smelled in the darkness, exciting him, pleasing him. A summer straw hat, roguishly tilted, completed the picture: he looked almost as if he were going on a trip—to Richmond perhaps.

He had eluded them cleverly, going directly home. He had seen no one. He hadn't gone to supper, but for a while—stretched out in the dusk on his bed—he had slept. Two orange-juice glasses of whiskey from Amy's bottle—stuff she used for her asthma—had assuaged his hunger somewhat and one more, an hour later, had inspired the yellow tie. In his den, quite giddy, he had tried to memorize a few lines from Swinburne—something to recite to her—but when Amy and Julia entered the house, wondering in small worried voices where Daddy was, he had slipped quietly out the back door. No one had seen him at all.

Fireflies like luminous raindrops flickered in the darkness. He watched, waited, and heard the bedtime bell ring across the lawn. *Sticks and stones,* they sang—boys' bare feet padding on the floors, boy's voices hoarsely shouting: 'Night, Lew . . . 'Night, Holly . . . 'Night, Lew . . . *hey* . . . 'Night . . . 'Night . . . 'Night. Would she never come?

Sudden light flooded the steps. She was there in the room. Fearfully he drew back into the shadows, watching her. She was gone for a long time and then she returned, dressed in her faded housecoat. She sat down in front of her mirror and began to brush her hair. Long dusky coils fell around her neck and face. He was so close that he could hear the whisper of the brush across her hair, the faint creaking of the chair as she moved. He was afraid to breathe, afraid, too, she would hear the dreadful beating of his heart. Endlessly she brushed her hair. Pale arms, pale hands glowed softly in the light, and it seemed that if he didn't rush to her now, press her close to him, he would be lost forever.

Then she paused, holding the brush in mid-air. She gazed at herself in the mirror. A look of infinite sadness and regret came into her eyes. A forlorn look, reflecting despair—longing, he knew, for him. She had never looked so beautiful. He leaned forward and upward so he could see. Pale monstrous blooms of honeysuckle obscured his view but, frantic now, he was bending forward, palsied hands fretting at the vines, witless with desire . . . *Oh I love you,* he tried to say.

Something gave way beneath him. He came crashing down, spread-eagled against the rotting stairs. Dazed, he looked upward and it occurred to him that she had seen him, for she had flown to the window and looked down for a moment into his face. Then, with a little cry of horror, she had banged the window closed, shutters, blind and all.

His straw hat lay crushed beneath his arm. He knew something was wrong, but curiously he couldn't even think where he was. A prayer formed in his mind—*Christ*—but the word trembled on his lips, a broken wisp of air, and in that terrible silence the only thing he could hear now, it seemed, were the thousand tiny blades of inchoate laughter that swarmed about him, shattering the air like fallen glass.

V

On the dusty dark road that leads through the woods he passed Jeffries, who was returning late from the river, a damp bundle of sails under his arm. Jeffries told the story again and again: how it had frightened him so at first, meeting Mr. Jones there, who appeared like a ghost out of the woods. He was dressed in clothes that Jeffries had never seen before, but these seemed dirty. He smelled of perfume. The strangest thing of all, though, was the way Mr. Jones had grasped him fiercely by the shoulders, peering into his eyes. "Sex!" he had cried wildly. "Faith, boy!" and then had wandered off down the road, muttering, "Love, love, love," many times.

American Vanguard (1950): 71–89.

Index